THE COMFORTS
OF UNREASON

*A Study of the Motives
behind Irrational Thought*

By

RUPERT CRAWSHAY-WILLIAMS

GREENWOOD PRESS, PUBLISHERS
WESTPORT, CONNECTICUT

Originally published in 1947
by Kegan Paul, Trench, Trubner & Co., Ltd., London

First Greenwood Reprinting 1970

Library of Congress Catalogue Card Number 71-98217

SBN 8371-3398-X

CONTENTS

PART I

INTRODUCTION

PART II

MOTIVES FOR IRRATIONALITY

PART III

METHODS OF IRRATIONALITY

PART IV

MOTIVES WHICH SHAPE OUR PHILOSOPHIES

PART I

INTRODUCTION

. . . the so happy and yet so unhappy existence which seeks its realities in unrealities, and finds its dangerous comfort in a perpetual escape from the disappointment of heart around it.
—Charles Dickens, in a letter to John Forster.

Those who would think correctly must resist considerable temptations.
—Aldous Huxley.

NUMBERS of books have been and are being written on the art of thinking. Some of these have dealt with the objects and purposes of thought ; but the more valuable, though perhaps less attractive, have been those which, in dealing with the mechanics of clear thinking, have pointed out the fallacies which obstruct the process and have laid down rules which nearly every sane person accepts as valid. The quantity and horrifying quality of the examples of bad thinking which these books are able to produce is demonstration enough (if such is needed in this world) that muddled thinking is far commoner than clear thinking. The writers of these books quite obviously accept this fact ; it was probably the chief reason which drove them to write. But it is only incidentally, if at all, that they examine the question of why it should be so.

If it were only a matter of laziness (i.e. of unwillingness to make the effort to think clearly) the problem would be much less complicated than it is. For, though laziness adopts the most ingenious disguises in order to avoid being recognized as such, it is, once recognized, susceptible to the exercise of determined will-power. The merely lazy man, in fact, would only have to be decisively persuaded of his own laziness and of the advantages of rationalism ; his progress towards clear-thinking would then depend on his own will-power and on his assiduity in reading books on logic.

(I am, it will be noticed, taking for granted the view that the ability to think clearly is acquired only by long practice and considerable effort, and that it is as much a thing to be *learnt* as is the ability to design a bridge or to navigate an aeroplane by night. There are, I am afraid, many people who will disagree with me, but I do not intend to start an argument about it.)

Is it conceivable, however, that mere laziness can account for the virulence of the irrationality which fills the world ? I do not think so. I believe that the explanation is to be found in the fact that the average man's attitude towards clear-thinking is by no means merely passive; it is actively though unconsciously *against* clear-thinking. And the reason for this (which I hope to demonstrate in detail later on) is that he dislikes most of its immediate results. It is this active and unconscious resistance which renders abortive most appeals for sound sense and good judgment. It is not much good telling people to think rationally if, in their heart of hearts, they would rather not. It is even less good if they are entirely unaware of the possibility that irrational urges may exist.

I propose, therefore, to try and demonstrate that during the greater part of our lives we, as human beings, tend to prefer unreason to reason and that, the more important the question, the greater is this tendency. At the same time I hope to show, by indicating its causes, that there is no reason whatsoever for feeling either worried by or ashamed of this tendency, provided we acknowledge its existence and provided we are aware of its dangers and of its peculiar temptations.

I find myself uncertain at this point whether I should proceed as if this were a startling and revolutionary idea or whether I should take it as being almost a platitude. It will not seem startling to anyone who realizes how firmly modern psychological investigation has established the existence of (what may roughly be called) the " unconscious " and of the inner unrealized motives that spring from it. Psychological knowledge has, however, only comparatively recently begun to spread beyond the confines of the text-books, and it has spread very unevenly. Large numbers of people have had no opportunity to learn more than the popular catchwords, and it is they who will find the ideas I am suggesting not only startling but repugnant—or, more likely, just rather silly. The ideas may be wrong, but I do not think they are merely silly. There is, as I hope to show, too much evidence in their favour.

It may be asked: " Why bother with these ideas at all ? If we prefer to think irrationally it must be because it gives us some satisfaction, and if we can get satisfaction in so easy a manner why not let us do so ?" The answer, that it is selfish and anti-social, is not the only answer. There is also one which should appeal even to egotism. For the desires which we satisfy in this way are only *immediate* desires, and being largely unconscious they are not necessarily the ones which will give us the most satisfaction in the long run. And, when we give way to them, we are like a man who stays in bed on Monday morning because he feels lazy, forgetting that in the end such behaviour will probably lose him his job. An important incidental point, made by Bertrand Russell in his essay, *Can Men be Rational ?*[1] is that stupid egotism is much more anti-social in its effects than intelligent egotism. " If all men," he says, " acted from enlightened self-interest the world would be a paradise in comparison with what it is."

In the same essay Bertrand Russell points out that psycho-analysis would be of value in enabling " men to become aware of a bias which has hitherto been unconscious ", and in pro-viding a " technique for seeing ourselves as others see us, and a reason for supposing that this view of ourselves is less unjust than we are inclined to think ". It follows that psycho-analysis would help us to understand why we are reluctant to think clearly, since this is largely a matter of understanding our inner motives and biases. But the methods of psycho-analysis are abstruse and seldom easily applicable to oneself. And, in default of them, it is probably worth indicating some of those inner motives and biases which can be said to apply in general to the great majority of people, and which affect their processes of thought. It is I think safe to assume that there are such general motives, in our society at least, since our mental environment is roughly common to all of us. The Trobriand Islanders would be, and in any case are, outside my picture.

These general motives obviously will not apply in every individual case, and even when they do apply their applica-bility will not always be recognized. But, even so, an understanding of them will have its uses ; for anything which makes it easier to understand *why* we are reluctant to think clearly will immeasurably help us to overcome that reluctance.

---

[1] Included in *Let the People Think*, Thinkers Library. The whole book is of course full of the most valuable sense on this subject ; and the essay referred to treats, in more general terms, the particular aspect I am concen-trating on.

At the least it will help us to detect the motes in other people's eyes, if not the beams in our own.

*   *   *

I propose first to deal with the desires or inner motives which, being common to nearly all of us, are relevant to our subject, and then to give some indication of the particular types of irrational thinking which are most often used in conjunction with them and which may be said to be the methods by which the inner motives distort our picture of reality to their own ends. I will then suggest that these motivated distortions of reality will be likely to tempt people into adopting beliefs and theories of varying kinds about such questions as what the universe is, why we are in it, and, in particular, what we ought to do about it. Such beliefs are as popular today as they have ever been; they are, in fact, growing more popular. And the fact that they exist at all is often taken as evidence in their favour, the argument being that people would not believe them unless they had *some* reason for doing so. My argument will, I hope, show that there is a possible explanation for their existence—an explanation which does away with the necessity for anything which could be called a " reason ". The explanation will be repugnant to many minds. But it will be found that this fact is, if anything, evidence in its favour.

Lastly, I will suggest some danger signs which usually indicate, in the person who exhibits them, an unconscious motive for irrational thinking, and which are therefore *prima facie* evidence that that person is talking through his hat.

REALITY, FANTASY AND DEFINITIONS

The hypothesis upon which I am working in this book is this: that there is in every adult a natural, though unconscious, tendency to think irrationally rather than rationally. This hypothesis is based on what has been called the Pleasure-Pain principle (but which would perhaps be more appropriately called the Satisfaction principle). This principle assumes that we tend to want to do things which satisfy our instinctive desires and to avoid things which run counter to these desires. Almost everyone will accept this as a platitude so long as its scope is limited, but a good many people dislike the idea that it applies to all human activity, and will wish to exclude such things as altruism. While it is true that it applies only indirectly to some of our consciously thought-out actions, it nevertheless *does* apply; these actions are satisfying *some* impulse or other. Moreover it applies directly to all our more spontaneous actions, and with rigid directness to our unconscious actions. (I am here including thought processes among "actions".) It is through the operation of the Pleasure-Pain principle that our two chief instincts, the reproductive and self-preservative, and their derivatives, are able to fulfil their functions. It is only because excessive heat produces pain and because we try to avoid pain, that we do not die of burns.[1]

A commonplace of life is that we do not get what we want all the time; i.e. our instincts, and the desires that derive from them, are constantly being frustrated. For instance, let us take the case of a child who wishes to drive—or even to be— an engine. Neither desire is likely to be satisfied in reality. So, in order to avoid the pain of frustration, he *pretends* to drive (or to be) an imaginary engine. From this activity— this indulgence in fantasy—he obtains positive satisfaction.

A child has plenty of time for such fantasy-thinking; moreover it does not matter in the least that his engine goes no faster than his own legs. An adult on the other hand has to deal with reality—his engine must get him somewhere on time. His fantasy-thinking is therefore to a large extent replaced by what I shall call "reality-thinking". And in dealing with the everyday world (rather than with his emotions) his success will depend on how often his thinking is "real" rather than "fantastic". But, since fantasy-thinking is still quite natural to him, he will always be in danger of allowing it to influence him more than he realizes, especially as it seldom appears in easily recognizable forms (i.e. as conscious and consecutive day-dreaming) but disguises itself as isolated, semi-conscious and largely unsubstantiated beliefs.

For those of us who can afford them, drugs or alcohol may

[1] I am purposely ignoring such complications as are raised, for instance, by a consideration of our apparent physiological need for occasional doses of fear. They do not affect our general argument. I am also using the words "instinct", "desire", "satisfaction", etc., rather loosely, in the hope that the reader will understand well enough for my purpose what I mean, and will not assume that my use of them implies adherence to any particular school of psychology. The only question I am begging is the question of the existence of such desires, instincts, impulses or whatever you like to call them. Their existence is material to my argument; the questions of whether they are innate or acquired, and of how they may be explained or classified, are not.

provide excellent defences against unpleasant reality, but most of us are reduced to reliance on our own processes of thought. If these processes can, by any sort of ingenuity, twist the evidence of unpleasant reality into a semblance of pleasant and satisfactory fantasy, they will invariably do so—*unless* we are forewarned and forearmed.

By this time the reader is probably wondering impatiently why I do not just say " wishful thinking " and have done with it. I have avoided this expression for as long as possible for two reasons: (a) it has become a popular catchword and, in consequence, has such a vague meaning that it is practically useless ; and (b) what meaning it has seems to be applied to such comparatively easily detected forms of fantasy-thinking as " Modern wars never last more than four years, therefore this one will be over quite soon." Thus, although one can say that irrational thinking is essentially " wishful ", it shows itself in so many and diversely disguised forms that the expression " wishful thinking " is quite inadequate as a label for it.

The rest of this chapter is devoted to tedious but essential definitions of one or two expressions which will recur throughout the book. These definitions will serve, not only to tell the reader roughly what I am talking about, but—more important —to ensure that he does not give such words as " irrationality " a different meaning from that I am intending—nor a wider one. For example, if he were to associate with " reality-thinking " the various philosophical associations of the word " reality ", he would probably misunderstand much of what I say. Again, there would be confusion if he were to take it for granted that the words " fantasy-thinking ", when used in this book, mean what *he* may mean by them, rather than what *I* mean. (If, further, he were to object, " But I think ' fantasy-thinking ' *does* mean so-and-so ", he would be providing a first-hand example of an attitude which is analysed in Part III.) Such words as these have been used in many senses, and the confusion could have been avoided if I had coined new words as labels for the particular concepts about which I am writing. But this would add so greatly to the labour of reading and understanding that its disadvantages would outweigh its advantages. In order to minimize confusion as far as possible, I have avoided the conventional method of giving definitions, which is to say, for example, " Reality-thinking can be (or will be) defined as so-and-so."

Instead I have used a method which makes it clear that the words are being used as labels for certain specific concepts and for no others.

In giving these definitions I shall have to anticipate a number of points which will emerge more fully and less dogmatically in the course of the book and which will be seen to be of fundamental importance.

" Reality-thinking ", then, is the name I am giving to a technique of thinking specially adapted to the specific purpose of enabling us to deal successfully with the objective world and its phenomena, by forming correct opinions about these phenomena and about their causes and effects. In the course of this book it will I think become clear that in most circumstances there is only one technique which has the slightest chance of fulfilling this purpose. This technique is in principle the scientific technique, though it is in practice seldom recognized as such, with the unfortunate results—(a) that other techniques of thinking are often assumed to be as efficacious, and (b) that the scientific technique itself is often assumed to be some special kind of mystery which is no use to the ordinary man.

Among the phenomena of the objective world must be included emotions and even opinions—when once they have manifested themselves as behaviour observable by outsiders. Thus my emotions and opinions are informative only about my own character; they have no objective value as *statements about the world*. On the other hand, they *can* have objective value as phenomena to be studied by someone who wishes to form correct judgments about my behaviour. They are therefore phenomena to which reality-thinking may be applicable. In dealing with them, psychologists, anthropologists and sociologists use the scientific technique as being the most accurate and objective method. But as yet the emotions of men are too complex for a scientific description to deal with concisely and stimulatingly. When, therefore, we wish to understand human emotion, we often get a sharper, more evocative and thus " truer " picture from imaginative or poetic writing, since this uses words with emotive associations which will induce in us—indirectly—emotions similar to those which are being described. It is in these circumstances that the arts may be of more use to reality-thinking than the scientific technique. For though the scientific technique still

provides the most accurate and completely verifiable knowledge, it is prevented by its prolixity from being of practical use
in giving a comprehensive emotional picture. For example,
if we wish to know what it is like to be a Jugoslav in a country
village, we will get a more apprehendable and useful picture
from one hour's reading of well-written fiction than we would
from twenty hours' reading of the most accurate statistical and
psychological analysis—even if this were available, which it
generally is not.

The point which must be emphasized is that reality-thinking
is designed for a special purpose. The knowledge which it
affords us is a special kind of knowledge and is only a part of
all that which is, or can be, called " knowledge " ; it has, for
instance, relatively little to do with the arts and nothing whatsoever to do with what are known as " the higher things of
life " or the "ultimate realities ". It is knowledge merely of
what is going on outside our own brains, and the reality with
which it deals is the reality only of the objective world. Thus
it is clear that reality-thinking is of no use for some purposes,
and it will later become clear that, conversely, knowledge of
such things as the " ultimate realities " is of no value whatsoever as a contribution to reality-thinking.

This restriction of the function of reality-thinking is, from
another point of view, very comprehensive. For it means
that reality-thinking provides us with *all* the knowledge which
is rationally usable as a basis for action, and all knowledge
which is such as to afford a basis for discussion ; in other words
the opinions and judgments which are based upon it are the
only opinions and judgments which, when stated by one party
to a discussion, are potentially verifiable or confutable by anybody else. This would, at first sight, seem an obvious enough
fact, especially when it is re-stated in the form " knowledge of
objective phenomena is verifiable by observation of objective
phenomena and other knowledge is not so verifiable ". But
in spite of its obviousness when looked at in this way, it is a
fact which is constantly ignored, and it will be harped upon in
this book almost *ad nauseam*.

This leads us to the definition of irrational thinking—which
incidentally by no means includes all thinking that is not
rational. In the first place irrational thinking includes all
attempts at reality-thinking which, owing to unrealized biases
and inner motives, produce incorrect beliefs or opinions. (It

can thus be distinguished from purely erroneous thinking, which reaches a wrong conclusion in all honesty.) Irrational thinking also includes fantasy-thinking which purports to be reality-thinking but which is in fact nothing of the sort. An important corollary is that fantasy-thinking, even when it is unconscious, *need* not be irrational, but only becomes so when it imagines itself to be reality-thinking.

"Fantasy-thinking", in its turn, is the name I am giving to "thinking which seeks to evade reality", or, to put it another way, "thinking which results from a wish to gratify desires which cannot be satisfied in ' real ' life." (It must be distinguished from that kind of random speculative thinking which does not seek to evade reality but is independent of it. A working hypothesis may often be selected, by reality-thinking, from a number of alternative hypotheses which have been presented to the mind during such speculation.) Whether fantasy-thinking is conscious or not, its object in fact is to give pleasure or to allay anxiety. When it is conscious, it takes some such form as day-dreaming, in which the pleasurable object is usually achieved without much difficulty or danger —we pretend, for the moment, that the wish is gratified and, although we know it is only a pretence, we induce in ourselves some of the pleasurable emotion which would accompany the real gratification of the wish. Examples are the day-dream about winning the Irish sweepstake and the day-dream in which—afterwards—we flatten our controversial opponent with our masterly arguments. In either case the disappointment we feel if the day-dream is interrupted is evidence that the induced emotion was actively pleasant. With unconscious or unrealized fantasy-thinking, on the other hand, the partial satisfaction which comes from pretending is out of the question. Since we are unaware of the fantasy we cannot even trace its existence except by reference on the one hand to the ungratified desire which motivates it and on the other hand to its effects. Sometimes these effects are irrational, as when the fantasy-thinking achieves its object through a distortion of reality, i.e. by making us believe in the fantasy. Sometimes they are extremely indirect and are neither rational nor irrational, as in the case of the complex satisfactions which we get from such things as poetry, painting and music, or the less complex satisfactions of watching films, dirt-track racing, football and fighting.

We see then that irrational thinking is one of the *means* by which unrealized fantasy-thinking attains its object, this object being to gratify some desire which cannot be satisfied without distorting reality. In the majority of cases the desire takes the form of a wish to believe something. This wish to believe something is in turn motivated either by the fact that a pleasurable emotion (e.g. excitement at a dramatic rumour, or pride in the exaggerated exploits of one's child) will accompany the belief, or by the fact that the belief will make it possible to avoid experiencing an unpleasant emotion (e.g. anxiety over money, or sympathy, which can sometimes be very depressing, so that we avoid feeling it about Negroes, Jews, Germans, slum-dwellers, or foxes—according to taste—by persuading ourselves, for instance, that " they are not so sensitive " or that " they really enjoy it ").[1] Unfortunately we are as a rule unaware not only of the fantasy-thinking but also of the desire behind it. We need not, however, always be unaware of this inner motive. And if we can train ourselves to recognize its surreptitious workings, we have much more chance, as I have suggested, of resisting its temptations.

Not that these temptations need always be resisted. We are not made of such stuff that we can consistently keep up a rational attitude. For one thing, it is too much of a mental strain. For another, it is boring and dull ; it is inclined to put a damper on enthusiasm and thus to restrict that flow of energy which makes difficult tasks so much easier and more enjoyable. For yet another it allows us no escape from the world as it is. In fact, without fantasy-thinking we should be deprived of mental recreation, of the tonic effects of optimism and enthusiasm, and of all those thoughts which, for some reason, are usually called the " higher " ones. Nor can there be much harm done if occasionally we allow our fantasy to lead us into mild irrationality—if we sometimes get pleasure from embracing with reckless ardour some good cause or even some good woman by whom we are at the moment sexually attracted and whom we believe to be the most beautiful, the most virtuous and the cleverest in the world.

This is all another way of saying that it is not only the child who cannot do without fantasy-thinking. The adult's need may not be so great—but it exists and it will not be denied.

[1] See Freud's *Psychopathology of Everyday Life* for instances of forgetting, and of slips of the tongue, which are the result of a desire to avoid disagreeable memories.

PART II

MOTIVES FOR IRRATIONALITY

(1) INTRODUCTION

THERE is some controversy among psychologists over the terminology of emotions and instincts. I should therefore explain at the outset, without entering into the rights and wrongs of the case, that for simplicity I am assuming three broad fundamental innate impulses (hereinafter called "instincts" for short)—the self-preservative, the reproductive and the gregarious, and that I am going to call "desires" those mental phenomena (such as the desire for self-assertion) that can be said to derive indirectly from these three fundamental instincts. There are psychologists who extend their list of instincts to cover some of these desires as well, but it is after all only a matter of classification. The person who believes that there is one, and one only, true meaning of the word "instinct" will perhaps want to quarrel with me. If so, I hope he will read further, for I will try to show that his belief is inspired by fantasy-thinking—that it is the result of a widespread and very natural desire to believe in anything which appears to simplify the unfortunate and baffling complexity of real life.

One may take it that any desire is capable, when unsatisfied, of inspiring irrational thought. But because a comprehensive survey would be too diffuse for mental comfort, I have selected five desires which are continually manifesting themselves and are almost continually being, at least in part, unsatisfied. I think they are common to most of us, and they account for the great part of irrational thinking.

Before beginning I must make a point which seems obvious enough in itself but which has such an important bearing that it is worth emphasizing. This is that we all tend to take the line of least resistance whenever we are acting or thinking without a conscious purpose. This is merely an extension of the pleasure-pain principle; we avoid something which is difficult or uncomfortable unless we have decided that it is justified as the means to some end. There are of course many people who will say that they enjoy the overcoming of an obstacle for its own sake (e.g. mountain climbers, cross-word puzzle addicts), but this experience does not affect the point, for, without going into the causes of such enjoyment, one can say that the obstacles are merely the means to an end which justifies them—the end being the feeling of a "deed well done" or "mastery" or whatever you like to call it. In any case these obstacles are consciously approached *as* difficulties. It still remains true that in the absence of a conscious object even the "obstacle" addict will naturally take the line of least resistance.

The fact that we automatically avoid something which is uncomfortable has its bearing on the question of mental habits. A mental habit may be said to be a process of thought which we have repeated sufficiently often for it to have become easy and comfortable. Habits enable us to get through the day with the minimum of mental effort, e.g. in dealing with such things as cleaning our teeth, dressing, etc.—witness our discomfort if our tooth brush has been put on a different shelf or our handkerchiefs in the "wrong" drawer. Prejudices, taboos, all the paraphernalia of conservative *status quo* thought—these also are partly the result of the formation of mental habits. This is why we tend to evade any new ("wrong drawer") ideas which may upset our preconceived ones; we even go so far as to deny to ourselves that these prejudices and taboos *are* preconceived ideas, for any such suggestion would automatically undermine our confidence in them—would threaten to oust us from our comfortable rut. The man who says he has no prejudices is probably more noisomely infested by them than the man who, having admitted their presence, is equipped to control their tendency to breed and multiply.

It is necessary therefore to realize that, in addition to any positive desires which may tempt us to irrationality, there is always present in our minds a negative desire—a sort of mental laziness—which not only acts on its own as a tempter, but also can modify the action of the positive desires. In particular it plays an important part in helping to confirm the hold upon us of any irrational opinion to which we may have succumbed.

(2) THE DESIRE TO UNDERSTAND

Mankind has to realize that it does not understand, that it cannot express, that it is purblind.—H. G. Wells.

As keenly as they desire to behave well—or at least to be thought to behave well—men desire to understand. To live in a world that makes no sense is intolerable to them.—Aldous Huxley.

This is the most important and the most formidable of the desires which act as tempters. It is formidable because its motive force is that same force which inspires us to systematize our knowledge of the world—to adapt ourselves to reality and reality to our needs. In fact one may say, paradoxically, that it is the desire to be rational which leads us as often as not to be irrational. This is not such a paradox as it seems, for an analogous situation holds good throughout the whole of our subject; that is to say, though any of our desires may lead to irrationality, none of them is irrational in itself. It is our method of satisfying them, or trying to satisfy them, which is so often irrational.

The key to the paradox is to be found in the reasons why we want to understand—or at least to believe we understand. Clearly enough unless we understand—to some extent—the objective world, we will be unable to keep ourselves alive ; we have to know what are likely to be the results of our actions. What is more, we feel safer in proportion as we are *certain* that we understand the things with which we have to deal. But unfortunately few of these things are as simple as we would like. Though the constitution and workings of such things as cars, bridges, houses and even wireless may be clear enough, there are innumerable other things—and complex combinations of things—which are still far beyond our comprehension. The resources of the world are now generally agreed to be sufficient for the comfort and well-being of all its inhabitants. But we do not understand how to deal with them—how to alter a state of things in which work, food and peace are never secure. Our desire to understand is in fact continually being frustrated, and as continually it is being augmented by the inescapable anxieties of life.

If we take it then that the desire to understand is connected with the desire to have control over our surroundings we see that it will tend to express itself as a wish to have the *same* assurance of understanding all our problems as we have in the

case of the simplest and easiest ones ; it can thus take the form
of a wish to avoid doubt and uncertainty, because these are
incompatible with a feeling of safety, and it can also turn into
a desire to arrive at some solution (preferably a pleasant one)
of a problem without having done the work necessary to ensure
that this conclusion is reasonable.

At first sight one would think that such a complex of
desires, however strong, has little chance of leading us into
irrationality, if only because it seems difficult to be mistaken
over the question of whether we understand a problem or not.
This is certainly true of the simpler problems, not only because
they are simple, but also because most of them demand a
correct solution on pain of immediate physical discomfort, so
that we very soon find out if we have failed to understand
them.   But these are only a small proportion of the problems
with which we are faced, even though they include such things
as whether we can afford to buy a Rolls-Royce, whether it is
safe to cross the road, whether rhubarb leaves are poisonous
and whether our house is likely to fall down.   The great
majority of our problems are much more complex and, what is
more significant, an incorrect solution of them does not have
immediately unpleasant consequences, nor can its incorrect-
ness be demonstrated with inescapable clarity.   All such
problems provide excellent opportunities for people to believe
erroneously—or at least with excessive confidence—that they
understand them.   And when the opportunities are there, they
are usually taken.   One has only to think of such-and-such a
political or moral or aesthetic controversy and of the number
of disputants who believe with passionate conviction that they
understand the problem involved, to realize that most of them
must be sadly mistaken in their belief.   There are of course a
number of possible motives behind their passionate conviction,
some of which will be suggested later, but one of them is,
clearly enough, the desire to avoid the discomforts and uncer-
tainties of that fundamentally sceptical attitude which remains
constantly aware of the fact that opinions on such subjects can
seldom be more than opinions and that few things are as
simple as we would like them to be.

As a matter of fact it would, I think, be true to say that
nothing in the objective world is as simple as we would like it
to be ; at any rate our whole understanding and knowledge of
this world is dependent on simplifying its complex phenomena

in such a way that they become manageable and apprehendable by our relatively limited mental powers. It is therefore by no means irrational to act and to reason *as if* things were simpler than they really are. Irrationality comes in only with the tendency to forget just how far this simplification has gone. But this tendency is unfortunately reinforced at every moment of our daily lives. Unless we stop to think, we seldom realize how much less accurate and certain (strictly speaking) is most of our knowledge of the world than it seems to be. In particular we forget—because there is no practical reason why we should not—how little our conception of even the most familiar objects and ideas is comprehensive.

One can divide knowledge of the objective world roughly into two broad categories: first—knowledge of Things, which consists in understanding them well enough to be able to classify them according to their qualities, i.e. according to their usefulness for various purposes, and, secondly—knowledge of the Laws which control these Things, which consists in understanding them, with their causes and effects, well enough to be able to predict with fair accuracy what is likely to happen in any particular circumstances.

Take knowledge of Things: We shall of course be compelled to take as our example a Table, since this appears to be the only piece of furniture which philosophers recognize or possess. If then I say, "This table is made of wood" (a simple statement about a relatively simple object), I have said something which, though correct enough for most purposes, is inevitably more or less inaccurate, more or less vague and more or less simplified. In the first place, the word "table" is a general word used to describe a number of different objects which resemble each other in certain useful respects sufficiently for us to have found it convenient in practice to put them in a class and give them a common name. The word "wood" similarly is a label for a class of substance. Thus neither "table" nor "wood" is a definite description of the particular object or substance in question. In the second place, to say that a table is made of wood is seldom strictly accurate and never strictly comprehensive; it is a simplification, again for convenience, of the real facts which are (say) that it is made of nails, screws, varnish and polish as well as wood. Furthermore, these words "varnish", "nail", etc., are themselves vague generalizations. "Varnish", for instance, what is that? If we were trying to be accurate (rather than trying to make life easy) we would have to explain that it consisted of such-and-such chemicals in such-and-such proportions, *approximately*. A scientist might be able to tell us these proportions with fair accuracy, for it is his job to diminish the inaccuracy of most of our knowledge. But even he would never be able to tell us with absolute exactness what they are, for the concept of exactness is an ideal—a comforting mental fantasy; in the objective world there is, as far as we know, no exactness (i.e. no two things have been proved to be devoid of any difference between them) and in our observations of objective phenomena we can do no more than approach exactness. " Although this may seem a paradox, all exact science is dominated by the idea of approximation. . . . Every careful measurement in science is always given with the probable error, which is a technical term, conveying a precise meaning."[1]

The situation is analogous, as will be seen, in the case of all our knowledge of objective phenomena. Every statement we make about things is analysable down to an attempt to place these things, in virtue of one or other of their qualities, in a category appropriate to the particular purpose we have in view at the time. Our simple classifications of phenomena into " tables ", " cheeses ", etc., are thus similar in object and method to those of scientists who, with the object of increasing our power to deal with the world, have arbitrarily divided up a large part of its phenomena into categories and have called these categories " metals ", " arthropods ", " mammals ", " nerves ", and so on. Even in these scientific categories there is no absolute exactness; the mammals all differ in various respects; there are even animals which fit so badly into any one category that there is argument as to where they belong. More important, it depends on the particular purpose in view into which category a particular phenomenon is placed, e.g. some chemicals may be poison for one purpose and tonics for another, while killing may be murder for some purposes and war for others.

However, although these categories are not exact in conception—although they do not give us an accurate picture of the objective world—they are sufficiently differentiated to be of immense help in systematizing our knowledge. The naming

[1] Bertrand Russell, *The Scientific Outlook*.

of things and the placing of them in categories is thus a sort of simplification (inaccurate but useful all the same) of the extreme complexity of "real" life. We can never understand this full complexity; as a rule we do not even need to. But we need to understand it to an extent which will help us to deal with it—to survive. We therefore simplify it.

Knowledge of Things is, however, according to our present classification, only a part of our knowledge of the world. We have also to understand the laws which control these things. (There is, strictly speaking, no sharp division between knowledge of Things and knowledge of Laws, but I make the division—in the same way as all such divisions are made—for the sake of convenience.) In other words, we have to know such facts as that water boils when we heat it enough, and that apples, and other things, fall to the ground when their support is withdrawn. These pieces of knowledge, when stated in a more precise form, are applications of " laws " (in the scientific sense) in that they predict what will happen in certain circumstances. And in fact all such knowledge is of the same type, though the laws which it invokes vary greatly in the wideness of their application. The application of the law about boiling water is relatively restricted, while that of the law of gravitation is relatively very general.

Such laws, however narrow in their application, are strictly speaking matters of probability, not of absolute certainty; for, in the objective world, the concept of absolute certainty is, like that of absolute exactness, an ideal only—a comforting fantasy. Though we can be absolutely certain of our own sensations, as I can be certain that I feel hot, we can never be absolutely certain—in the sense of there being no possible doubt—about anything outside our own minds and sensations. I might, for instance, *feel* hot, but I cannot be logically certain that there is, in the objective world, an object emitting heat-rays which has caused my sensation. I may have a temperature, or I may have had some whisky; it is even possible that I am suffering from delusions and that the fire I think I see is not really there at all.

I am belabouring this point in order to emphasize the distinction between two common usages of the word " certain ". In ordinary life it usually means " certain for all practical purposes ", i.e. " so highly probable that it is worth taking as certain " But it can also mean " logically certain " or

" absolutely certain ", i.e. capable of indubitable proof in the same way that two plus two can be proved to equal four.[1]

This lack of absolute certainty makes it impossible in any case to prove *logically* that a law is sound. However, this can hardly be said to matter, for the law's value lies, not in its logicality, but in the fact that it enables us to predict what will happen. And if the predictions we base upon it are sufficiently often correct we can in practice ignore the element of uncertainty. A law is in fact a possible hypothesis or generalization which will explain certain observed facts. It is never certain that some other hypothesis might not explain these facts just as well. But if the chosen hypothesis is correct, other facts should be deducible from it. If these new facts are then found by observation to exist, their existence confirms the probability that the hypothesis is valid; and every such confirmation increases this probability until, as in the case of (say) the laws of motion, the probability becomes so extremely high that the hypothesis is made the basis of scientific research and prediction. The laws of statics, for instance, enable us to build a bridge and to predict with " practical " certainty that it will not fall down. Similarly our semi-automatic understanding of natural laws enables us to predict with practical certainty that it is safe to cross the road when we have looked to see that there is nothing coming.

Note however that, in addition to the theoretical element of doubt in the laws themselves, there is a further element of doubt in the predictions based on them. Such a prediction says, in effect: " It is highly probable that, given certain specific conditions embodying certain causative elements, such-and-such will happen." And the correctness of the prediction depends on the conditions being in fact what they should be in theory. But this again is never certain, for, as we have seen, even scientific measurement can never be exact, and there may always be some obscure but important causative element (usually—while still unnamed and unclassified—called the

---

[1] Such splitting of hairs has only incidental relevance here. But, as will be seen later on, the failure to notice the distinction often leads to the tempting but erroneous belief that it *must* somehow be possible to attain logical certainty in our knowledge of the objective world, i.e. in our reality-thinking. The search for this mare's nest of logical certainty is of course a favourite occupation of philosophers. The fact that propositions like " 2 plus 2 equals 4 " and " All A is A " can be logically certain is, as will also be seen, no evidence in favour of the mare's nest's objective existence, since these propositions do not give us any knowledge about the objective world, but merely express our community's agreement to use certain words in a certain way.

element of chance) which we are unable to identify. Thus, however certain I may feel in predicting that it is safe to cross the road, there is always the chance that there may be a subsidence which will collapse when I put my weight on it. Whatever we do, in fact, we can never get away from the possibility of the " element of chance ". (When its effects are sufficiently startling we get—if we want to—a miracle.)

We see then that all our knowledge of the world—even that which seems most accurate, comprehensive and certain—is strictly speaking only approximate. It is a mixture of simplifications and assessments of probability. In practice of course this does not matter; most of the knowledge is perfectly good enough for us to act on. I have however emphasized the point at such length for two reasons: (a) as I have already suggested, the theoretical implications will be shown later to be of fundamental importance to our subject; and (b) unless we stop to think we hardly ever realize that our habit of simplifying reality (at the expense of accuracy) is not merely a result of laziness of mind but is the necessary basis of all reality-thinking. And if we do not realize this we tend to underestimate the full strength of our desire to simplify, with the consequence that we are not sufficiently on our guard against it on occasions when—unlike that of the wooden table —the simplification may be misleading. Thus, to say that a table is made of wood usually has the simple purpose of differentiating it from a tin one. But to talk of the " economic man ", who has nothing but rational economic motives and is able to follow them, is a simplification which has so little relation to the facts as to be nonsense. For example, the " economic man " will sell his labour in the highest market. The ordinary man however will probably be prevented from doing this by the facts that he has not enough money for his train fares, nor for obtaining another house, that he cannot leave his old mother, nor his married daughter who is expecting a baby, nor relinquish his secretaryship of the Bowling Club.

The desire to understand is almost synonymous with the desire to simplify, and it is closely bound up with the desire for certainty—for assurance. But, when we find we have over-simplified, this does not necessarily imply that our conclusions are wrong. It implies merely that they are less right than we thought, or that we have exaggerated their comprehensiveness. All the same, this tendency to over-estimate our grasp of complex subjects is dangerous enough in itself, however comforting it may be. And it becomes disastrous if we forget that reality-thinking will never provide us with absolute certainty in our beliefs about even the simplest of our problems, while the more complicated they get the greater is the scepticism required. In practice, in the world as it is today, the over-estimation *is* disastrous, for, contrary to all reason (but very naturally), the general tendency is for people to be more certain they are right in proportion as the problem they are dealing with is more complicated. "It is an odd fact," says Bertrand Russell,[1] "that subjective certainty is inversely proportional to objective certainty. The less reason a man has to suppose himself in the right, the more vehemently he asserts that there is no doubt whatever that he is exactly right." And, as we shall see, the greatest certainty of all is achieved, again very naturally, in relation to those problems where the objective truth can never conceivably be ascertained. There appears to be no limit to the ingenuity of the methods which we employ to make ourselves believe that we understand things better than we really do. Nor is there a limit to the harm that can be done when these methods are carried to extremes. The most important of them will be summarized later with examples under the heading of The Adoption of Comfortable Concepts.

(3) THE DESIRE TO FEEL GOOD

And virtue, tho' in rags, will keep me warm.
                        —Dryden. "Imitations of Horace."

The word "Good" has so many meanings that I must roughly define the way in which I intend to use it in this context. As the capital G suggests, it indicates the kind of goodness which results from cultivating as many as possible of those qualities which are generally regarded in our community as virtues, even though in other communities and at other times, they may not have been so regarded. (Certain actions, for instance, will in some communities be called kindness while in others they will be called weakness.) Even this is a vague enough definition; for no two people would agree

---

[1] *The Scientific Outlook.* See also Wilfred Trotter, *Instincts of the Herd in Peace and War*, particularly chapter on Sociological Applications of the Psychology of the Herd Instinct.

exactly as to which qualities are virtues and which are vices. However, it is clear enough for our particular purpose and its most important aspect is its implication that " being good " leads our acquaintances to approve of us.

This does not mean that the only object of the lover of virtue is to win approval. Virtue is its own reward—as Cicero, Claudian, Silius Italicus, Dryden, Prior, Emerson, Gay and Vanburgh assure us. The majority of people will, I think, agree that a desire for virtue as such exists in them— that they enjoy the feeling that goes with a good deed well done. There are apparently a few people who, rebellious through some twist of upbringing, self-consciously reverse the categorical imperative of conscience. But they are, I think, in a small minority and in any case they acknowledge by their behaviour the existence of that conscience—of what Julian Huxley calls " the absolute categorical, and other-worldly quality of moral obligation, on which moral philosophers lay such stress."[1] It is this quality of moral obligation—this " feeling "—which makes many people believe that there must be some corresponding absoluteness about the things in the outside world that are called good and bad. A " feeling " about the world, however strong, is of course evidence of the existence of the feeling, but of nothing else. However, for my present purpose, the feeling is what matters.

As Julian Huxley says, our modern knowledge helps us to understand this feeling and leads to the conclusion that " the absoluteness of moral obligation turns out on analysis to be no true absolute, but a result of the nature of our infantile mental machinery, combined with later rationalization and wish-fulfilment ".[2] This point will be returned to later in the chapter on Morals. In the meantime, it must be noted that the moral sense is reinforced in us by the workings of the gregarious instinct. Since we are members of a herd, it is essential that we obtain enough of the herd's good opinion to prevent it from doing us any harm. And in fact the herd itself will not survive the evolutionary process unless its members develop some impulse which makes them tend to work with the herd rather than against it. Wilfred Trotter, in *Instincts of the Herd in Peace and War*, has shown how such an impulse may lead to an " innate " conception of morality and may explain

[1] *Evolutionary Ethics*, page 14.
[2] Op. cit., page 15.

altruism. But explanations of our moral impulses are outside
my scope. I think I can safely assume that the great majority
of us do have a sense of right and wrong and that, quite apart
from considerations of expediency, we have a powerful desire
to be assured of our own Goodness.

Considerations of expediency do in fact add considerably
to the strength of the desire, though it is of course the non-
rational rather than the rational element which usually exerts
the greater influence. Living in a herd or group gives us an
extremely reasonable motive for wishing at least to be *thought*
good. Even those people who say defiantly that they do not
care what other people think are as a rule either lying or
deceiving themselves. In any case their nonchalance would
soon disappear if the other people began translating their
thoughts into action. Moreover, if we wish to be thought
good, we have a further reason for self-deception. For, the
more sincere our faith in our own goodness, the easier we find
it to convert others. We can then receive the approval of our
neighbours with an easy conscience.

Once again I have had to emphasize with apparent redun-
dance the strength of a desire—in this case the desire to feel
good. I have done so in order to contrast it with the reality,
in which this desire is continually being frustrated by the
practical difficulty of *being* good.

It is no part of my argument to deny that mankind is
capable on occasion of great virtue—of altruism, of courage,
of self-sacrifice, of " kindness in another's trouble, courage
in his own ". On the other hand it must be admitted that
" courage in another's trouble, kindness in his own ", is as
often as not the true picture of his behaviour. No one except
a saint (and he is probably suffering from very recherché
repressions unattained by most of us) is consistently good.
Most of our motives, particularly the unconscious ones, are
selfish in the very broad sense that they are designed to bring
us satisfaction of some sort. And, in the short run, many of
our individual desires are incompatible with the interests of
the community in general. So, once again, we are faced by
temptation ; if we can, by thinking irrationally, make ourselves believe that our everyday actions are really good and
unselfish, we shall continually do so. To quote Julian Huxley
again,[1] we shall build up " an idealized ethical mask, strangely

---

[1] *Evolutionary Ethics*, page 31.

compounded of moral aspiration, spiritual conceit, and hypocrisy, in which we can disguise ourselves from ourselves, or which we can present to the world to enhance our self-respect and our apparent moral stature ".[1]

The chief methods which we use in building up this admirable picture of ourselves are Selection of Evidence and Rationalization. I hope to show later how all-pervading these methods are in our daily lives.

(4) THE DESIRE FOR EXCITEMENT

Two things only the people anxiously desire—bread and circus games.—Juvenal.

We appear to have a physiological need for a certain minimum of emotional stimulation in our everyday lives. Whether we have or not, there is no doubt that the sensation of excitement on the whole is a pleasurable one. I need not therefore go into the reasons why we like excitement nor into the various emotions whose stimulation can be so pleasurable, beyond pointing out that there are some apparently unpleasant emotions (such as fear, grief and sympathy) which, though painful when violently stimulated, can be quite pleasant when the stimulation is gentle. This is sometimes true, in the case of fear, even when the danger is personal, as in car-racing, mountaineering, etc. It seems almost universally true when the danger is vicarious, i.e. when the sensation is a combination of fear and sympathy—when our emotion of fear is aroused sympathetically by observing someone else's danger. Witness to this fact is the popularity of dirt-track racing and of the more horrifying turns at circuses. A less obvious but none the less reliable witness is the popularity of thrilling novels. Similarly, tragedy can give pleasure by vicariously, and therefore gently, stimulating the emotion of grief.

It might be supposed that in any nation at war the desire for excitement would be fully satisfied. I do not however think that this is the case. It is true that those who are

---

[1] There appears to be a small minority of people in whom the herd instinct is very weak, who consequently have little vanity, who define goodness in terms of what is expedient, and whose incomes are independent. These people have virtually no need to feel good or to be thought good. But, as I have said, they are very few. Ivory castles, being no longer impregnable, are becoming obsolete.

engaged in active service or who live in much bombed areas suffer from no lack of emotional stimulation. (Even for them, moments of boredom can be almost painful by contrast.) But those who are not are apparently little less avid for excitement than they would be in peace time. There is perhaps not quite the same rush towards the scene of a fire as in palmier days; there is not quite the same keen sense of disappointment when two cars narrowly escape a crash. But no one could say that such symptoms of the desire for excitement entirely disappear. Even air-raids have their potentialities. For those who suffer them the excitement is unpleasantly violent and direct, though there are, I believe, some people who experience a compensatory exhilaration. For those who hear of them, on the other hand, the emotion is vicarious; the stimulation is, by comparison, extremely gentle—gentle enough to have just a touch of pleasurable excitement about it, whether or not this excitement be mixed with sympathy for the injured.

At this point I expect to be accused of being unduly cynical. It must be remembered, however, that I have *not* made the dramatic and exciting statement that we always derive pleasure from the spectacle of other people's tragedies, but the much duller—and I believe truthful—one that we sometimes do. One has only, for example, to think of the occasions when eager country ears have caught the distant sound of an explosion. The possessors of those ears would almost sacrifice them for assurance that it really was a bomb and not just someone blasting a tree stump. If the rumour arrives that in fact it *was* a bomb, the rumour is instantly believed. It is quite simple—a foreign bomb, terrible as its consequences may be, is more exciting than a merely home-made and harmless explosion.

The desire for excitement appears to be stronger in childhood and youth than in age. The child can largely satisfy it by conscious fantasy-thinking; the youth, if fortunate, by adventurous living. But, at any age, if unsatisfied, it will make us tend to believe something which is untrue but dramatic rather than something which is true but dull. The irrational processes which this tendency encourages are very mixed, but are most evident among those dealt with under the headings of Selection of Evidence and Emotive Suggestion.

(5) THE DESIRE FOR SELF-ASSERTION

He is a poor creature who does not believe himself to be better than the whole world else.—Samuel Butler. "Note Books."

This desire is in many ways similar to the desire to feel good ; it could, for instance, be stated as " the desire to be or to feel superior—in the sense of stronger, more efficient, cleverer ". Moreover, the two desires are often found to go together, as in people who believe that honesty of purpose is proof of efficiency of method, or, conversely, that might is right. But I have separated them because, in what might be called their pure forms, the two desires are quite distinct, and because they can lead to different types of irrationality.

The desire for self-assertion in its pure form has nothing to do with ethics. It is a matter, one might say, of the survival of the fittest, and is therefore related to expediency rather than to goodness. As such it is probably a direct product of the instinct of self-preservation—if one is stronger and cleverer than one's fellows one will survive, or at least one may make more money. It seems also to be reinforced, particularly in men, by the instinct for self-reproduction; if one is stronger and cleverer than one's fellows one will get the pick of the women. However, whatever its causes, the desire for self-assertion is a very reasonable one and is fairly powerful. Unfortunately it is even more often unsatisfied than are the other desires we have been examining.

Sometimes we can improve matters by trying to impress others with our superiority, whether this superiority be real or imagined. We wish to assert ourselves, and, unless we have been well disciplined by our upbringing—or if we have broken down such discipline by getting drunk—we boast, we bound, and we become snobs. But, however successful our boasting, it remains true that the desire to *believe* that we are at least no weaker or stupider than our fellows is continually present in our minds.

There is an allied desire for self-submission, which is probably traceable partly to the sex and partly to the herd instincts. This does not cancel out the desire for self-assertion though it sometimes complicates its action. But though it is a powerful factor in the Fascist mentality, I need not deal with it here since it goes hand in hand with the Desire to Conform.

(6) THE DESIRE TO CONFORM

*In interpreting into mental terms the consequences of gregarious-
ness, we may conveniently begin with the simplest. The conscious
individual will feel an unanalysable primary sense of comfort in the
actual presence of his fellows, and a similar sense of discomfort in
their absence. . . .*

*Slightly more complex manifestations of the same tendency to
homogeneity are seen in the desire for identification with the herd in
matters of opinion. Here we find the biological explanation of the
ineradicable impulse mankind has always displayed towards segrega-
tion into classes. Each one of us in his opinion and his conduct, in
matters of dress, amusement, religion, and politics, is compelled to
obtain the support of a class, of a herd within the herd.*

—W. Trotter.

*An idea which emanates from the herd to which we belong bears
the stamp of the imperative, and we tend to accept it unquestioningly.*

—R. B. Cattell.

Though this desire leads to more irrationality than almost
any other desire, it is in a different category from the desires
with which we have dealt so far. Satisfaction of these *can* be
obtained without irrationality; they lead to irrational thought
only on those (numerous) occasions when they cannot be
satisfied except in fantasy. The desire to conform on the
other hand is, although in most circumstances very easily
satisfied and in many ways socially useful, fundamentally
unreasonable in that it impels us to adopt opinions without
evidence—to regard them as " self-evident " merely because
they are prevalent among the community in which we live.
This does not necessarily mean that the opinions themselves
are wrong; it only means that to accept them without evidence
is irrational.

The existence of this desire (it would perhaps be better
called impulse, since it is largely unconscious) in individuals
of the gregarious species called man is now generally accepted
among sociologists, though its potency is usually much under-
estimated among laymen. Like the desire to feel Good, it
springs partly from the herd instinct; the herd would not have
survived the course of evolution unless there were a powerful
impulse in its individuals which made them conform in matters
of general welfare.

" The cardinal quality of the herd is homogeneity. It is
clear that the great advantage of the social habit is to enable
large numbers to act as one, whereby in the case of the hunting

gregarious animal strength in pursuit and attack is at once increased to beyond that of the creatures preyed upon, and in protective socialism the sensitiveness of the new unit to alarms is greatly in excess of that of the individual member of the flock.

" To secure these advantages of homogeneity, it is evident that members of the herd must possess sensitiveness to the behaviour of their fellows. . . .

" The original in conduct, that is to say, resistiveness to the voice of the herd, will be suppressed by natural selection; the wolf which does not follow the impulses of the herd will be starved; the sheep which does not respond to the flock will be eaten." [1]

There has in many herds to be a leader, but, in the nature of things, the leader type must be a very small proportion of the whole. The great majority will—and does—find mental comfort in conforming. In primitive times it also found physical safety as well; but civilization has altered the conditions unfortunately without perceptibly diminishing the primitive impulse. Thus the disproportionate power of this impulse has impaired the efficiency of democratic government through lack of intelligent and constructive criticism of the *dicta* of authority; in some cases even it has allowed democracy to transform itself into fascism, with paradoxical effect on the physical safety of the majority of the herd.

The impulse to conform, together with that for self-submission, can probably be traced also to the desire to escape anxiety. Erich Fromm, in *The Fear of Freedom*, traces the mechanism in great detail, with mention of obscure mental processes involved (e.g. projection, sado-masochism), which are beyond my scope. He points out, incidentally, that the desire to escape from a feeling of aloneness has been increased during the last century or so by the breaking down of the individual's traditional anchorage in society.

I need not produce here any detailed evidence as to the potency and pervasiveness of the impulse to conform, since it surrounds us on all sides in our everyday life. It would, however, perhaps be as well to give some hints for recognizing its manifestations, since, like the postman in one of G. K. Chesterton's Father Brown stories, they are so much taken for granted that they are seldom seen in their true colours.

1 Trotter, *Instincts of the Herd in Peace and War.*

One has only to examine any of the following with a fresh and innocent eye; table-manners, wedding ceremonies, polite conversation and small talk with its conventional restrictions of subject—" Good morning; looking better today, isn't it? "[1] " the conventions " (" What will people say? "), fashions in clothes, and so on almost *ad infinitum*. In the field of opinions the manifestations of the impulse are more noticeable as condemnations of those who do *not* conform. This is naturally so since it is the behaviour of the one abnormal sheep which stands out from—and endangers—the rest of the flock. In human communities the non-conformer represents danger, not so much to physical safety as to the inviolability of common opinions. Thus it is regarded by many people as " wrong " to try and find out the facts about some phenomenon of which the herd disapproves, as for instance, birth-control or (before June 1941) Soviet Russia. In the 1920's and 30's, to be found with books such as the Webbs' on *Soviet Communism* or the *Encyclopedia of Sexual Knowledge* was accepted by large classes of people to be tantamount to proof that one was already a pervert and a Bolshevic. It was of no use to argue that it might be sensible to find out all the facts—to examine the evidence—before forming an opinion. The herd did not care about facts, nor about any opinion but its own; its feeling was akin to that so carefully (and so comparatively easily) instilled into the German people by Dr. Goebbels, that to listen to wireless broadcasts from foreign countries is listening to the voice of the Devil.

In times of danger to the community the whole tendency to conformity is greatly strengthened; the herd huddles together and becomes more intolerant than ever of " cranky " opinion. Thus, in retrospect, the 1914-18 war seems an excellent example, and so perhaps may the present[2] war.

It is of course true that the suggestibility of the individual human being to herd opinion has its advantages. It is a potent factor in rendering any community stable. But it can be too much of a good thing, since it prevents the acceptance of a new idea irrespective of whether this idea is good or bad.

---

[1] As Trotter points out, the human greeting with its accompanying small-talk is largely a mechanism for making sure that the person encountered conforms to the standards of one's particular class and thus will not upset one by making provocative remarks or by exhibiting alien and dangerous opinions.

[2] This book was written in 1944.

Feudalism continued, long after it was outworn, to be regarded as the only imaginable order; the earth, until quite recently, was the centre of the universe; and evolution, during the last century, was immoral nonsense. In any case, whatever its advantages, the impulse to conform is irrational in so far as it accepts opinions without independent evidence. Indeed, it is sufficiently powerful to make a large number of people accept opinions in deliberate opposition to the evidence.

Once again, the nearest we can get to cure or prevention of the trouble is awareness; our only chance of minimizing the effects of our impulses is to recognize them and as far as possible to discount them. " To maintain an attitude of mind which could be called scientific in any complete sense, it is of cardinal importance to recognize that belief of affirmations sanctioned by the herd is a normal mechanism of the human mind, and goes on, however much such affirmations may be opposed by evidence, that reason cannot enforce belief against herd suggestions, and finally that totally false opinions may appear to the holder of them to possess all the characters of rationally verifiable truth. . . ."[1]

Since the impulse to conform seldom needs to employ elaborate methods of thought for gaining satisfaction, it is of secondary importance in the scope of this book. As will be seen, there are however some occasions when it is frustrated, and the individual then tries, by subtle use of words, to persuade himself that the herd conforms to *his* ideas—or at least that it ought to. There are also occasions when the impulse produces extremely irrational effects in conjunction with the desire to understand. These will be examined in the chapter on Rationalization.

(7) MISCELLANEOUS DESIRES

For each man has (besides the generic aberrations belonging to his human nature) some individual cavern or den which breaks and corrupts the light of nature.—Francis Bacon.

Any desire which is unsatisfied is a potential danger to reality-thinking. From the many which goad us through our

---

[1] Trotter, op. cit., page 39. If anyone feels impelled to disagree with the views here expressed, I hope he will examine, before finally making up his mind, the evidence provided by W. Trotter, by J. H. Robinson in *The Mind in the Making* and by Pareto in *The Mind and Society*. The latter will keep him quiet a long time, even if it does not convince him.

lives, I have selected five which appear to me to be common to most people. These five:

The Desire to Understand,
The Desire to Feel Good,
The Desire for Excitement,
The Desire for Self-Assertion, and
The Desire to Conform,

we have already studied at some length. Except in the case of the first (where the irrational effects are so paradoxical), I have made little attempt to explain *why* the desires exist. For one thing, their existence can I think be assumed. For another, no amount of explanation would help us to decrease their strength, even if we wanted to, whereas explanation of how these desires may affect our thinking should help to make that thinking clearer.

Although the multitude of other desires with which we have not dealt are perhaps individually less important in this connection, this does not mean that they are collectively harmless. There are a number which tend to be largely unsatisfied in real life and which I will summarize here because they appear occasionally as motives for irrationality later in the book. Among these are:

The Desire for Order.

This is possibly an off-shoot of the self-preservation instinct and of the desire to avoid anxiety. Its satisfaction can often be perfectly rational, and it also appears to enter largely into aesthetic pleasure. On the other hand, it can lead to such ideas as that there *must* be justice in the world and consequently that apparent injustices or illogicalities either do not exist or are irrevocably ordained for a special purpose. It is also connected with what Pareto—unfortunately—calls the "instinct for making combinations". This expresses itself in a tendency to believe that phenomena which appear unrelated (e.g. stars and human life, pyramids and dates, palms and the future, vests and pants, etc.) *must* be somehow related in a way which is simple enough to be grasped by the human mind. It has therefore an important bearing on opinions about gambling, coincidences, astrology, etc.

The Desire or Impulse to Translate Emotion into some sort of Action.

This is familiar in such forms as flight, pugnacity, screams, laughter—even in talk, as when the lover cannot resist the temptation to bring the loved one somehow into the conversation. In civilized conditions the more extreme manifestations of this impulse are continually unsatisfied.

The Desire to Conserve Inviolate our Pre-conceived Opinions.

This is an off-shoot of the desire to understand, as is also:

The Desire to Persuade Others to our own Opinion.

This is the mainspring behind the remarkable ingenuity with which we invent linguistic disguises for unsound arguments. Perhaps the vainest of all human hopes are those induced by this desire—the hopes implicit in every serious conversation —and (if the talkers are much over thirty years old) almost inevitably doomed to disappointment.

The Sexual Desire.

Its manifold irrational expressions are too obvious to mention, even when this is possible.

In addition to these and many others, there are the desires and impulses which spring from repressions, complexes, inhibitions, etc., and which are peculiar to each individual. One person may have a "thing" about dirty ash-trays, another may have a "thing" about blue-chinned running-champions or about blue-behinded apes. There are people who have extraordinary likings for (say) certain types of voice, certain shapes of houses or of rooms. Again, one will find people who have an impulse to behave in some special way (sadistic or masochistic or provocative or rebellious) towards their friends, their superiors and their inferiors. All these may be signs of potentially unsatisfied desires. But it is important to remember that repressed desires are so common that they may be regarded as normal and therefore do not *as a general rule* give rise to what we should call extraordinary behaviour. It is never safe to assume, from the fact that one cannot trace any motive behind one's thoughts and actions,

that such a motive does not exist.   There are inner unrealized
desires which infest the dark corners of all our minds.   However, these are hardly amenable to classification since the only
thing they have in common is that our attempts to justify the
actions and opinions to which they give rise may lead us into
rationalization.

Finally, there are all those impulses which remain as
heritages from our remote and barbaric selves, who wanted to
feel safe in a very unsafe world.   These impulses affect our
attitude towards kings, great men, the aristocracy, etc.,
towards doctors and their medicine, towards genius and
abnormality, towards darkness and thunderstorms, myths and
legends, and towards all the ceremonious appendages of birth,
marriage, and death.   They are perhaps the most pervasive
of our irrational impulses and they will continue to be vital
factors in our ways of thinking so long as incalculable or
incomprehensible factors continue to affect our ways of living.
There may be less of these incalculable factors in our lives
now than there are in the lives of primitive peoples, but there
are still enough to make us think often in the same way as does
the primitive native.   The point is put neatly though inversely
in the following passage from an essay on " Magic Science
and Religion " by B. Malinowski[1] which summarizes part of
what he has to say about the attitude of the Melanesians
towards knowledge and magic.   " They (the Melanesians)
have . . . a whole system of principles of sailing, embodied
in a complex and rich terminology, traditionally handed on
and obeyed as rationally and consistently as is modern science
by modern sailors.   How could they sail otherwise under
eminently dangerous conditions in their frail primitive craft?

" But even with all their systematic knowledge, methodi-
cally applied, they are still at the mercy of powerful and
incalculable tides, sudden gales during the monsoon season and
unknown reefs.   And here comes in their magic, performed
over the canoe during its construction, carried out at the
beginning and in the course of expeditions and resorted to in
moments of real danger.   If the modern seaman, entrenched
in science and reason, provided with all sorts of safety
appliances, sailing on steel-built steamers, if even he has a
singular tendency to superstition—which does not rob him of
his knowledge or reason, nor make him altogether pre-logical

---

[1] In *Science Religion and Reality*, edited by Joseph Needham.

—can we wonder that his savage colleague, under much more precarious conditions, holds fast to the safety and comfort of magic ? "

As the general pattern of human behaviour makes some myths more acceptable than others, so the forms which irrational thought and non-rational emotion take are largely conditioned by the culture pattern of a particular society. Our society will therefore tend to think fairly uniformly in these respects. But all the same I need not do more than mention this body of non-rational and irrational thought. For one thing, it does not *tempt* us to irrationality; it is, when irrational, directly so. For another, most of its manifestations have a common method of diagnosis and cure, which consists in carefully testing the grounds for our beliefs, while being specially on our guard against bare assertions disguised as axioms. The significance of axioms and the validity of various types of ground for belief are discussed later.

PART III

METHODS OF IRRATIONALITY

(1) INTRODUCTION

We all appear to ourselves to be thinking all the time during our waking hours, and most of us are aware that we go on thinking while we are asleep, even more foolishly than when awake.
—James Harvey Robinson.

We have now studied five main, and various subsidiary, desires; and it has become clear that they are continually being frustrated. How, then, do we deal with these frustrations? We may imagine sometimes that we accept them passively. But they are much too alive and kicking for this. We cannot annihilate them by our stoicism, nor ensure that they have no repercussions on our thinking. We are forced, therefore, to make some effort to avoid the pain they bring.

The mental writhings—the twists and distortions—which result from this effort to avoid pain, are the " Methods of Irrationality " examined here.

In its worst manifestations the type of mental process which is commonly called Wishful Thinking dispenses entirely with anything that one might call a method; the wishful thinker merely believes whatever he wants to believe without recourse to reasoning of any kind. In consequence his conduct cannot in fairness be called irrational—it is more like plain lying. This sort of wishful thinking is thus in any case out of our province. Moreover, it can be easily diagnosed, if not by the patient himself, at any rate by his friends.

It is with the more elaborate thought-processes that we are concerned. In fact, one can almost say that the man who is in the habit of complicated thinking finds his very skill in manipulating those complications of the greatest help in the task of distorting reality to his own ends. This is merely to point the fact that it is not the tool but the workman who is to blame—that irrationality results from the abuse of those very mental processes which are the intrinsically neutral tools of rationality itself, and that the greater the skill the greater the potentialities for abuse. This may seem an exaggeration— until one thinks of the philosophers, whose emphatic disagreements prove that at least some of them must be thinking with quite wild irrationality. The matter is probably one of relative forces. Long practice in thinking will as a rule produce rational results *unless* the desire to distort is overpoweringly strong. "When a man is running out of the right road," said Francis Bacon, "his superior skill and swiftness will lead him proportionally further astray."

It is impossible, as Miss Stebbing has remarked,[1] "to discuss in an orderly manner the mistakes into which we are prone to fall in our efforts to think to some definite purpose. These failures are evidence of disorder in our thinking; they cannot be rigorously isolated nor classified in a neat logical manner. There are many ways of being wrong, but only one way of being right." Miss Stebbing is, I think, referring here to thinking which consciously strives to be rational. But her observation applies with equal or even greater relevance to my present subject—to thinking which unconsciously strives to be irrational. For the latter type of thinking not only makes use of all the fallacies and distortions that the former is prone to, it also presses into its service a number of little dodges of its own.

In Miss Stebbing's book, and in others on the same general subject (particularly *Straight and Crooked Thinking*, by R. H. Thouless, which gives an invaluable list of thirty-four dishonest tricks of argument), most of these fallacies, distortions and dodges are of course examined in detail. It is to such books that one must go for a comprehensive review of the processes of muddled thinking. However, these books do not examine the processes from the particular point of view of their adaptability to the purpose of satisfying the fantasy-thinking which springs from frustrated desires.

I have selected a few of the more common offenders in this respect and have re-classified them so as to fit the new purpose. But I must emphasize Miss Stebbing's reservation that no such classification can be logically exact, nor can its limits be sharply defined.

[1] *Thinking to Some Purpose.*

(2) SELECTION OF EVIDENCE

The human Intellect, in those things which have once pleased it (either because they are generally received and believed, or because they suit the taste), brings everything else to support and agree with them ; and though the weight and number of contradictory instances be superior, still it either overlooks or despises them, or gets rid of them by creating distinctions, not without great and injurious prejudice, that the authority of these previous conclusions may be maintained inviolate. And so he made a good answer, who, when he was shown, hung up in the temple, the votive tablets of those who had fulfilled their vows after escaping from shipwreck, and was pressed with the question, "Did he not then recognize the will of the gods ?" asked, in his turn, "But where are the pictures of those who have perished, notwithstanding their vows ?" The same holds true of almost every superstition—as astrology, dreams, omens, judgments, and the like— wherein men, pleased with such vanities, attend to those events which are fulfilments ; but neglect and pass over the instances where they fail (though this is much more frequently the case).
Francis Bacon. "Novum Organum."

It is a curious commentary on the limitations of the human brain that one should so often hear the phrase, "I pride myself on being able to see both sides of the question." What a depressing view of our capabilities is implied by that word "pride"! And what an odd assumption is suggested by the word "both"!

This chapter is intended, not to point the obvious fact that we tend to select the evidence in making our judgments, but to emphasize how great is the temptation to do so, how inevitable the process is, and how pervasive are its effects. In particular it is intended to bring out the fact that we hardly ever realize the extent to which we are forced—by circumstances and by the limitations of our brains—to select only the evidence which suits us.

In the chapter on the Desire to Understand we saw that our view of the world is inevitably more or less simplified. Similarly, when we collect a body of facts on which to base a proof, belief or judgment, we cannot help overlooking many of the available facts and—as a rule—many of the relevant facts. Theoretically there is no limit to the number of facts available and in consequence there is no way of describing or even comprehending all the true facts.[1] Luckily there is also

---

[1] Or the complete "reality", as it is sometimes called. This incidentally shows how futile are the attempts of people who try to describe and define this kind of "reality". Cf. the section below on Hypostatization.

no need to do so. In practical life all we need to do is to select *sufficient* of the evidence to justify a judgment which will enable us to deal adequately with the phenomenon in question.

There are numbers of things, such as tables, and some relatively unimportant problems, such as whether a table is made of wood, of whose many aspects we neither want nor need to grasp more than a few, and about which we are unlikely to have any strong pre-conceived opinions. On the other hand there are many things somewhat more complicated (such as our neighbour's behaviour to his wife, or his views on democracy) about which we may need to grasp as many aspects as possible. Our necessarily restricted view of the evidence will be unbiassed—though possibly still mistaken— only so long as we have no desire to believe one aspect of them rather than another. And this will only be so when they are unimportant to us. The danger in fact is greatest just when it is most necessary for us to be careful. And unless we remember the existence of all the evidence which we are perforce ignoring, we will be continually deceiving ourselves as to the validity of our opinions.

Our continual selection of evidence is not only inevitable. It is also to some extent advisable. Life is too short. We cannot spare the time to examine all the evidence before we form each opinion. We have to make a compromise between leaping in the dark and looking so long before we leap that we leap too late. The situation is thus analogous to that which we found when we were dealing with name-words and classification of knowledge as generalized and necessarily inexact aids in coping with the world.

The conclusion from this is that, *even when we genuinely wish to see all sides of a question*, we are as often as not debarred from doing so. Let us take a common example from domestic life. Imagine a long-standing relationship between two neighbours which culminates in a quarrel. Mrs. A. says she has done a great deal for Mrs. B., ever since Mrs. B. first came to live there. And now why does Mrs. B. show herself so ungrateful, refusing to lend her the mowing machine ? Mrs. B. says: " Well, Mrs. A. is really expecting a bit too much. She comes round and bosses me about and tells me what to do. Of course she *has* done a lot in the past ; I suppose she meant it kindly. But she forgets what *I've* done for *her*." The setting is familiar enough to everybody. The chief obstacle to a reconciliation is, paradoxically, the long-standingness of the relationship. For, by now, so many things have happened between Mrs. A. and Mrs. B. that neither of them can possibly remember them all—much less can remember all the aspects of each event.   However genuinely Mrs. B. (say) may wish to remember *all* the times that Mrs. A. has been kind or good and all the times that she herself has been the opposite, she just cannot do so.   On what principle then will her mind act in choosing which evidence to remember and which to forget?   On the pleasure-pain principle, inevitably.   She will select the evidence which helps her to believe what it pleases her to believe.   And what it will please her to believe is that she has been Good—that she has been generous and grateful.   It is unfortunate that this entails believing—and trying to make everyone else believe—that Mrs. A. has been ungenerous and ungrateful ; but it cannot be helped. The same processes will occur in Mrs. A.'s mind, with the result that, whatever the real truth of the matter, neither of the two is likely to get within miles of it.   The quarrel indeed has little chance of ever being resolved unless Mrs. B. becomes aware of the fact that she has a desire to feel Good which conflicts with her desire to be rational.   In such a case she will still have a distorted view of the question, but at least she will realize that it is distorted—and that she cannot rely upon it. It hardly needs emphasizing that Mrs. B. will have to be an exceptional woman to do anything so uncomfortably harmful to her self-confidence and her self-esteem, though the fact remains that in the long run both she and Mrs. A. would almost certainly benefit.   On the other hand, what probably does need emphasizing is the improbability of Mrs. B. wanting to be rational at all.   In most differences of opinion the parties concerned are so passionately absorbed in the effort to remember all the evidence in their own favour that they have no room in their minds for any other considerations.   As the argument goes on the effort becomes more and more feverish, until sometimes tempers rise to the point that they can only be properly satisfied by action.   Then matters are pretty hopeless.   For, even if the parties are sufficiently civilized to restrain themselves from violence, they are left with a quivering surplus of unspent energy, which usually goes on, for hours after the shouting is over, selecting further pieces of evidence and eagerly feeding them to the flames of anger and hatred.

This is a domestic example of the way the Desire to Feel Good uses Selection of Evidence as an irrational means to its own satisfaction. There is a curious corollary to this which is very common and which might be called Invention of Evidence. This consists in regarding as evidence of one's own goodness something which, in fact, is not evidence at all. In home life the method is to start a conversation by stating " I never wish to say unpleasant things about other people, but I do think that so-and-so ought not to have done such-and-such ", and then to continue with the comfortable feeling that somehow one's generosity of spirit has been proved. It is a method which comes in very useful when there happens by some mischance to be no actual evidence at all in one's favour. In political life the method takes some such form as " No one could have the interests of the nation closer to his heart than I "—a statement for which as a rule no evidence whatever is offered and which is a pure waste of the audience's time. Incidentally, it is often the prelude to a common fallacy, which links up the desire to be thought good with the desire to be thought efficient, and which consists in the assumption by a statesman that his (assumed) exalted patriotism automatically confers on him a divine freedom from error. " I am an upright and honourable man," he asserts, " and therefore you must trust in the correctness of my judgment." The converse fallacy, equally popular, is that anyone who disagrees with the statesman's opinion is foully impugning his honour—is, in fact, not playing the game.

Selection of evidence is a mental process which operates not only on the facts which make up a phenomenon (whether it be a quarrel, or " unemployment ", or Soviet Russia), but also on the facts which are the causes of phenomena. One of the commonest and most pernicious results of injudicious selection of causes is the finding of scape-goats. And the reason why it is so common is that it springs not only from the desire to understand but also from the desire to feel good and to convert anger (which has not been satisfied by action) into righteous indignation. The rise of anti-Semitism is an obvious example. There are a number of quite strong motives (as opposed to reasons) for thinking that the Jews are the cause of various troubles: We would like to be able to understand why the world is in a mess. But the causes are so complex that we have to select a few from the many.

We would also like to believe that *we* cannot be blamed—that we are Good. Therefore we reject any cause which might point towards us. We are made angry and irritable by the mess, and we want to be able to direct our anger towards something, in the form either of action or of righteous indignation. We have already ruled out ourselves as that something. We therefore need to find something else—something, or preferably some person or persons[1] which is not of us, but is among us, and which is as near to being a simple entity or individuality as possible. These specific needs are fulfilled by the Jews.

This statement of the case is itself a simplification, for naturally the workings of our minds are much more complicated than that. But this does not matter very much so long as we are aware of how much it simplifies.

The favourite domestic sport of finding scape-goats is motivated roughly in the same way, that is to say, by the desire to give vent to irritation and to believe that anyone rather than oneself has been behaving foolishly or selfishly. It depends partly on the ability to select evidence of someone else's bad or foolish behaviour—to pick on the other person's faults. It also depends to some extent on rationalization, which is dealt with later. The irritation itself, by the way, can be caused by general malaise or indigestion or sometimes by suppressed guilt over one's own laziness or misdemeanour. In the latter case, one has an extra motive for scape-goat hunting in the desire to cover up the memory of one's own fault by concentrating on someone else's. The finer points of the sport are of course to be observed not so much in the family as in the small group—the boarding house, the factory shop, the school, the university college.

When the desire to understand combines with the desire to keep our prejudices inviolate, it finds selection of evidence a most convenient tool. If we have formed an opinion about a subject, we find it a nuisance to have to re-form it later on, especially when it is based on a sentiment formed in childhood.[2]

---

[1] The reason for this preference is dealt with later under Hypostatization.

[2] "Many of our strongest sentiments are formed in childhood. . . . And once a strong sentiment has been formed it is very tenacious of existence and very resistant to change. Evidence which runs counter to it is usually rejected by the mind; evidence in support of it is sought and may be manufactured." Henry A. Mess, *Social Structure*, page 35. Mr. Mess quotes Bernard Hart's definition of a sentiment or complex as "a system of connected ideas, with a strong emotional tone and a tendency to produce actions of a certain definite type." *The Psychology of Insanity*, pages 61-2.

Once an opinion is formed, the strong temptation to hold on to it at all costs makes us forget how much we originally simplified the issue. The result is that in making our selection from all the myriad facts which are presented to our attention day by day and which are nearly all of them evidence for or against some opinion of ours, we tend to ignore those which do not " fit in ". If this happens in the case even of rational opinions, founded originally on some evidence, how much more must it happen in the case of opinions which were never anything more than comfortable distortions of reality ? With such opinions there is a great increase both in temptation and also in the amount of evidence to be avoided. There seems to be practically no limit to the amount of evidence that a man can ignore when he feels sufficiently strongly disposed to do so. The bigot is by no means rare, and the older and more authoritative he becomes the more bigoted he gets. For when an opinion has in the course of years so guided the selection of evidence in its favour and has forgotten, if it ever realized, the humble simplification of its origin, it turns into a prejudice and fights like a die-hard for its existence.

It is obviously impossible to give examples of all the varieties of irrational belief based on selection of evidence. For any belief whatsoever, provided that it is satisfactory to the holder, can fulfil the conditions. The more fantastic types of rumour, for instance, probably owe their vitality to the fact that the desire for excitement will tempt us to remember the rumours which are dramatic (" But people actually *saw* snow on their boots ") and to forget the dull, but possibly true, facts which contradict them. It is, however, worth emphasizing that, the more desires a belief satisfies, the more tempting it is and the more dogmatic it becomes. Many dogmatic beliefs about morality appear to gain strength because they are inspired not only by the desire to understand but also by the desire to feel good, by the desire for self-assertion and, as Bertrand Russell suggests, by the desire to inflict cruelty with a good conscience. But ideas of morality are usually based on some philosophical or ethical system. And, since such systems can, and often do, incorporate every variety of irrational mental process, they will be dealt with later.

I hope that I have not appeared to suggest that it is impossible to form a considered and rational opinion about a complex subject. I am concerned only to point out that to do so requires more caution and more trouble than we usually exercise. In particular, we must search our minds beforehand, find out what we would *like* to be true—and, having got this clear—constantly discount our natural tendency in that direction.

(3) ADOPTION OF COMFORTABLE CONCEPTS

"Self-determination," one of them insisted. "Arbitration!" cried another.

"Co-operation?" suggested the mildest of the party.

"Confiscation!" answered an uncompromising female.

I, too, became slightly intoxicated by the sound of these vocables. And were they not the cure for all our ills?

"Inebriation!" I chimed in, "Inundation, Afforestation, Flagellation, Transubstantiation, Co-education!"

—Logan Pearsall Smith. "More Trivia."

The word " concept " has been defined as " an abstract general notion or idea ; also, any notion combining elements into the idea of one object ". The " idea ", say, which any one person has of what he calls " democracy ", is thus a concept. And the word " democracy " itself is, accurately speaking, a label we give to this concept in order to be able to refer to it conveniently in thought and conversation. But, although there is deceptively just the one word for our use, the number of different concepts which it denotes seems almost as large as the number of people who use the word. Even if one narrows the meaning of the word down to " the system of government in Great Britain today ", it remains a surprisingly promiscuous label, in that there are innumerable divergences of opinion among individuals as to which parts of the system are " truly " democratic. This promiscuity of words—a most useful tool in distorting reality—is discussed in the next chapter. In the meantime, the fact remains that the whole subject of how government works in Great Britain is one of those things of whose innumerable aspects we can never hope to grasp more than a few. It follows that the idea of it in any one person's mind must necessarily be more or less of a simplification. As such, there is of course nothing irrational about it; for, as we have seen, a certain amount of simplification of complex phenomena is a necessary basis for the systematization of knowledge. One may say, therefore, that any one person's idea of democracy is a conveniently simplified concept.

However, because it is satisfactory to feel we understand things, we are always being tempted to forget how far this simplification has gone. When this happens—when we have managed to persuade ourselves into complacent acceptance of some simplification as being true and comprehensive, we have allowed a convenient concept to turn into what, for want of an accepted term, I am calling a " Comfortable Concept ". The epithet " comfortable " is, I think, an appropriate one because it expresses the satisfaction we get from feeling that such a concept is rounded, just and complete—that there are no tiring or worrying mental reservations attached to it.

The temptation to adopt a comfortable concept is naturally greatest when it will help us to believe something that we would like to believe. " Nazism " for instance is, like democracy, a concept. Or rather, to be more accurate, the word " Nazism " is a label for several concepts, with a certain amount of confusion as to which concept it is referring to at any one time. Sometimes it is used for " the ideology of the German National-Socialist Party "; sometimes for " the behaviour of the members of this party " (not necessarily conformable to its ideology); sometimes for " the system of state organization in Germany "; and so on. Each of these concepts (or meanings of the word " Nazism ") is itself almost as complicated a subject as democracy; each must therefore be conveniently simplified in our minds. A very comfortable version of the last of them was the basis of a political belief which enjoyed some popularity in respectable English circles between September 1939 and June 1941. " Of course," it was said over the tea-cups, " there's practically no difference between Nazism and Communism." (Before 1939 Nazism had not yet become the enemy and was thus not yet a Bad Thing. While after June 1941 the belief was not so often put into words, though it is probable that it still nestles cosily in respectable and circular minds.) The only possible basis for such an opinion appears to be a skilful selection of the evidence so as to form two similar comfortable concepts about Nazism and Communism—a process which I imagine operates somewhat on the following lines: First; in Germany there is a dictatorship which allows only one political party and which stringently controls industry. Therefore, Nazism can be adequately and comprehensively described by saying that it consists of a dictatorship which allows only one party and which stringently controls industry. Secondly; in Russia there is a dictatorship which ditto and ditto. Therefore Communism also is adequately described by saying ditto, ditto and ditto. "Why there's just no difference at all. One's as bad as the other." I hasten to add that I am not forgetting the many other similarities which can be traced between Nazism and Communism (as also between Nazism and British Imperialism, for that matter). But they must of course be set against the innumerable differences. In any case, I am only concerned to point out the essential irrationality of imagining that a short, simple and easily grasped comparison between two such complex organizations has any appreciable value.

The type of Comfortable Concept just illustrated is very common, though perhaps not in quite such an extreme form, and is surprisingly varied in its application. Further examples are dealt with fully and entertainingly under the heading of " On being misled by half, and other fractions ", in Miss Susan Stebbing's *Thinking to Some Purpose*. There is, however, one important but depressing general conclusion to be drawn. This is that, in considering a subject of any importance, we should always beware of an opinion which dresses itself up in engagingly simple disguise. For, unfortunately, conciseness and objective truth are temperamentally incompatible, and it is only by the exercise of the utmost skill and delicacy that they can even temporarily be reconciled.

The pattern of truth is complexity; but complexity is structurally incompatible with the pattern of our understanding, so that truth has inevitably to be lopped into conciseness before it is digestible. It is futile to try and encompass the whole truth if it is too voluminous for us to grasp it; and a three-quarter truth, or even a half truth, in the hand is worth more than a whole truth in the bush, always provided that the part is seen to be less than the whole.

There is no end to the usefulness—and potential danger—of fractional truths. For example, there are " poetic truths " —not only in poetry but also in prose and painting—which are not purely subjective. At their best they provide us with one of the most valuable kinds of simplified concept—the kind that illuminates the world for us by communicating emotional associations (as well as objective facts) in a rhythmic or formal context which makes us receptive, and in a sufficiently concise form to be relatively easily grasped.

In much pure poetry it is clearly a mistake to regard the poet's statements as being intended to convey objective truths. Orpheus with his lute did not—as a matter of fact—make trees bow themselves. Nor did a little birdie say, " Let me fly, Mother, let me fly away." Statements such as these are a form of nonsense. But what about statements like Shakespeare's that all the world's a stage, or Keats' that truth is beauty and beauty truth? These get nearer to objective truth. But all the same they remain what I. A. Richards calls " pseudo-statements "—they remain statements which must be believed in a different way from those which are intended to be objective. " It is only when we introduce inappropriate kinds of believing into poetry that danger arises," says Mr. Richards.[1] Coleridge pointed out the reason for this in his *Biographia Literaria* ; " A poem is that species of composition, which is opposed to works of science, by proposing for its *immediate* object pleasure, not truth."

Of course to get a true view of any situation there are emotional aspects that must be taken into account. Even a stone wall, when we look at it, has associations in our mind—some of them peculiar to that particular wall, most of them peculiar to us. A poet who is trying to communicate some of his own emotional associations will be prized as a poet in so far as his associations are sharable by others. And if he does succeed in making others feel something of what he feels, he will have illuminated a new aspect of the " whole truth " about his subject. But it will be only a fractional truth. In addition, in so far as the poet's emotions are personal and are not objective, they cannot provide a basis for discussion on the plane of reality-thinking. No one can say that what he feels about things is what we *must* feel.

However, a " poetic " truth does succeed in giving a

[1] *Science and Poetry* (1935), page 67.

picture—or communicating an experience—which is very often unobtainable by any other method. In the case, for instance, of a stone wall, a scientific analysis of the wall and a psycho-analysis of the mind of the beholder might get nearer to the objective truth, but what a long time it would take and how boring it would be !

Keats' famous aphorism is an excellent example of a poetic truth which sounds quite objective and which has all the conciseness of a convenient concept. " Beauty is truth, truth beauty." This is a statement which, says Keats, " is all ye know on earth, and all ye need to know ". It is certainly a pleasant concept; it comes at the end of a profoundly moving ode, and it illuminates what might be called a fractional truth, the whole truth being very roughly that some things which are true are (according to *some* definitions of the word " beauty ") also beautiful. Keats himself tells us that this convenient concept should be taken as all we need to know ; i.e. as a comfortable concept, and there is no way of telling whether he believed what he was saying. Some of his readers have certainly believed him.

To summarize, the kind of convenient concept that may be called a " poetic truth " is invaluable because it makes it possible to state an idea in an illuminating (though relatively short and inaccurate) form and because this form will fire the reader's imagination in a way that an accurate (and therefore long and boring) statement would not do. Keats' examination of the meaning of the word " beauty " takes a dozen lovely words. C. K. Ogden and I. A. Richards' scientific examination of the same subject (in the *Meaning of Meaning*) takes seven thousand utilitarian words.

The concise form of Keats' statement almost makes it an epigram. And epigrams, because they usually underline a new and surprising aspect of what we already feel we know, have a peculiar fascination of their own. When they pretend to have a universal application, this fascination can make them doubly dangerous. It is true of course that one can usually recognize an epigrammatic simplification as such when one sees it in isolation. But it so happens that one of the most persuasive tricks of the public speaker consists in stating a half-truth in epigrammatic form, while at the same time choosing words which have sufficiently strong emotional force to carry us away and make us incapable of rational scepticism

" Save us from epigrams," says H. G. Wells. " The world
has gone out of its way time after time through simplifications
and short-cuts." I could easily diverge at this point into a
chapter on the Dangers of Emotive Oratory as designed to
make us swallow Comfortable Concepts. But such books as
Miss Stebbing's and R. H. Thouless' have already done the
job for me. All I need add is one small warning. Everyone
knows the sharp pleasure that one can get from a witty and
epigrammatic remark. But what happens if one analyses
that pleasure? How much of it is occasioned by the wit and
how much by the fact that the remark has bolstered up a
pre-conceived opinion? And how often one answers the
question by saying to oneself, " That puts it beautifully—its
just what I think myself."

A Comfortable Concept can, in favourable circumstances,
be manufactured from any simplification of reality. And,
since the circumstances nearly always are favourable, the
number of possible examples is enough to make one's mind
boggle. It boggles even more when one thinks of the number
of comfortable beliefs that can derive from any one Comfortable Concept—and of the even greater number that can derive,
by permutations and combinations, from two or three Comfortable Concepts gathered together.

Nearly all popular opinions about medicine and disease,
for instance, are simplifications which the patent medicine
advertisers help to turn into such comfortable beliefs as that
headaches are " simply " a matter of stomach-acidity and that
therefore they can be cured by taking so-and-so's brand of
powder, or that " inner cleanliness " is the royal road to outer
spotlessness. It is very natural; we should all be delighted
if it really were a simple and easy matter to cure our ailments.
Such comfortably simplified beliefs lead their users into various
further labyrinths of irrational thinking and bad-tempered
argument. These are fully analysed and clarified with the
aid of examples under the heading of " Potted Thinking " in
Miss Stebbing's *Thinking to Some Purpose*, to which again I
should like to refer the interested reader.

There is yet a further type of Comfortable Concept which
acts upon language—the basis of most reasoning—and which
is a great favourite because it can be a powerful support for
any kind of irrational opinion. It is considered in the next
chapter.

(4) COMFORTABLE CONCEPTS ABOUT THE
MEANINGS OF WORDS

The belief that words have a meaning of their own account is a relic of primitive word magic, and it is still a part of the air we breath in nearly every discussion.—C. K. Ogden.

There is a peculiar tedium, a special kind of boredom which seems inseparable from books on words. . . .

—Logan Pearsall Smith. "Words and Idioms."

At the beginning of the last chapter I suggested that there was no correct definition of "democracy". Similarly, in discussing Keats' attitude towards "beauty", I suggested that this word could be defined in a number of different and incompatible ways. To some these statements may have seemed rash and I now propose to try and defend them. This involves an excursion into Semantics, the science which deals with the evolution and function of language and which, according to taste, may be regarded either as an unsettling and irritating exercise in hair-splitting or as one of the most exciting and illuminating of modern intellectual adventures.

Broadly speaking, my contention is that no word of the type of "democracy" or "beauty" or "instinct" or "sin' can be regarded as having one, and only one, true meaning. As it happens, this is a situation which can I think be shown to hold good with the great majority of words—with all words in fact which act as *labels*, whether for concrete things like houses or for sense perceptions (e.g. qualities such as "blue", "hard", etc.) or for actions (e.g. "move", "think", etc.) or for attributes such as "good", "crooked", "just", etc., or for the abstractions from these qualities such as "democracy", "beauty", and "redness". But for our purpose the words that matter most are the abstract ones, especially those that have acquired an emotional or ethical value; e.g. *justice*, which has a "good" value; *tyranny*, which has a "bad" one; *heroism* and *atrocity*, which are variously emotive, and the words which are unmentionable because they have a sexually emotive value. There is, of course, no sharp distinction to be made between emotive and ethical words. *Sin*, for example, combines both qualities. And any word with an emotive effect tends to acquire bad or good associations depending on the moral views prevailing in the group which uses it. The words " Bolshevik " and " reactionary " have both acquired " bad " values through being used emotively in political argument.

The belief, or unthinking assumption, that such words have a one and only correct meaning is, I think, a comfortable concept. And once adopted, it makes it almost impossible for the user to detect the irrationality of the arguments which are based on it. " But ", you will perhaps say, " that is all nonsense ! Of course there is such a thing as beauty. I know just what it is. It's—er—let's see . . . it's all a matter of significant form . . . and harmonious relations . . . and then there's the beauty of nature. . . . Naturally it's difficult to put it precisely into words. But that doesn't prove it can't be done. After all there must be some quality—or essence or whatever you like to call it—that is common to all things which are beautiful. It's this essence that I'm talking about. The philosophers and aestheticians, whose job it is to do so, will have defined it."

They have indeed !—in at least sixteen different and mostly incompatible ways. You have only to consult them, or better still, to consult Messrs. Ogden and Richards (in their chapter, to which I have already referred, on the meaning of beauty in *The Meaning of Meaning*) to find out just how different these various definitions are—so different and, in some cases, so incompatible that there is no possibility that there can be any property common to them all, and there is no way of deciding that one definition is more correct, more " true ", than the others. The answer in fact seems to be not that there is such *a* thing as " beauty ", but that there are numbers of different concepts, or emotions, which have all been given the same label, sometimes because there is an actual similarity between them and sometimes, on the basis of a fancied similarity, because there just aren't enough labels to go round. That is to say, since it would obviously be impracticable to invent a new label for each and every one of the infinite number of emotions, fictions and facts which constitute our experience, and of which none is, strictly speaking, identical with any other, it is inevitable that the great majority should be referred to by using already existing labels, which, though they may not fit exactly, will fit well enough for practical purposes, the chief of these purposes being of course to help classify them according to their use value.[1]

Naturally, since the speaker hopes to make somebody else understand what he means, he must choose a label which has already been applied to something which is reasonably similar to the thing he is now concerned with. *But that is as far as the similarity need go.* This is a most important point, and is worth amplifying because one of the arguments in favour of the belief that a label-word has one essentially true meaning is based on the erroneous assumption that, since the fundamental purpose of such words is to identify similar things, *all* the things identified by a single word must therefore be similar. Suppose that the label " beautiful " has been applied to a quality " A " of a work of art. Then " B ", another quality which is similar to " A " will also be called beautiful. And so will " C ", because it is similar to " B " . . . and " D ", because it is similar to " C " . . . and so on, up to (say) " Q ". All of these different qualities will have been called by one person or another " beautiful ". And each will have been similar to those immediately before and after it in the sequence. But there is no reason whatsoever why " A " and " Q " themselves should be similar. After that series of changes they may have nothing in common at all, and it may be almost impossible to imagine how the same label could have been applied to two things so different from each other— indeed quite impossible, unless one is aware of the fact that this label has also been applied to the dozen or so other things from " B " to " P ". If one is not aware of this fact, if one finds it too inconvenient to grasp the complexity and diversity of meaning of such a word as " beauty ", one will naturally take it for granted that the qualities " A " and " Q ", because they are both " beautiful ", cannot really be so very different —that there *must* be some essence which is common to both of them.

But, as I hope I have shown, there need not be—and in practice often is not—anything whatsoever common to them. The common factor is to be found in the attitudes or emotions of the users of the words, not in the outside objective world. One may quite legitimately say that " A " has beauty and that

---

[1] See above, page 16. Cf. also *The Psychology of Reasoning*, by Eugenio Rignano (1923), pages 109 ff., for a demonstration of the theory that we classify things according to their value in satisfying our emotional or instinctive needs.

"Q" has beauty, but these two words "beauty" may refer
to two quite different and incompatible things, as different and
incompatible as the book that a turf accountant makes and the
unwritten book that is shaping itself in some author's mind.

The situation is the same in the case of other words, such
as "justice", "sin" and "humour", which are used, like
the word "beauty", to refer to qualities separately from the
objects they qualify. It can also be shown to be analogous,
as I have said, in the case of other types of abstractions and
in fact in the case of any word which acts as a label.[1]

Sometimes the situation is so obvious that no one questions
it and the word is in consequence called ambiguous. The
most easily recognized ambiguities occur when at least one of
the meanings of the word is concrete. Thus one can nearly
always tell from the context whether the word "table" is
referring to a solid object or to a mathematical abstraction.
But these are very simple ambiguities. The less concrete
a word is the more ambiguous it tends to become. "Dis-
crimination", "enterprise", "shock"—there are thousands
of such words whose vagueness is generally acknowledged.
And it seems only to be expected that, as one gets away from
concrete and scientific words, these ambiguities should become
progressively more complicated. For the more comprehensive
and old-in-years words become the more varied and confused
are the meanings they acquire, until finally there begins even
to be wide variation between the *kinds* of things they refer to.
As Mr. I. A. Richards points out,[2] "They are the servants
of too many interests to keep to single clearly defined jobs.
Technical words in the sciences are like adzes, planes, gimlets
or razors. A word like ' experience ' or ' feeling ' or ' true ' is
like a pocket-knife."

As it happens, this increasing ambiguity, or rather multi-
guity, seems to be recognized by most people. But it is only
recognized up to a point. It is recognized, for instance, as far
as (say) "nation" in such a scale of increasing abstractions
as "table", "house", "village", "country" and so on.

1 Scientific words may be said to be the exceptions which test the rule,
since by definition they are of no value to specialists unless their meanings
are confined within narrow limits. But directly a word ceases to be purely
"scientific" it ceases to be an exception. Such words as "gas" and "reflection" were once scientific; they now have sufficient diversity of meaning to
be useless to the scientist unless they are first carefully defined, i.e. unless the
scientist indicates which of their various meanings he intends them to refer to.

2 *How to Read a Page* (1943), page 23.

But when one goes farther up the scale, via " government ",
" fascism " and " tyranny " to such advanced abstractions as
" justice " and " sin ", there is an odd tendency to relapse
into the belief that the many meanings have become one. The
reason for this is probably that, beyond a certain point, the
varieties of meaning become too numerous to be easily grasped
and, in consequence, it is more comfortable to believe that the
resultant confusion masks a simple " essence ", than that it
covers up a multitude of different meanings, all claiming by
right of usage a certain validity.[1]

This plethora of meanings, unfortunate in itself, is rendered
doubly unfortunate by the fact that it always attaches itself
to those words which, in acquiring during the years their
" richness of meaning ", have inevitably acquired as well a
pronounced emotional or ethical value. No one is likely to
feel strongly about any subject concerning tables or chairs,
or about (say) " biometry " which, being a comparatively
new scientific word, still has a very well defined meaning and
still lacks any emotional associations.[2] When experiments
in biometry are being discussed no one gets heated, but when
abstractions like " beauty ", or " sin ", or " justice " are
involved in argument the situation becomes pregnant with
irrational and irascible possibilities.

I have here stated one side of a controversial question in a
very bald and simplified manner. The whole question is of
course much more fully examined in the (comparatively few)
books that deal specifically with the function of language,

---

[1] For an amplification of the point, cf. J. S. Mill, *A System of Logic*,
Book IV, Chap. III and IV, " Of Naming " and " Of the Principles of
Definition ". " Aristotle and his followers were well aware that there are such
things as ambiguities of language and delighted in distinguishing them. But
they never suspected ambiguities in (certain) cases. . . . Accordingly they
wasted infinite pains in endeavouring to find a definition which would serve for
several distinct meanings at once. . . ."

[2] In confirmation of this it may be noted (a) that poets do not find scientific
words of any value until they have become so widely used as to cease to be
scientific ; and (b) that a large number of euphemisms owe their popularity
to the fact that they replace a direct Anglo-Saxon (and therefore long-estab-
lished) word by a medical, scientific, or foreign word ; that is to say, they
replace a word which has an embarrassingly powerful emotive force by a word
which has practically none. This is incidentally why the euphemisms for
" privy " have rung such remarkable changes, from lavatory, via W.C., bath-
room, cloakroom, " geography of the house ", retiring-room to the latest but
not least delightful American example, " comfort-station ". As each new
word began to lose its freshness and innocence, it had to give way to another
as yet uncontaminated.

such as the *Meaning of Meaning*, already mentioned, *Communication*, by Karl Britton, and, in a less abstruse vein, *The Tyranny of Words*, by Stuart Chase. I have, however, risked this bald statement of opinion because it vitally affects our attitude towards those elements of language whose manipulation forms the basis of all discussion and nearly all reasoning, and because, if one allows the correctness of the view I am advocating, it follows that the widespread misunderstanding of its implications is at the root of a great part of the irrationality which is rampant in the world.

In outlining this view I have followed the fundamental plan of my whole subject by emphasizing the unrealized motives which would tend in any case to make people reluctant to admit such a view. It certainly seems clear that the belief that there is one, and one only, true meaning to a word fulfils all the conditions of a Comfortable Concept. Though this does not prove the belief to be wrong, it does at least show that the belief should be suspect. Moreover, even when consciously repudiated, its magical power is such that it may remain as a concealed assumption actively influencing a man's thoughts.

I have tried at the same time to emphasize the undeniable fact that, whichever view is correct, people are in practice continually using the same words to refer to different things—a fact which, when over-looked, is fatal to rational and calm discussion. Moreover, it often happens in argument that a person manages without realizing it to make one word refer *simultaneously* to two different things and in so doing makes confusion worse by confounding his opponent. I will however return to this point later. For the moment I need only point out that the tendency to ignore how many meanings a word may have is naturally greatest in those who have a settled conviction that it should only have one.

The arguments that result when two people are using the same words, but mean different things by them, obviously have no chance of coming to a peaceful conclusion unless at least one of the protagonists wakes up to what is happening. Even then, if one of them happens to believe that *his* meaning of the word is the only correct one, the argument merely alters its focus and goes on with unabated ardour and increased fury. Arguments of this sort—as to what is the *true* nature of "reality" or "knowledge" or "life" or what you will— are a favourite diversion of adolescents and metaphysical philosophers and, if one accepts the theory I am advocating, are clearly an expense of thought in a waste of irrelevance.[1]

I think that many of the people who argue about Free-Will and Determinism, for instance, do so because they fail to define exactly what they themselves mean by these words and omit to ask their opponents how *they* are defining them. The difficulty is increased by the fact that the expression "Free-Will" has a very common meaning which is slightly and confusingly different from that which it is given in the Free-Will-Determinism controversy. In the accepted common usage it implies freedom of the human being to make a choice between alternatives, which is independent of any external force and is conditioned only by his own reasoning powers and by his own inborn or acquired impulses and preferences. In the other usage it is contrasted, for want of another expression, with Determinism, a belief in Determinism implying that there is always an antecedent cause of any impulse, emotion or action. In this latter case, therefore, Free-Will is taken to imply that the human being is able to make a choice which—on occasion at least—is entirely independent of any previous cause, which is in fact a sort of *Deus ex machina*.

Thus, in a discussion, I may say that men have no Free-Will—that human actions are determined—using (but omitting to state that I am using) the expression "Free-Will" in its second sense. I will be intending to imply roughly the following: Though a man is able, uninfluenced by any external predestination, to make a choice between two alternatives, this choice is not completely a matter of chance but depends on one of the alternatives seeming preferable (if only for the slightest of reasons) to the other; and the things that will influence the man in preferring one to the other (i.e. that will determine his choice) are, not an immaterial will or soul, but his present desires and impulses, which in turn are conditioned by his heredity, upbringing and environment.

If you, arguing with me, were to find out what I really meant, you might or might not agree with me. However, you are hardly likely to find out what I really mean, for such a long and boring definition would unduly clog the easy flow of talk. There is nothing more profoundly boring—as the opprobrious flavour of the word "pedantic" shows—than a

[1] This statement will be developed in Part IV, and will then I hope seem less dogmatic.

conversation which takes care to be accurate and rational. With things as they are the discussion is in any case doomed to futility. But worse is to follow. You take it for granted that what I must mean by " Free-Will " is what you mean by it. And what you mean is perhaps as near as damn it to the first usage given above. In fact we are—if we only knew it— very near to agreement. And yet we are very far. You have just heard me apparently denying the power of a man's own " personality " to make a choice. " But there *must* be Free-Will," you expostulate. Soon both you and I are busily but unconsciously using all our important words in two senses at once, and the argument becomes so involved that there is no chance of our ever getting back to the beginning and down to definitions.

Of course you may all along have been using Free-Will in its second sense. In that case we will be disagreeing fundamentally and not much harm is done, unless the argument degenerates into an argument about what the words *should* mean. As I hope to show later it will then depend for its heat on the passion with which we respectively hold our preconceived opinions.

Although there appears to be no rational basis for asserting that one rather than another of the various meanings a word has in practice acquired is the " true " meaning, one can of course assess the relative validity of the various meanings as depending directly on the wideness of their acceptance. This is, incidentally, what compilers of dictionaries do. But even then, especially in the case of abstract words, one can do little more than indicate the *kind* of meaning that is most generally used, as witness any dictionary definition of any abstract word. " Democracy ", with which we have been concerned, provides a good example. According to one dictionary the kind of meaning that is most commonly used is stated as " Government directly by the people collectively ". This definition itself is so vague that one could argue for days about it. To take only one point: what precisely is the meaning of " the people " ? Does it include *all* the people ? The answer is vague, sometimes it does and sometimes it doesn't. In the Greek democracy it did not include slaves or women. In the England of 1830 it did not, according to Brougham, include the working classes. The " people " were the middle classes —the working class was the " populace ". In early twentieth century England, which was widely called a democracy, it did not include women, though nowadays it does so. In some states of the U.S.A. today it does not include those who cannot afford to pay a poll-tax. And so on. If anybody is disposed at this point to object that past democracies were not " true " democracies they may be asked what .evidence they can produce to back their denial. Attention can also be turned to the further question of the precise definition of " collectively " or " government " or to comparisons between the actual organization of present-day "democratic" states. And at the end of the argument the result will be seen to be the same as it is with the word " beauty ", in that there are numbers of different meanings. It is true that some kinds must be more generally accepted than others. But, apart from that, what it boils down to is that some meanings are used by some people and others by other people. That appears to be all there is to it. For, in order to alter the situation, one would have to postulate some criterion with a divine rightness which is quite independent of mere personal opinion. This is of course what is done by people who believe in a Divinity. But, since the arbitrary nature of Divinities is to act in a way which transcends rational explanation, a rational discussion has perforce to ignore their laws. In any case it must be admitted that there is in the world a certain amount of disagreement as to which Divinities and which absolute laws *are* the absolute ones. In other words—and to come back to the subject—the words " sin ", " good ", " bad ", etc., have many different and incompatible meanings.

I feel I shall probably be accused at this point of having reduced my argument *ad absurdum*. If, it will be objected, the meanings of all the words we use are really as vague as all that, we might as well give up talking at all. But does this, in fact, follow ? Only, I would suggest, in the mind of the sort of idealist who produces his desire for perfection *ad extremum* —who persuades himself that a thing is no use whatever unless it is perfect. (I would further suggest that this attitude is derived from an overpowering desire to believe that things *can* be perfect. It is basically the attitude of the fanatic and the lover—neither of them outstandingly rational types.)

The meanings of words may be so vague that the world is full of deadly misunderstandings, but this does not mean that if there were no words at all the number of misunderstandings would decrease. Our words may in fact be imperfect labels but, so long as they do not pretend to be more than that, so long as we take the trouble to define them when necessary with care, they are invaluable aids to mutual understanding. If, on the other hand, their imperfections are unanalysed, they transform themselves from convenient and unassuming labels into magic talismans with the power of producing, in our fantasy-thinking, all the pleasures of poetry, but in our reality-thinking, all the pains of discord, denunciation and death. For, in spite of civilization, the human race does not appear yet to have overcome its primitive tendency to invest words with an almost magical power. Its attitude towards swearing provides an obvious but comparatively unimportant example. However, I must refer anyone who is interested in this aspect of the subject to the specialist writers on Semantics.

Mankind's irrational desires will naturally seize every opportunity to misuse language in the pursuit of their own ends. The belief that there is one correct meaning of a word is, as I have suggested, a Comfortable Concept motivated by the desire to understand. But when it comes to deciding what that one meaning shall be, other desires may become involved as well, especially when the word in question has an ethical value. For example, if I am convinced that there is only one correct meaning of the word " justice ", I will be tempted to believe that this meaning is one which not only includes in its scope those aspects of the law that I personally approve of but, even more important, *excludes* those aspects that I dislike. To put it the other way round : when a word has an admirable aroma about it, I will want to grab it as a label for something I personally like, in the hope that this something will then begin to smell as sweet. This is after all only to be expected. There is nothing essentially irrational in my disapproving of (say) the English divorce laws, nor in my saying that in consequence I think the word " justice " should be definable in such a way that it would exclude these laws. The irrationality only comes in when, under the pressure of my emotions, I assert that this definition is the only correct one and then adduce it as evidence for my statement that the divorce laws are therefore " bad things " (i.e. unjust). In fact, as can be seen, it is not evidence at all ; it is only an elaborately camouflaged re-statement of my own opinion. " But," I say indignantly, " Justice would never allow two people to be tied together who both wanted to be separated. It's inconceivable. After all, one's only got to think what Justice means. . . ."

The same thing happens when people talk about art. " But you can't seriously call that a work of art! It's not in the least beautiful. After all, to be beautiful a thing must have *some* resemblance to nature "—or poetry, " That isn't poetry; it's got no rhythm "—or politics, " You can't seriously suggest that that should happen in England. Why, the whole essence of democracy is . . . "—or about morality, " But it's wrong, I tell you ! "—or even about themselves, " I am no prude but . . . ", or, in fact, about anything in the world, so long as there is available some word with an ethical or emotive force whose one correct meaning can be assumed by the speaker to be what *he* wants it to be.[1]

In each case, the argument which has been so ingeniously camouflaged can be quite simply stated in the words, " I don't (or I do, as the case may be) like it, and therefore I am right. No other evidence is needed ! "

This camouflage is as a rule so successful that it bamboozles not only the user but also, with luck, his opponent as well. It seems therefore worth restating it so as to show up more clearly the fallacious use of one word in more than one sense (sometimes called the Utraquistic fallacy or the fallacy of Equivocation) upon which it depends. My argument about justice, for example, can be analysed thus : " Justice " (with a capital J) is a label for an abstract and undefinable concept that everybody approves of. I approve of Justice. You approve of Justice.

I disapprove of the divorce laws. I therefore decide to apply the label " justice " to a concept which excludes from its scope laws of the type of the divorce laws, and which excludes in particular the idea that two people must be forced to remain married when neither of them want to.

---

[1] In the *Biographia Literaria*, Coleridge sees the pitfall and, after being kind enough to point it out to us, falls straight into it himself: " Controversy is not seldom excited in consequence of the disputants attaching each a different meaning to the same word ; . . . If a man chooses to call every composition a poem, which is rhyme, or measure, or both, I must leave his opinion uncontroverted. The distinction is at least competent to characterize the writer's intention. . . . But if the definition sought be that of a *legitimate* poem, I answer, it must be one, the parts of which mutually support and explain each other. . . ."

Then, because I am taking it for granted that the word "justice" can have only one meaning, I conveniently overlook the fact that I myself have actually used it to refer to two quite different things; one, the Justice (with a capital J) of which everybody approves; and two, the things that I personally approve of. "True" Justice, I assume, is the same as "justice". "There you are!" I say, triumphantly using the word with both meanings at once, "the divorce laws are incompatible with justice. Therefore I'm right to disapprove of them." I drive my point further. "You say you approve of Justice; it follows that you ought also to disapprove of the divorce laws. And if you do not, you are either a fool or a knave!"

Only in a small proportion of arguments is this last sentence said out loud. But, as everyone can testify from their experience, it is often implied. When the argument is about politics or ethics, it is usually implied with considerable force —and inevitably so, because the motive involved is as a rule the powerfully tempting desire to believe that what one wants for oneself is what mankind in general wants. This desire is tempting because, as often as not, it can only be satisfied in fantasy; and, because, when satisfied, it has the inestimable advantage of dispelling all doubts as to one's own altruism and of satisfying inversely the desire to conform. When questions of aesthetics are involved, the temptation is perhaps not quite so great. The motive is more usually a mixture of the desire to understand and the desire for self-assertion. Not only do we want to believe that what we like ourselves is admirable, we also want to believe that we can understand and appreciate all forms of beauty. Similarly, if someone else professes to appreciate something which we cannot appreciate ourselves, we are reluctant to believe that he is our superior in intelligence —much better to assume that he doesn't know what beauty means.

I have belaboured this point because it does, I hope, show how Comfortable Concepts about the meanings of words can help to establish and consolidate irrational opinions about almost anything under the sun. The way they do so is, incidentally, seldom as obvious as in the instances I have given up to now. We will try later to unravel more complex examples.

The very natural tendency to grab a sweet-smelling label

for something one personally likes (and conversely to grab one which stinks for something one dislikes) shows itself in almost every argument that is not purely scientific. It is, after all, a favourite controversial and oratorical trick, since it enables the user to beg the question he is discussing. In the Spanish Civil War Franco's forces were called Rebels by some people and Nationalists by others. And, to give a famous example from history, when newspapers were fighting for their rights, one side talked of the " freedom "—while the other side talked of the " licence "—of the press. Again, nowadays the opportunity for a rich man to send his son to a public school—to educate him beyond the age of 14—is called a " privilege " by those who have not the opportunity, and a " right " by those who have. Such examples can be multiplied indefinitely and are particularly prolific in arguments which try to prove that such-and-such a thing is wicked and something else is good. In themselves they can be dangerous enough to peaceful and useful discussion. They provide also an additional motive for the belief that a word has a true meaning which suits the user's purpose. For, if he is challenged, he is tempted to try and justify himself by asserting and believing that his special definition exercises a divine right which shall exclude all other definitions. (" But they weren't really *rebels;* they were trying to establish a proper government. They were Nationalists in the true sense of the word.") He may of course be able to marshall independent evidence for his opinion. My point is that, only too often, he imagines that, by using a derogatory (or reputable) word and assuming that he has used this word in its only true sense, he has already started to prove the badness (or goodness) of the thing he is talking about. He has, of course, proved nothing except his own opinion.

It seems possible that the workings of this mental process provide the reason why words with an ethical or emotive value have in practice acquired so many meanings. Each time someone has wished to bolster up an opinion, he has selected an appropriate word and added to it a new meaning specially suited to his present purpose. If then, by virtue of his intellectual, moral or political eminence, he has been able to get a sufficiently wide hearing for his opinion, his additional meaning has gradually become accepted as part of the language. But, unlike Humpty Dumpty, he has usually been

unconscious of what he was up to.   For Humpty Dumpty
" glory " meant " there's a nice knock-down argument for
you ! "—and " impenetrability " meant even more.   But,
when Alice objected, he was quite frank about it.

" When *I* use a word," he said in rather a scornful tone, " it
means just what I choose it to mean—neither more nor less."

" The question is," said Alice, " whether you *can* make
words mean different things."

" The question is," said Humpty Dumpty, " which is to
be master—that's all."

(5) HYPOSTATIZATION

Mankind in all ages have had a strong propensity to conclude that
wherever there is a name, there must be a distinguishable separate
entity corresponding to the name ; and every complex idea which the
mind has formed for itself by operating upon its conceptions of
individual things, was considered to have an outward objective reality
answering to it.—J. S. Mill.   " A System of Logic."

Words are wise men's counters, they do but reckon by them, but
they are the money of fools.—Hobbes.   " Leviathan."

The Fascist State has a consciousness of its own, and a will of its
own, on this account it is called an " ethical " state.
                              —Mussolini on the Doctrine of Fascism.

This mental process (sometimes alternatively called
" reification ", i.e. making into a thing—as distinct from
" personification ", i.e. making into a person) may be defined
as " assuming that the meaning of an abstract word stands for
something which is an entity—a definite single thing existing
somehow on its own ".   Its effects manifest themselves most
often in the field of what one person will call " religion " and
what another will call " superstition ".   This field is, however,
less a field than a quagmire of controversy, and I will keep off
it for the moment.

But, since unrealized hypostatization can render any
reality-thinking abortive, it should be mentioned briefly,
especially as it comes all the more easily to those who believe
that abstract words have one true meaning.   In the case of
words like " beauty ", " justice " or " evil ", which are
abstractions of qualities, the assumption that there is such *a*
thing as beauty or justice or evil would be equivalent to the
assumption that there is such a thing as roundness existing
somehow quite independently of round tables or ponds or heads.

As the word " beauty " is a label used for convenience in

thought when we want to refer to a quality separately from the object it qualifies, so other abstractions are labels for the concepts of qualities which have no objective meaning except as they apply to concrete things or people. For example, the verb " to move " has no objective meaning unless we know what it is that is moving; the word " think " presupposes something that thinks; the word " healthy " is a name for the bodily condition *of* some person or animal or plant; the word " between " describes the spatial relation *of* three objects— one is between two others; and so on. From the last of these words one could abstract the word " betweenness ". As it happens it expresses an idea we seldom wish to talk about, though it might be quite useful if we were trying to describe the functional position of a piece of meat in a sandwich. In any case we should hardly feel justified in hypostatizing it— in assuming that there is such a thing as " betweenness " which exists on its own.

Similarly, from the other words one abstracts the expressions " movement ", " thought " and " health " And there is in these cases as little justification for assuming that they exist apart from things that move, think and are healthy. The assumption is on the face of it so absurd that it is in fact seldom made—except in the case of those high abstractions such as Good and Evil, whose complexity of meaning is so baffling that it is artificially reduced to an essence. One often comes across references to Ultimate Reality or statements that the evil in the world seems to be something that cannot be explained away purely as a product of human agency. More-over, there are some schools of philosophy which base most of their systems on hypostatization of abstract words. In asserting that there are such *things* as Reality, Justice, Similarity, etc., they attempt to avoid the obvious difficulty by stating that these abstractions " subsist " (rather than " exist ") and they are conveniently vague as to what " subsist " itself means. We will deal later on with the resultant confusions. Here we need only remark that such hypostatizations cannot have much value unless it can be assumed that the words hypostatized have each a " true " meaning. And as I hope I have shown, this cannot be assumed.

It seems possible that the tendency to hypostatize words is tied up with primitive beliefs about language. According to Jung, hypostatization is a natural process in the primitive, uncivilized mind. In his *Psychological Types* he says, " the ' reality ' . . . of the abstract idea is no artificial product, no arbitrary hypostatizing of a concept, but necessary by nature ". For to the primitive mind a mental image has a sensuousness which makes its perception almost as real a sensation as the perception of an actual object. " When the primitive ' thinks ' he literally has visions, whose reality is so great that he is constantly mistaking the psychic for the real." The primitive belief in the magic of words must also be involved with hypostatization. If, as has been suggested, this is connected with the infant's discovery that the pronunciation of the formula "ma-ma " produces an apparently omnipotent genie, the foundations of belief in word-magic are laid in all of us. Certainly it is significant that there should be so many religions in which the utterance of the name of a thing created that thing; i.e. the word comes before the thing rather than the thing before the word, with the corollary that if there is a word there must somehow be a thing to correspond to it.

We are inclined to forget how powerful, even in civilized communities, is the aftermath of these primitive beliefs. For example, the Romans did not dare to call the avenging dieties by their real name, Erinyes, but instead called them Eumenides (well-meaning or soothed goddesses). And we still retain traces of such combined flattery and avoidance of dangerous names in our custom of addressing kings and other eminent persons indirectly. We do not utter their names but talk obliquely to their auras: " Your Royal Highness—Your Grace," we say, with deference.

It is also significant that, as Comte and the Positivists suggested, progress in human knowledge seems to be divisible into three main stages, of which the second is typified by advance from the belief that phenomena are to be explained by supernatural agencies to the belief that they are to be explained by metaphysical abstractions (i.e. what we are here calling hypostatized abstractions). Thus, in the second stage, " Nature " was said to abhor a vacuum ; magnetism was regarded as " effluvia " of " souls " in magnetized bodies; gases in flames were taken as examples of " levity "; the phenomena of living bodies were (and sometimes still are) regarded as due to a " vital force " ; and so on. According to this view the second stage is imperfect and should ideally give way before the advance of (real) science. Naturally these three stages cannot be sharply separated ; they overlap. There are phenomena to-day which are explained in all three ways according to the point of view and to the completeness of our knowledge of them.   For example, ghosts are explained sometimes as supernatural spirits, sometimes as the effect of " electrical fields " or " auras " left behind by past events, and sometimes as vivid projections of the subject's mind.

In any case, however " natural " or not it may be to us, it is fairly understandable that we should sometimes be tempted to take it for granted that if " table " stands for an existing entity, then " nature " also stands for an existing entity.   The temptation is yet more insidious in the case of those less obvious abstractions which are formed from words which are labels for a collection of objects or concepts.   Hypostatization here consists in simplifying a miscellany down to a single entity, and functions as a type of Comfortable Concept.   For example, the word " Germany " can, in one sense, mean merely the expanse of land which is labelled Germany on the map ; while in its wider and more abstract sense, it can mean a collection of diverse people, pieces of land, institutions, ideas, emotions, etc., all roughly centred in the piece of land called " Germany ".   In this second sense, it is clearly not the name of a *thing*—it is a convenient label for a large collection of things.   Again, the word " mind " is used in one sense as a label for the innumerable and almost infinitely complex actions, re-actions, inter-actions, reflexes, sensations, instincts, etc., etc., which go on in the grey matter called the brain and nervous system.   These innumerable things cannot possibly be severally detailed every time we want to talk about them, and we therefore use the label " mind " in order to be able to refer to them collectively.   This label is naturally used in the singular ; we do not talk about " those things called mind " ; it would be too cumbersome.   We talk about " the mind " as we talk about " the digestion ", and, carrying this convenient simplification still further, we think of the mind as *a* thing.

Up to this point the whole process is merely an example of that simplification of complex reality that I have shown to be the necessary basis of rational thought.   It is beyond this point that hypostatization comes in.   We forget that our word is a simplified label and unthinkingly take it for granted that, because the label is a single thing, what it refers to must also be a single thing, i.e. an entity.   There may perhaps be some one thing which could appropriately be labelled a "mind" or "personality" or "soul". Many people think so; though as Sir Arthur Keith says,[1] "the conclusions reached by all anatomists, physiologists and nuerologists who have made a first-hand acquaintance with the human brain in its living and in its dead state . . . (are) that there are no grounds for regarding the soul as a separate entity". The existence of such an entity is of course a pre-requisite for belief in human immortality, and the fact that we talk and think *as if* it existed is taken by many people as an indication that it does exist, whereas this is obviously no evidence at all.

Similar considerations apply to such words as "instinct", "character", "country", "conscience" and "England", which all might be called collective abstractions. An abstraction is, in short, an empty linguistic convenience, which, unless it remains empty, is apt to develop into a public nuisance. For, to uplift the metaphor, unless such labels are firmly tied down to their complex and cumbersome meanings, they begin to fly away out of the reach of reason, and in so doing, they carry any discussion which hangs on them up into aery wastes of fantasy.

Hypostatization, when it is combined with other irrational processes, produces some remarkable results. We shall deal with these in Part IV. In the meantime, here are a few illustrations of the fields in which it works. Take such a word as "generosity" or "courage" or "memory". Unless we stop to think, we often tend to accept a statement like: "It was his generosity which led him to provide such a wonderful tea for the Scouts," as a full and complete explanation of someone's behaviour. In fact, it is of course a sort of redundancy, equivalent to saying, "It was his kindness which made him so kind." This tendency does not matter at all in small affairs; it even makes social intercourse easier. But if it extends into serious reality-thinking it can become dangerous. For of course a person's behaviour is not fully explained until the motive for it is uncovered, and this motive must have a connection with the satisfaction of some impulse or instinct. The worst dangers of such points of view are perhaps shown in dealing with children. A child's tendency to steal or to be unduly destructive is too often put down

[1] In an article called *The Creed of Two Anthropologists*, printed in the Rationalist Annual for 1942.

merely to his "naughtiness" or to his "instinctive destructiveness", with the result that the real reason is never uncovered and the child is perhaps permanently prevented from making a proper adaptation to life.

The situation is similar with such a concept as "memory". "Memory" is a collective abstraction acting as a label for a complex mental function with an impetus of its own. As K. Koffka has said in his *Principles of Gestalt Psychology*, "Nothing is more dangerous to scientific progress than such a single word which tends to become reified, to be taken as an entity which produces all the different effects."

The type of hypostatization which probably has more potentialities for good and evil than any other is that connected with the concept of Nationality. As we have seen, the words "Germany" and "England" are collective abstractions. As such they are useful and convenient simplifications. But when they are hypostatized they become indefinable and powerful entities whose paramount quality (especially in wartime) is that they act as a focus of devotion. Mr. A. is fighting for the preservation of those institutions in present-day England that *he* considers the best; he is also fighting for his own and his friends' happiness, for his own economic interests, for his stomach. Mr. B. is fighting to preserve, perhaps, other institutions and for the sake of other economic interests. Mr. C. is perhaps fighting for quite new institutions—and so on. It is true that all three are fighting for a number of the same things—that their interests have much in common. At the same time they are fighting for many things which are more or less different and which would be very hard to define concisely. But, since in each case the name given to these things is "England", Mr. A., Mr. B. and Mr. C. can all feel that "really" they are fighting for almost exactly the same thing. And the more this thing is hypostatized—is simplified into an entity—the greater is the patriotism, the sense of common purpose, that it can inspire in those fighting for it. For, as Bertrand Russell has said, "in times of excitement simple views find a hearing more readily than those which are sufficiently complex to have a chance of being true". This is all very well in war, for at such times the advantages of cool reason are outweighed to some extent by the advantages and the power of hot passion. But when peace comes, and it is once again possible to negotiate the tight-rope between reason and treason, the well-being of the millions of individuals who constitute part of the abstraction "England" depends very directly on how soon they realize that this abstraction means nothing whatsoever apart from them.   Only then will they be able to discuss rationally what is the best thing for the future of "England"; for they will know that what they are discussing is, not just the preservation of an institution or an idea, but the welfare and happiness of living men, women and children.

When nations are hypostatized they are often personified as well; that is to say they are clothed with the emotions and attributes of an individual person, as when we talk of a nation's "honour" or "dignity".   Thus there are many people who will discuss the relations between Great Britain and India as if they believed that "Great Britain" was an entity capable of behaving unselfishly and of doing whatever it does "for the sake of the Indians".   On the other side, there are people who will talk as if this personified Britain were cruelly and maliciously intent on causing suffering. Whatever the viewpoint taken, this assumption of consciously human intent on the part of Britain does nothing but envelope the issue in a damp fog of revolting hypocrisy.   (The careful reader should here smell a rat.)   Similarly, patriots of all races will be shocked by the suggestion that their country may be capable of "breaking its word".   (Their attitude is of course largely excused by the fact that their history books have failed to mention such breaches of good taste unless some other nation has committed them.)

The irrationality in such points of view is classifiable as a sort of false analogy.   For example, it is of course true that many of the individuals in a nation will take up an emotional attitude on some current issue, as when vocal opinion in England swung from approval of the North American States before the Civil War to disapproval during the war.   But the mechanisms of such opinion and its effect on government are so far different from the mechanisms of emotion in individuals that no valid analogy is possible.

In practice, and among reasonably sensible people, this personification of nations is seldom consciously taken to its logical conclusion; if it were (as for instance in the statement of Mussolini's quoted at the head of this chapter), it would at once be recognized as nonsense—except by a Fascist.   But the fact remains that much political thinking—even among non-Fascists—is seriously affected by irrational assumptions derived from unrecognized habits of personification. Perhaps the most memorable example is provided by the way in which numbers of people believed in 1931 that Great Britain must economize in its internal finances, apparently on the assumption that, because it is sensible for an individual to economize in difficult times, it must also be sensible for a nation to do so. There is of course no valid analogy.

The Fascist ideology is not meant to be rational. Consequently no person who is able and willing to follow a reasonable discussion of its hypostatizations is likely to need to do so. On the other hand, those to whom it has appealed are precisely those who do not want to be rational themselves and would never think of listening to a rational discussion. They are unconvertible by such methods, for the sufficient reason that they have no desire to be converted.

(6) EMOTIVE SUGGESTION

Language does express thought, but not primarily, nor, at first, even consciously. The primary motive for language is to influence (through the expression of desire, emotion and thought) the activity of others; its secondary use is to enter into more intimate sociable relations with them; its employment as a conscious vehicle of thought and knowledge is a tertiary, and relatively late, formation.
—John Dewey. "How We Think."
With words we govern men—Disraeli.

The heading, Emotive Suggestion, is designed to include all those mechanisms of thinking which rely on persuasion through the emotions rather than through the intellect.

In the section on the Meaning of Words, we saw that almost any word which has a good or bad association tends to be used as a question-begging label. Franco's followers in the Spanish Civil War were called Nationalists by those who approved of them, largely because the associations of the word "nationalism" are much less opprobrious than those of "rebel". If someone who has called Franco a Nationalist is challenged, he has to fall back on an attempt to prove that the "true" meaning of Nationalist is what he wants it to be. But the chief danger of such question-begging terms is that in practice they seldom *are* challenged. They are so common that their special function is seldom appreciated and, even if it is appreciated, the man who interrupts a conversation to question them is merely regarded as an insufferable bore. In addition, the user himself is of course nearly always unconscious of the inner motives for his particular choice of word, and consequently is indignant at the implied suggestion of bias.

The chief reason for the commonness of question-begging terms is probably that a very large part of everyday writing and talking is not intended to be reality-thinking, but is intended to be persuasive or emotive in some way or other. As such it quite legitimately makes use of emotively tinged words and phrases. We thus become so used to these words and phrases that their presence seems quite acceptable in any type of statement. We do not notice (and until lately we have certainly not been taught) that they have no legitimate place in reality-thinking. In fact, the whole question of the distinction between informative and emotive statements appears to be a development almost of the last fifty years.

Significantly enough, perhaps the best illustration of the difference is to be found in a question set in the English B. paper of the Common Entrance Examination for June 1940, this being the first appearance of a question of this type. The question quoted three passages from the same page in a daily newspaper. The first two of these passages were:

(a) "Mr. Harry Woodring, who is expected to announce to-day the U.S. Government's decision to release American 'secret' fighter 'plane models for the Allies, has been Secretary for War since 1936."

(b) "During this same week the German High Command has emphasized its powerlessness against the Allies' mastery of the sea by a ferocious onslaught upon neutrals. Eight of their ships have been sunk and many neutral seamen murdered."

The third passage referred to Turkey and, with such words as "far-sighted", "resolute" and "benefit" appropriately used, indicated approval of Turkey as clearly as the second indicated disapproval of Germany. (Note, incidentally, that even the word "neutral" ceases to be entirely neutral in such a passage.) Out of the hundreds of thousands of people who must have read these statements in their newspapers, extremely few will have noticed the difference in function between them. It needs the juxtaposition—and the questioning—for the difference to become apparent. And even then it seems unlikely that many would have been able to indicate what *kind* of difference was involved. The examinees (aged about 13—almost the age at which education ceases for the great majority of our population) were asked to choose three words from each of (b) and (c) which made clear the feelings of Great Britain towards Germany and Turkey, and to explain why there were no such outstanding words in (a). I understand that it was regarded as quite a difficult question.

The point here is that the style of the second passage appears at first sight quite as reasonable as that of the first. We are so used to such writing (and talking) that we do not appreciate the effect that words like " mastery ", " ferocious ", " onslaught ", etc., have upon us, especially when they are used in statements which, like this one, purport to be merely informative. We *expect* to be moved or persuaded by poetry or by certain kinds of advertising ; we are not expecting mere information and we would therefore seldom make the mistake of thinking that what we were being told was objectively true.[1] On the other hand, when we are expecting objective statements, we tend to take it for granted that our agreement or disagreement with what is being said depends only on the objective evidence produced. Emotively charged words like " ferocious " and " murdered " are thus able to pre-condition our state of mind without our noticing it ; they induce in us by suggestion the emotion felt by the speaker. And that is just what the speaker wants. If he were to produce objective evidence of the Germans' behaviour together with quotations from experts on International Law, he could probably make us agree on reasonable grounds that this behaviour deserved disapproval. But it would take a long time and we would be bored. It is much easier to induce, from the beginning, a *feeling* of anger, for then we do not realize that we are basing our judgments on the speaker's opinion alone.

The spoken word is of course a much more efficient vehicle for emotive suggestion than the written word, since the tone of voice can augment the emotion. Hence the remarkably small proportion of informative statements to be found in political speeches and in wireless propaganda. But the unspoken and unwritten word is in itself efficient enough to

---

[1] Some people do get confused over this aspect of poetry. Cf. *Science and Poetry*, by I. A. Richards. Many people are also taken in by pseudo-scientific advertisements.

serve as a potent aid to irrationality—to the satisfaction of desires unsatisfiable in reality. For we find that we have only to think of (say) a left-wing politician as a " Red " or a right-wing politician as a " reactionary " to feel already that our disapproval is somehow confirmed. The basis of this kind of satisfaction is thus the consolidation of pre-conceived opinion. If we want to believe that capitalism is a Good Thing, we will tend to think of private ownership of the means of production as private " enterprise " and of state ownership as state " control ". We will then unthinkingly assume that " enterprise " in the one case and " control " in the other case are the proper and correct words to use, and the two forms of ownership are automatically differentiated in our mind before ever we come to consider the question of whether in fact there is more enterprise and less control in private than in state ownership.

Still another factor comes in here which has been touched on before. We feel more comfortable if we can conform to group or herd opinion. When this comfort cannot rationally be obtained we will be tempted by any mental device which helps us to feel that group opinion *ought* to agree with us. To call those people who agree with our opinion " sincerely patriotic " is to suggest to ourselves that they have some inherent quality, independent of their fortunate agreement with us on matters of politics, which makes them the sort of people whom all " right-thinking " men should follow, and whom only " unpatriotic " men will oppose.

Examples of this method of irrationality will be analysed in the Supplement. A few are, however, given here because I think that those who have not been taught at an early age how to make the distinction between informative and emotive statements are as a rule surprised when they discover how much emotive writing and speaking they are daily swallowing whole. The first example is perhaps more obvious than most. Lieut.-General Sir William Dobbie (quoted in the *News Chronicle* of October 28th, 1942) spoke of " the sort of amusement and entertainment which some misguided people think should be provided for the Forces. I resent most strongly," he said, " the imputations that are made by those who think that, in order to entertain the Forces, something beastly and horrid should be provided." Of course, such a statement is not in itself irrational. There is no reason why the speaker should not try and persuade others to his own views. But I cannot help suspecting him of believing that his own opinion was one which was objectively valid—that what *he* thought beastly and horrid *was* beastly and horrid—with no question about it. And, in fact, the paragraph goes on to say, " He was certain that this form of entertainment was distasteful to nine-tenths of the Forces." Not only ought the group to agree with him, but it jolly well does. Could self-persuasion go much further?

Here is a much more subtle example, taken from *The Beveridge Plan: A Symposium*, published by the Individualist Press (the section by James W. Nisbet): " If a person is out of a job through sickness, it is possible that the liberal disability benefit, with the other allowances proposed, will occasion a distinct tendency to malinger." The eminent reasonableness of that word " possible " sets the tone nicely on an impartial basis, so that the faintly sarcastic emphasis of the word " distinct " can produce its effect without arousing suspicion.

Finally, an example with a pleasantly contradictory sting in its tail. It is taken from a letter to the *News Chronicle* of May 10th, 1944, on the subject of the Incitement to Strike regulation. Notice the use of " cocksure " rather than " sure " and the pre-conception implicit in " despicable ": " If Mr. Bevin is so cocksure of the support of the trade unionists of this area, or elsewhere, why not come into the Ebbw Vale division and meet Aneurin Bevan in debate and try to convince us of the desirability of this despicable regulation? We guarantee him a fair hearing."

(7) RATIONALIZATION

True or false, solid or sandy, the mind must have some foundation to rest itself upon and . . . it no sooner entertains any proposition but it frequently hastens to some hypothesis to bottom it on ; till then it is unquiet and unsettled.—John Locke.

Nous sommes si accoutumés à nous déguiser aux autres, qu' enfin nous nous déguisons à nous-mêmes.—La Rochefoucauld.

Hunting is really kindness to the fox. Instead of being the scum of the earth—as low in the opinion of man as the rat—he has become almost a king, respected by nearly everyone.—Major V. D. Williams, Chairman of the Institute of the Horse and Pony Club.

Irrational opinions are the result of unrealized fantasy-thinking ; in other words, they are the means by which desires (which cannot be satisfied in reality) attain an illusory satisfaction.

Once an irrational opinion has been formed, any or all of the methods which have been used for forming it can be used also for consolidating it—for strengthening it against disturbing opinions from outside. There is, however, one further mental process which acts solely as a consolidator. By its means we persuade ourselves that the grounds for our opinion were *really* quite rational all the time. Clearly there is only one way of doing this: since what grounds do exist are usually unrealized and in any case irrational, new ones must be invented which, to ourselves at least, seem to be rational. The process of inventing them is usually called " rationalization "—a term which might be translated as " manufacturing reasons for our opinions which may or may not be rational in themselves but in any case are not the real ones ".

There are, of course, people who are so set in their prejudices that their own opinions seem completely self-evident. And there are in most communities some superstitions and taboos which have been instilled so early into the childish mind that they are never afterwards questioned, even by otherwise reasonable people. It naturally does not occur to the holders of such opinions to try and rationalize them, whereas their very " unquestionableness " is a sign that they should be questioned without delay. For the only statements that can be said to be self-evident are axioms, whose function (as I will attempt to show later) is merely to re-state a definition. Any other kind of statement needs evidence to support it.

This applies even to such a statement about the objective world as that " pornographic literature is injurious to the welfare and happiness of human beings." And yet some people take it for granted as self-evident. " It is obvious," they will indignantly assert. " No decent person would deny it." And if some indecent person, without specifically denying it, were to ask them on what grounds they based their opinion, they would immediately put up a barrier of expostulation designed to forestall any attempt to question it in their own minds. There seem only two conclusions to be drawn: either the grounds for their opinion are too irrational to bear the light of day, or these grounds are too deeply embedded in their minds for it to be possible to unearth them.

Such an opinion may be right or it may be wrong. In

any case it is irrationally formed. I have chosen this most obvious and shocking example just because it is so seldom questioned, at least in public. But, particularly in the field of manners, morals and taboos, there are many others—some of them fantastic, a few of them fairly sensible—which, though questioned by a minority, are clung to by the majority with passionate tenacity. The most virulent of these have been wittily analysed in *The Future of Taboo in these Islands*, by Archibald Lyall, which I would recommend as a cold douche for the mind.

One of the distinguishing features of a taboo, pointed out by Archibald Lyall, is that it should not be recognized as such by the person who is subject to it. " A taboo ? Certainly not ! " he says, " That's just one of these things decent men don't talk about," or " Nonsense ! It's simply that it isn't done."

Anybody who has this sort of attitude towards an opinion feels no need to try and justify it—no need to invent grounds for it. However, it is only towards opinions that are generally accepted among one's own group that it is possible to take such an attitude. The majority of one's opinions are in continual danger of being questioned. And, for one's own peace of mind, it is essential to be able to produce apparently rational grounds for them.

The task is not so difficult as it might seem at first sight. For, since the inner motives behind the formation of an irrational opinion are often quite unrealized, there is, so to speak, a vacant space where they should be, waiting to be filled up. The situation is then similar to that in which somebody has been given a post-hypnotic suggestion. He wakes from hypnosis, remembers nothing of what happened, and then some time later feels a powerful urge (say) to turn an armchair upside down. When under hypnosis he had been told to do this—and he will not be comfortable until he *has* done it. But, as he does not know the real reason why he wants to do it, and as it is a sufficiently odd action to need explaining, he says that he wants to find out who the maker of the chair was—perhaps, he says, there is a name underneath. To quote William MacDougall (who gives, in his *Outline of Normal and Abnormal Psychology*, a number of similar examples drawn from actual experiments), " not knowing the nature and source of the impulse by which he was moved he invents an explanation and puts forward a plausible motive in place of the true one, *in perfect good faith*" (my italics).

The mental process is parallel in everyday life, as MacDougall himself points out: "We often act or believe from motives of which we have no understanding; but we always seek to explain our action or belief according to the principle of 'sufficient reason'."

Of course if the inner motive for some action is so obscure that there is no chance of our even suspecting it, there is nothing much that we can do to avoid rationalizing, beyond remembering that our ability to produce apparently rational grounds for an opinion is proof neither that they are rational nor that they are real grounds. If we are really sincere in our desire to be rational and are prepared to take some trouble, we can also turn to such a book as *Clearer Thinking*, by A. E. Mander, which devotes a chapter to "Testing our Grounds for Belief" However, a short analysis of the various forms which rationalization can take will probably make them easier to identify.

In the first place it must be emphasized that rationalization consists not only in inventing reasons but also in inventing motives, and that this applies both to actions and to opinions. The ostensible motive for the formation of an opinion is always the desire for truth—the desire to understand. And this of course is the only reasonable one; in fact, however, an opinion is often motivated by other desires. When we are rationalizing an action, on the other hand, we can reasonably and openly choose almost any motive—though usually we take good care to choose a respectable one.

But actions are, from this point of view, more complicated than beliefs. For, unless an action is purely spontaneous, not only has it a motive but also it is based upon one or more judgments or beliefs. Strictly speaking at least two judgments or beliefs are involved. For instance, suppose I want to cut up a table for firewood, there have to be, first, the judgment that the table is made of wood (it might be made of painted steel), and secondly, based on this first judgment, the further judgment that the result of hitting the table with an axe will be firewood, the motive of course being to *get* firewood (though it might conceivably be to work off a fit of temper).

Thus we have, in any one action, at least two judgments

or beliefs (each with its own motive) as well as the motive for the action itself—all susceptible of rationalization. The opportunities are enormous. In such an example as that of the table, it is hard to imagine there being much temptation to rationalize. But, to take another example, suppose that I hear a piece of scandalous gossip about a pretty woman who has spurned my advances. If I can believe the gossip is true, I will satisfy some of my frustrated desire for revenge and also, in an obscure way, may get a salacious pleasure out of it. I fall to the temptation and I believe the gossip. But, if I were asked to justify my opinion, I would rationalize by saying perhaps that my informant is a reliable witness, that it is just what I would expect, that there's no smoke without fire, and so on, it being all the time assumed that my only motive in forming my opinion was a desire for truth. Later I meet a friend and retail the story to him. This action is of course based on a complicated mixture of judgments and beliefs, some of them perfectly rational (such as that my friend will listen to what I say, that he will understand the language I use, etc.), and all of them summarizable into the general judgment that my speaking to my friend will spread the truth, this being based on the previous judgment that the story I retail *is* the truth. As to motive, the superficial one is the desire to communicate information. But why do I want to communicate this particular piece of information? What are my other motives? One can imagine a number of far from respectable ones: A desire to impress my friend, for instance, by making my conversation interesting; a desire to increase my own salacious pleasure by sharing it; even perhaps a desire to fortify my own conviction that the gossip is true by convincing somebody else as well.

It may perhaps be objected that these are all rather obscure and unconvincing motives. Precisely!—they are not the obviously sensible ones that we like to think control our everyday actions. But, as those who have studied human behaviour—the psychologists—will confirm, they are typical of the kind that in practice are often active. In any case, supposing that motives of this kind were the mainspring of my action, they would probably be unconscious—or at least they would be hurriedly stowed out of sight in the dark recesses of my brain, with the result that, if I were asked why I had retailed the gossip, I would invent—and believe—a number of thoroughly respectable motives. ("Else she'll betray more men.")

Here, then, is an example of an action which involves two or three separate rationalizations. It is perhaps a more unpleasant and petty one than the average; but its difference from the average is one of degree rather than of kind. For there is no escaping the fact that the rationalization of an action is usually a sort of petty hypocrisy, which is made no less unpleasant for being unconscious.

It is, I think, clear enough that, given an irrational or at least unacknowledged motive for a belief or action, the process of rationalization is not only possible but also probable. And, as in the case of all other forms of irrational thinking, our chances of avoiding it depend primarily on our being aware of its insidious temptations. This in its turn depends largely on how far we are able to recognize and discount the desires which it satisfies. These desires vary according to circumstances. But, in the case of the great majority of opinions, the motive for rationalizing is the desire to believe that we are being reasonable, that our belief is a correct one; and thus it may be said to be an offshoot of the desire to understand. In the case of actions, the same thing applies, in that we want to believe we have acted sensibly, i.e. with a correct understanding of the results of our action. But there is usually an additional motive; we want to believe that we have been Good as well as sensible.

Everyone will on occasion have noticed in someone else (if not in himself) a tendency to self-deception, the purpose of which is nearly always the invention of a "good" motive— —or at least one which is less disreputable than the real one. In domestic life examples will often be found in the reasons with which people justify their pet economies, or with which mothers justify restricting the freedom of their children, or which people give for drinking alcohol, or, and perhaps most often, in the reasons which people give for behaving snobbishly. Again, jealousy is well known to induce feelings of dislike for the person one is jealous of, and in consequence it often leads to very unpleasant and irrational behaviour. But one always takes care to persuade oneself that one has good reason for regarding the person in question as wicked, selfish and eminently deserving of all he gets. One's action, in fact, is supposed to have been inspired by moral indignation—an emotion which, by definition, is essentially altruistic and which, as Miss Rose Macaulay has pointed out, is very popular among English people. Undoubtedly it can be sincere and it can have its altruistic uses, but, on the other hand, it is a favourite with rationalizers, especially since, to re-quote Bertrand Russell, "the infliction of cruelty with a good conscience is a delight to moralists". Moral indignation is again the motive usually invented when a scape-goat is being punished. As we have seen, the finding of scape-goats is facilitated by selection of evidence and motivated as a rule by a mixture of rather disreputable desires. When we form our opinion that it is all so-and-so's fault, we believe that we are only interested in finding out the truth; and when we act on it, we believe that our righteous indignation is inspiring us to act in the interests of "justice" or humanity in general.

In business life rationalization is inevitably very common; for there are many people who try to avoid remembering that they are out to make money primarily for themselves. In political life rationalization is both commoner and easier to get away with, since the officially acknowledged purpose of a politician is to further the interests of his country—and of course of humanity in general, unless the latter are inconsistent with the former.

In the essay already quoted, Bertrand Russell acutely remarks that in the English-speaking countries the more public rationalizations are often of a type which would better be called "irrationalizing", since they consist of inventing irrational but altruistic grounds for an opinion or action which is really formed more or less unconsciously on rational but selfish grounds. "Having come to a sound egoistic decision by the help of the unconscious, a man proceeds to invent, or adopt from others, a set of high-sounding phrases showing how he is pursuing the public good at immense personal sacrifice. Anybody who believes that these phrases give his real reasons must suppose him quite incapable of judging evidence, since the supposed public good is not going to result from his action."

The scope of rationalization is not confined to those cases where there is an irrational motive to be exorcized, though these are the ones most pertinent to our subject. It also invades fields where the motivation, though non-rational, is not necessarily irrational. Thus our desire to believe that we always behave rationally is so strong that we often try to find extra justification for actions which could already be adequately justified as attempts to satisfy instincts and impulses. The pleasures of hunting and of listening to emotive oratory, for example, are non-rational. But there is nothing *irrational* about them. All the same, there are people who waste a lot of time in trying to persuade themselves that they do these things for other and " better " reasons than the mere satisfaction of impulse or instinct. Hence such statements as that of Major Williams' quoted at the head of this section. Hence also the shocked disapproval with which many people will greet any attempt to point out that a typical speech, such as the following, is not very informative. " To-day . . . youth will demand a voice in its own destiny . . . you have . . . a heritage of religious faith, of morals and of liberty. . . . You can lead our nation back to unity of purpose again."[1]   As members of a community or group we indulge in a number of amusements which, like listening to oratory, do us an immense amount of good, partly because they are in fact non-rational. Into this category come all the traditional customs which insist upon ceremony and upon there being a " right " way of doing things. To take a few examples from the many available, there are Lord Mayor's Processions, Royal Openings, conferment of the freedom of a city, wedding breakfasts, men's town clothes and the whole farrago of good manners. Some of these are clearly recognized by most people as being devices for assuring us that we are safely rooted in conformity, or for safeguarding us from the worry and indecision of continually thinking anew in our every-day lives. Some, on the other hand, are completely unquestioned, like the hat-raising and hand-shaking customs. But there are quite a few which we are reluctant to regard as " merely " traditional, because such a justification does not satisfy our desire for reason. As a result we tend to believe that there is, for example, some inherent quality in a king which makes it " only natural " that we should bow to him; or that the dishes which we traditionally eat at our meals are the best for our stomachs—or again that there is some peculiarity of women's brains which makes them less efficient than men in politics. (There may be, for all we know. But the point is, we don't know; we just assume that there is a reason for our traditional practice.)

[1] Speech by Herbert Hoover at the Republican National Convention, 1944.

The fact that irrational beliefs are often rationalized does not mean that they always need be. There are many occasions when we realize that we have formed an opinion under pressure of some emotion, such as anger, jealousy, fear, or simple irritation. Sometimes we even manage to modify the opinion in the light of reason. But, if we have already acted upon the irrational opinion, such heroic modification has much less chance of taking place. For then we have, so to speak, staked something on the opinion and we do not like to feel we have lost the stake. Far better to persuade ourselves that we really acted reasonably and respectably, especially if there is a danger that someone may ask us to justify the action. A further complication is introduced by the fact that our actions are often impelled by strong emotion. Strong emotion is more than non-rational; it is to some extent anti-rational, so that opinions and actions based on it are particularly tempting fields for rationalization.

In the same sort of way action may sometimes tempt us to rationalize (or rather to over-rationalize) an opinion which was quite reasonable in the first place. As already pointed out, we have no time to consider as carefully as we should like the judgments upon which we act. We have to compromise between the extremes of Hamlet-like indecision and bull-necked impetuosity, emulating Pericles and the Athenians who prided themselves on being "at once most adventurous in action and most reflective beforehand". It is thus inevitable, even in favourable circumstances, that we should often base our actions on very meagre evidence. There is of course no irrationality in this, so long as we remain aware of the provisional nature of the judgment and are prepared to reconsider it if necessary. All the same, the very fact that we have acted makes it at once more important that we should have been correct in our judgment. In some cases, of course, it is impossible to avoid the realization that we have been wrong; as, for instance, it would be for me if I had judged that it was safe to cross the road and then got run over. But in an enormous number of cases our action brings no definite indication as to whether the judgment was correct or not. For example, the owner of a business judges that an employee is not worth his wages. Finally, on the basis of this judgment, he sacks the employee. Originally the judgment may have been more or less consciously a tentative one—an assessment of probabilities from selected evidence. But, once he has acted, the owner will probably be more comfortable in mind if he can over-rationalize the judgment by forgetting exactly how much it was a simplification of the issue and, if necessary, by inventing further evidence to justify it.

If it is accepted that we are beset by powerful motives (and numerous opportunities) for rationalization, there is a conclusion to be drawn which is at first sight repugnant. This is that our sincere belief in our own virtue and good sense, even though it appears to us to have full justification, may be eyewash. In other words, the world might be a more rational place if each individual were prepared to take a more cynical view of his own character and intelligence. If he were to do so, he would merely be taking the view that has been confirmed by recent psychological studies. For it is now a common-place of knowledge that people continually deceive themselves about their motives, though it is one of those common-places that is rarely applied to particular cases —to you—the reader of these words, and to me—the writer of them. And yet the adoption of this view need not entail any sudden loss of faith in human nature, as so many people have suggested. Why should it? It is a sign, not of original sin, but of mankind's having survived the evolutionary process —of his having, in T. H. Huxley's phrase, " ascended from monkeys rather than descended from angels ". It is also a sign that, if he is to survive now that civilization has altered all the rules, he must make greater efforts than before to be reasonable and virtuous.

There is one particular result of rationalization which has a bearing on this. If I (that is to say, any individual) want to believe that the majority of my actions are Good, I shall find it much easier if I can as often as possible persuade myself that what *I* happen to want is also what humanity in general wants—or ought to want. The best way of doing this is, of course, to rationalize my beliefs—to invent evidence designed to show that such and such a thing (which I want) will benefit the community. If I do this often enough, I shall gradually come to identify my own and the community's interest so closely that it will never occur to me to separate them; in consequence, I shall be unlikely to come to a reasonable and objective conclusion on any question of politics or economics whatsoever. The dangers of this sort of rationalization are naturally greatest in the case of people who belong to a class which is economically in the minority. The upper middle class of England, for instance, is quite a small minority of the total population.[1] Yet how often does one find a member of this class to whom it occurs, even occasionally, to make a distinction between his own interests and those of the majority ? After all, in any discussion which implies the question, "What is the right thing to do?" the word "right" is, unless specifically defined otherwise, usually taken in the sense of "most likely to be generally beneficial". Consideration of the interests of an individual or of a minority can thus add nothing of value to the discussion, unless, again, these interests are acknowledged as having only a limited bearing on the subject. And a discussion which does not acknowledge this is almost as useless an occupation (apart from its value as a friendly way of passing the time) as an argument about whether Sophonisba is a nicer name than Hortensia. Again, how often does one find an American or an Englishman or a Frenchman who discusses politics without unconsciously assuming that what is best for his own country is best in the widest sense of the word, i.e. is best for the world in general?[2] (Fascists and Nazis do not pretend, except sometimes in propaganda for foreign consumption, to care for anything but themselves.)

The main temptation of rationalization lies in its power to produce immediate mental comfort. But, as with most forms of muddled thinking, the pleasures of the immediate effect are inclined to be outweighed by the probable—but unforeseen —pains of the ultimate effect. There is an old-established platitude which says that anticipation is better than realization and which appears for many people to be borne out by their experience. I would like to make the tentative suggestion that, if it were not for the widespread tendency to rationalize, this platitude would lose most of its meaning. Let us consider

---

[1] Among those *assessed for tax* in the British Isles for 1941/42, people with incomes of over £1,000 a year numbered 315,000 out of 15 million, or just over 2 per cent. Those with incomes over £2,000 numbered only 105,000, or ·7 per cent.

[2] "If she (England) enters into conflict in a righteous cause—if the contest is one which concerns her liberty, her independence or her Empire, her resources, I feel, are inexhaustible. . . ." Disraeli. Speaking in 1875 at the Guildhall.

"The idea of treating with Mussolini is preposterous. He is not a moral being at all. His wants cut right across our interests. . . ." Letter in the *News Chronicle*, quoted in "This England" Column of the *New Statesman*.

it this way. If I am deceiving myself as to my real motives for my actions, I am, in effect, keeping myself ignorant of what it is that I *really* want and imagining that what I want is something quite different. The very fact that I have been impelled to conceal my real desire is a sign that it has considerable strength, probably abnormally increased by repression. On the other hand, the invented desire cannot in the nature of things be very urgent. This is all very well when I actually succeed in getting what I really want; the fact that I may fail incidentally to get what I thought I wanted is obviously of secondary importance. But what happens if I rationalize so successfully that I get what I thought I wanted, and fail to get what I really wanted? It is surely only to be expected that I will find the sensation of pleasure inadequate as a recompense for the trouble I have taken.

Yet this is what may happen. An obvious example of this kind is provided by the classical antithesis of sacred and profane love. Everyone has met, either in life or in novels, the young man who thinks that what he wants from somebody of the opposite sex is spiritual companionship only. He rationalizes so successfully that he actually attains what he thought he wanted, unfortunately failing to attain the other thing. This generally makes him very uncomfortable and bad-tempered. Even if he gets both at once he is sometimes disappointed by the spiritual side of the relationship, because his anticipation of its pleasures has been unduly coloured by the urgency of his physical need.

The varied and unanalysed desires which express themselves in what we call "ambition" may easily include a number of unrecognized ones. Hence, perhaps, the proverbially bitter taste of success and the unhappiness of the self-made millionaires. And then there are the incomprehensibly complex motives behind the urge to create a work of art. I wonder what was hidden, even from himself, at the back of Robert Louis Stevenson's mind when he said, "it is better to travel hopefully than to arrive".

PART IV

THE MOTIVES WHICH SHAPE OUR PHILOSOPHIES

(1) FLIGHT FROM REASON

> . . . *the general public has derived the impression that physics confirms practically the whole of the Book of Genesis. I do not myself think that the moral to be drawn from modern science is at all what the general public has thus been led to suppose. In the first place, the men of science have not said nearly as much as they are thought to have said, and in the second place what they have said in the way of support for traditional religious beliefs has been said by them not in their cautious, scientific capacity, but rather in their capacity of good citizens, anxious to defend virtue and property.*
> —Bertrand Russell. "The Scientific Outlook."

In the foregoing chapters I have examined a very small selection of the methods and devices which can be used by one desire or another for distorting reality. This selection was conditioned largely by the wish to emphasize those methods which pander particularly to the (likewise very small) selection of desires previously examined. A more accurate approach would have subdivided the broad categories of my classification ; it would also have included numbers of other categories. On the other hand it would, I think, have been even less easy to stomach.

In giving examples of irrational beliefs I have up till now been restricted to those which stem from a single method. Whereas the most important real-life examples stem from a mixture of methods and often from a very obscure mixture of motives.

It would take a long time to try and suggest all the varied and tempting mixtures which may lead a historian or an economist, for instance, to distort the facts he is dealing with. Similarly, it would mean delving much too far into psychology to analyse the desires which can be, and often are, satisfied by a belief in ghosts or numerology or astrology or the Serial Universe. I hope I have done something by suggesting that desires exist which can be satisfied more easily by irrational than by rational methods.

The one desire which is at the bottom of most beliefs, whatever other desires may be present, is of course the desire to understand, with its concomitant—the desire for certainty, for a lessening of anxiety. Under its influence we are continually being tempted to *believe* that we understand; and we will use every conceivable variety of irrational method to help us. Though some of the results are comparatively harmless and some are (literally) fantastic, many of them are dangerous.

The most dangerous of all, perhaps, is also at first sight the most paradoxical. It seems absurd to suggest that the tendency of the modern world to turn away from reason is due to the strength of its desire to understand. But it seems less absurd when one reflects that reason has sadly disappointed its old champions. Though the eighteenth century has been called the Age of Reason, it was the nineteenth century which really took reason to its heart. Scientific Rationalism and Materialism, it felt, were the long-sought answer to everything. Only a few more years of wonderful progress would pass and then mankind would find that the whole universe would be explained in terms of a formula that man (so small a part of that universe) could encompass with his mind. The nineteenth century, in fact, grew up into the twentieth century imbued with an optimistic belief that its desire to understand would shortly be satisfied. And what has happened? In whatever direction science has explored, it has failed to reach any finite boundary. On the contrary it has always discovered further vast and illimitable territories to be conquered—so vast and illimitable that we have long had to abandon the hope that any one man's mind could survey them all at once. Furthermore, this expansion of knowledge has swamped the minds of even the greatest scientists with an ever accumulating mass of unassimilable facts. And, what is worse from the point of view of the average layman, it has established only one thing for *certain*—and that is that it is impossible to be certain (in the sense of having no doubts at all) of any objective phenomena. For science is a method of assessing probabilities by experimental observation. A scientific law is no more than a statement that such-and-such a thing is extremely likely to happen in certain circumstances, and has never yet been observed *not* to happen in circumstances which, as far as can be judged, were similar. It is extremely probable that the sun will rise in the east tomorrow. It is not a matter of absolute or logical certainty (in the sense that two and two make four), though from the point of view of practical life, it is quite sufficiently certain for it to be worth acting upon.

In ordinary life there are of course many of these "practical" certainties—so many that it never occurs to most people that they are not absolute certainties. And since, in addition, most people are repelled by the idea that absolute certainty about the outside world is unattainable, they are naturally inclined to expect this absolute certainty from "reason" and scientific method. They want to understand and they want to be sure that what they understand is correct; it is so much more comfortable that way. But to quote Pareto: "Science tries to bring theory as close to facts as possible, knowing very well that absolute coincidence cannot be attained. If, in view of that impossibility, anyone refuses to be satisfied with approximate exactness, he had better emigrate from this concrete world, for it has nothing better to offer." Pareto's counsel is very drastic. In default, the only thing that can be done is to abandon the scientific attitude and fly off into the realms of abstract fantasy. In short, reason has disappointed our hopes of it; it has failed to make the universe into an apprehendable concept; it has markedly increased the discomforts of its devotees. And therefore it is No Good.

As Pareto suggests, anyone who genuinely feels in this way is at liberty to emigrate into fantasy or faith or philosophical abstraction. And, in fact, many people do so. Nor would this matter so much if it were not that, owing to their inveterate desire to believe that they have a rational understanding of the world, they continually forget that they have emigrated. They want to have the best of both worlds and in consequence they try to convince everybody that their own subjective beliefs and emotions and principles are applicable to the objective world as well as to themselves. As Francis Bacon said, referring to St. Matthew xxii. 21, "it is a very salutory thing, with all sobriety of mind, to render unto faith those things only that are faith's".

I must emphasize that I have here touched on one small aspect only of the modern flight from reason. There are of course innumerable other factors to be taken into consideration, both economic and spiritual. Some of these are connected with a desire to justify absolute systems of ethics and will be discussed in the section on Morals for the Masses. Again, some are tied up with recent signs of breakdown in the traditionally ordered forms of society and with consequent increase in basis anxiety (cf. again *The Fear of Freedom*, by Eric Fromm). Hence the remarkable recrudescence of explicit religious and mystical sentiment in the crisis years from 1938 onwards, with a spate of books—like those of Gerald Heard and Lord Elton—which try to persuade the public to abandon reality-thinking for fantasy-thinking in their dealings with the world around them.

In the past there have been many swings of the pendulum. But never has hatred of reason been frankly admitted, as it is at present by Fascist thought. Always before reason has at least been aped; only now is it denied.

(2) UNIFYING FORMULAE

The poor physicists, appalled at the desert that their formulae have revealed, call upon God to give them comfort . . . and the answer that the physicists think they hear to their cry is only the frightened beating of their own hearts.
            —Bertrand Russell. "The Scientific Outlook."

Thinkers, theorists, and individuals accustomed to logical medita-tion . . . are restless, annoyed, pained at certain apparent discords between theory and fact or between one theory and another, and do everything in their power to attenuate, eliminate or dissemble them.
            —Pareto. "The Mind and Society."

I don't believe in beliefs. I believe in knowledge—Evan Jones.

The implications of the present flight from reason suggest interesting speculations on the tendency of a few present-day scientists (born and bred in the hopeful nineteenth century) to postulate a surprisingly immaterial sort of Unifying Principle, such as a Pantheistic Principle which makes Evolution emerge, a Mathematical God, or an Underlying Purpose—a Unifying Principle which will help to make the scientists' conception of the universe less uncomfortably chaotic and amorphous. Such postulations have, I think, something to do with a desire to believe in Free-Will. But for the moment let us leave this aside. From another aspect, however, they seem connected with the search for a Unifying Formula—for some coherent explanation of the universe. This search has always been one of the avowed objects of philosophers. I do not want to suggest that such a formula cannot exist; though it seems to me more likely that, if ever we get as far as finding theories to fit all the facts of the universe, they will be too complex to be grasped as a whole, and thus will be useless as a " coherent explanation ".[1] What I do want to suggest is that the motives behind the search are not always as simple as they seem. The fundamental desire involved is naturally the desire to attain knowledge—to find out the truth. But what is this but the desire to understand—to feel that one has control over one's surroundings? From this point of view the long-sought Unifying Formula is a very tempting prize. If only it could really be found, what a mental comfort it would be ! The whole mass of knowledge could then be arranged into a pattern or, to quote Freud—a *Weltanschauung* (a world-view),[2] which he defines as " an intellectual construction, which gives a unified solution of all the problems of our existence in virtue of a comprehensive hypothesis, a construction, therefore, in which no question is left open and in which everything in which we are interested finds a place. It is easy to see that the possession of such a *Weltanschauung* is one of the ideal wishes of mankind. When one believes in such a thing, one feels secure in life, one knows what one ought to strive after, and how one ought to organize one's emotions and interests to the best purpose. . . . It is (also) easy to see that the qualities which, as we have shown, are expected of a *Weltanschauung* have a purely emotional basis. Science takes account of the fact that the mind of man creates such demands and is ready to trace their source but it has not the slightest ground for thinking them justified. On the contrary, it does well to distinguish carefully between illusion (the results of emotional demands of that kind) and knowledge."

[1] This needs qualifying in view of the fact that scientific theories have recently tended towards simpler assumptions. But these assumptions do not make a comprehensive understanding of the world any simpler. On the contrary !—as emphasized by the following passage from page 225 of *The Evolution of Physics* (1938), by Albert Einstein and Leopold Infeld : " To clear the way leading from theory to experiment of unnecessary and artificial assumptions, to embrace an ever-wider region of facts, we must make the chain longer and longer. The simpler and more fundamental our assumptions become, the more intricate is our mathematical tool of reasoning ; the way from theory to observation becomes longer, more subtle, and more complicated."

[2] See " A Philosophy of Life " in *New Introductory Lectures on Psycho-Analysis*.

The search for a Unifying Formula is thus mainly an attempt to find something which, whether it be objectively true or not, is certainly a form of Comfortable Concept. This is, I think, the reason why so many philosophers have never admitted the possibility that there might not after all be any such formula. It is also, I think, the main reason why some philosophers (among them, it seems, Freud himself !), having found a pattern into which they could manage to force an appreciable part of their knowledge, have fallen to the temptation to believe that this pattern is the perfect one into which *everything* will fit. They have, in consequence, clung on to it with passionate tenacity, distorting all the facts that don't quite fit and ignoring all those that don't fit at all. The real secret of the pattern's fascination has been hidden from them and, what is more, they would much rather it remained hidden. Far better for them to believe that they have found Truth than that they have merely found Comfort !

Even where philosophies have failed to construct a completely Unifying Formula, the urge towards it has tended to show itself in the components of the construction. Thus, Plato's theory of Forms postulated one ideal form which was " manifested " in all the particular members of a class ; in other words, there was an ideal or universal form of Man, of which all particular men were a sort of copy. In fact, one can say that idealist schools of philosophy in general postulate *a* reality behind the multitudinous phenomena of the world. This reality is given various names and described in various ways according to the particular school, but in each case it is regarded essentially as a unity. And the same thing applies to *the* Principle of Life which is postulated by various Vitalist systems. Sometimes, of course, philosophies have been forced to allow that there may be two fundamental stuffs in the universe. Again, there have been some, such as those of Heracleitus and Bergson, which have regarded everything as continually changing. But, even then, they seem to imply that " the only reality " is change. It is true that modern physics is leading us to a conception of the universe as consisting of a sort of interchangeable mass and energy. But, as suggested by the quotation from Einstein above, this does not help us to a Unifying Formula which will be of every-day use. In any case, the point is that philosophies tend to show a strong *pre-conceived* urge to find a Unifying Formula.

Among beliefs which do not now aspire to the dignity of being called philosophies, there are many which go wholeheartedly for unity. They range from those connected with the philosophers' stone and the elixir of life—now rather out of date—to those connected, as late as 1941, with Joanna Southcott's box. The advertisements of the Panacea Society, prominently displayed during the first years of the war, suggested that the box, which had been opened in 1928 and discovered to contain nothing of importance, was not the " real box " and that, when this real box was really opened, it would be discovered to contain the secret of the universe and its cure.

It would be a waste of time to analyse the fundamentally irrational philosophies—the ones that, at first sight, provide the obvious examples—as it would be a waste of time to analyse and expose the irrationalities of Hitler's or Mussolini's ideology. The people who see through them do not need an analysis; and the people who fall for them would find nothing more tedious than a careful semantic and psychological examination. In any case, it would be like enumerating the holes in a sieve.

A common method of persuading oneself that one has found a Unifying Formula or Pattern is to make it so amorphous that, instead of having to distort the facts to fit the Pattern, one merely stretches the Pattern to fit the facts. Then whatever shape the Pattern takes, it is still *called* the same and therefore is assumed to *be* the same. However, this kind of formula does not appear to be so dangerous as the other; for it does at least avoid distorting the facts—it only plays about with labels for facts.

In my opinion an example of this latter type of formula is provided by the philosophy of Dialectical Materialism. This formula is much less tempting than the average, because it is perhaps the least deistic and most material of the many formulae that have been postulated at one time or another (though, as Mr. Edmund Wilson points out in *To the Finland Station*, the triadic Thesis, Antithesis and Synthesis, derived from Hegel, is surprisingly like " the old Trinity, taken over from the Christian theology, as the Christians had taken it over from Plato "). What applies to it should therefore apply all the more to other formulae, and it is for this reason that I take it as an example.

Unfortunately, it is sometimes difficult to avoid being misinterpreted as saying more than one intends. I must therefore emphasize that, in my opinion, the methods of thought for which Dialectical Materialism attempts to provide a philosophical basis are the best so far devised for the purpose of reality-thinking about many problems of the world. Dialectical Materialism has therefore great practical value as a weapon of propaganda for clear thinking. I do not want to question its methods of thought as applied to specific sciences. I merely want to question the legitimacy of turning a useful classification into a universal explanation. I must also emphasize strongly (a) that the temptingness of Dialectical Materialism is not *proof* of its falsity; and (b) that its correctness or otherwise as a *Weltanschauung* has no bearing on the validity of Marx's observations in the restricted field of history and sociology. An observation may apply in a special field without applying universally. And, in fact, Marx himself was chiefly concerned to show that the dialectical process governed the relationships of social classes. It is true that, again as Mr. Wilson suggests, he can hardly have failed to find comfort in the way his belief helped to convince him that the social changes he desired must eventually come to pass.[1] And Marx was also naturally delighted when he thought he had found the Dialectic to apply to Higher Mathematics. But he does not appear to have had any violent urge to believe that it governed the entire natural world. On the other hand, some of his followers have spent a lot of time in trying to make everything " fit in ".

But what does this process of " fitting in " really entail? It appears to consist first of all in defining the " dialectical process " sufficiently vaguely for it to be said to cover a number of different classes of process (such as the " struggle of opposites ", the " negation of negation ", etc.), each of

---

[1] It is often pointed out that two of Marx's predictions have not been confirmed by history. These are, (a) that the class-interest of the proletariat would bring them to make a stand against the propertied class, and (b) that there would be a progressive absolute increase in proletarian misery. They appear to be the ones that follow most directly from the Marxian assumption that the process of history is a sequence of logical necessity tending towards a goal. Compare Thorstein Veblen's Essay on " The Economics of Karl Marx " in *The Place of Science in Modern Civilization*. Veblen contrasts the purposive, " teleological " basis of Marx's theory with the Darwinian scheme of thought with its " blindly cumulative causation, in which there is no trend, no final term, no consummation ". This latter appears to be much the more " materialist " view.

which, in turn, is defined vaguely enough to cover a fairly
wide variety of natural phenomena. Thus, by the law of
geometrical progression, the number of phenomena which can
be labelled " dialectical " is at once most satisfactorily large.
All that has then to be done is to pick out the examples from
nature and pin them down. For instance, the study of
evolutionary processes has shown that certain characteristics
of a species become so modified by the development of other
characteristics that they cease to be efficient instruments of
survival, and that the strain of that species which is most
likely to survive in future is that in which these inefficient
modified characteristics become gradually improved by the
process of mutation and selection. Professor J. B. S. Haldane
quotes an example in *Dialectical Materialism and Modern
Science:* " Man has recently developed a large brain which,
among other things, has cramped his teeth and bent his nasal
passages. The teeth and nose are among the weakest and
most readily infected parts of our bodies." He goes on to
explain that these inefficient characteristics will probably
improve in our remote descendents. Now, this process might
be more shortly—though more vaguely—called a process of
" beneficent progress " or an example of the " undulatory "
theory of nature, in which all phenomena rise to prominence
and then fall into abeyance.[1] On the other hand, by using
the word " negation " rather vaguely, it can, with equal
appropriateness or inappropriateness be called an example of
" the negation of the negation ", the former efficiency of man's
teeth and nose being regarded as negated by their present
weakness, and this weakness in turn being negated by their
future improvement. This is, of course, how Professor
Haldane sees it. " Natural selection ", he says, " is likely to
negate this weakness in our remote descendents."

What he has done, in effect, is to use the label " negation
of negation " as a convenient way of referring to a certain
class of natural process ; and there is no reason why he should
not do so. Nor is there any reason why he should not make
this class fairly comprehensive by using the same label for
referring to rather different kinds of process. It is after all
impractical, as we have already seen, to apply a different label

---

[1] The " Undulatory " *Weltanschauung,* now I come to think of it, fits a
lot of things beautifully. But, as I have just this moment invented it, I
have not had time to go into it deeply.

to each and every different phenomenon. But the processes to which Professor Haldane applies this particular label do in fact differ considerably. Compare the development of scientific theory and practice, for example, with that of teeth and noses. "At the end of the nineteenth century", says Professor Haldane, "the atomic theory in chemistry was generally accepted, though Ostwald and a few other chemists stood out. But the number of atoms in a gram was uncertain within a factor of a hundred or more. Then Thomson showed that electrons could be detached from atoms in a gas, and Rutherford that atoms broke up. This negated the atom as an "eternal brick", but made it possible to count atoms with great accuracy, since individual electrons or atomic explosions produce effects which are visible with a microscope." We can also compare Marx's own famous example, from *Kapital*: the process in which "the expropriators are expropriated. The capitalistic mode of appropriation, the result of the capitalist mode of production, produces capitalist private property. This is the first negation of individual private property, as founded on the labour of the proprietor. But capitalist production begets, with the inexorability of a law of Nature, its own negation. It is the negation of negation."

In my opinion these three processes are rather different. And there are, I think, equal or greater differences between the other processes that Professor Haldane cites (ranging from the breaking of a stick or metal bar which is over-bent to the modern geological theory of the formation of certain mountain ranges). Similarly, with the processes that are picked out as examples of "the unity of opposites", not only in the pamphlet already mentioned, but also in his more detailed study of the question, *The Marxist Philosophy and the Sciences* (1938) (cf. particularly page 97 and page 114). In fact, these expressions, as labels for classes of process, appear to be sufficiently vague to force the conclusion that the main similarity between the processes included in the classes lies in the label applied to them.

The use of such labels may be justified as an aid to a rough classification. But I do not think it can be regarded as a sound basis for the conclusion, implied by Professor Haldane, that because various processes are *called* "negation of negation" or "unities of opposites", and because these in turn are called examples of the "dialectical" process, there is some sort of unified conception which negates the actual diversity of natural phenomena and brings them into the party line. The Unifying Formula which he has established seems to me to indicate a fact, not about facts, but about words. The point is confirmed by the following passage from Eugenio Rignano.[1] He is discussing the theory of Hegel upon which the dialectic was founded. "This classification or ' framing ' of successive phenomena of reality in thesis, antithesis, and synthesis is always possible, owing precisely to the great vagueness of these concepts. So that, even if the evolution of the world had followed another course, the same classification would still have adapted itself without any difficulty. . . . This great vagueness of concepts . . . would be fatal for constructive reasoning, which aims at producing mentally and consequently foreseeing new *facts*. But it is of the greatest advantage for metaphysics, because it shelters the intentional *presentation* of the whole of reality, as it already exists, from any possibility of contradiction on the part of reality itself."

Professor Haldane himself answers this kind of objection in an article on "The Marxist Philosophy" (from *Keeping Cool*). His answer appears to depend on two arguments: (a) that "the human mind is so intimately dependent on matter that it really can mirror its behaviour ", and (b) that " the union of opposites, for example, is very often a hard physical fact ". The first argument seems to be deprived of validity by the Dialectical Materialists' own statement that reality (i.e. both mind and matter) consists of different classes of the same kind of process. In any case, if the ideas of the mind reflect reality, then not only must the unity of opposites exist—but so must God. The second argument begs the linguistic question.

The linguistic aspect of the matter is illustrated more directly by the Dialectical Materialists' use of the expression " transformation of quantity into quality and vice versa " as a label for yet another class of natural process—one which was regarded by Marx and Engels as a fundamental dialectical

[1] *The Psychology of Reasoning* (1923), page 244. Rignano uses the word " intentional" in the last sentence as suggesting that " the metaphysical reasoner aims solely at classifying phenomena or objects of reality, *existing and already known*, in some conceptual frame, with the object of presenting the world in conformity to his own desires ". This suggestion is fully worked out by Rignano in his chapter on Metaphysical Reasoning. I refer to it again in the next section.

process and which, as Professor Haldane admits, covers four slightly different facts or processes. The expression derives, like all the more metaphysical parts of Dialectical Materialism, from Hegel, the idealist, who originally discovered the law that "merely quantitative changes beyond a certain point pass into qualitative differences". But what is this law? Is it a law of nature, applicable to objective phenomena?—or of language, applicable to words? The implication of the dialectical approach is that it is a law of nature. But for this to be so, it must make a prediction of very high probability about objective phenomena, as a law of dynamics makes predictions about the movements of objects. Is a difference of quality an objective phenomenon? I would suggest that it is only an abstraction, i.e. a linguistic convenience for describing our own *attitude* towards two objective phenomena. (One person, from one point of view, will see certain differences between two things; another person, from another point of view, will see different differences or even none at all.) However, this is an obscure point of semantics and would take too long to elaborate, though it has been touched upon in the chapter on Hypostatization. The fact remains that the dialectical approach necessitates the assumption that the passing of a quantitative change into a qualitative difference indicates a definite process or event of some sort in the objective world; and this, in turn, rests on the assumption that the abstract words "quality" and "quantity" have each a one and only correct meaning, so defined that there is no chance of their overlapping. As I hope I have shown, this assumption is a form of Comfortable Concept and is unjustified. For instance, let us take a simple example: compare two wisps of hay with a billion wisps of hay. In the first place the qualities of the billion wisps depend on whether or not they are regarded as a haystack (e.g. the stack will differ in shape, pliability and heat from individual wisps); the qualities therefore are subjective aids to classification. In the second place, it depends on how the word "quality" is defined whether some of the differences are classed as quantitative or qualitative. For instance, size is a quality (the quality of largeness)—or, on second thoughts, is it a measure of quantity? *It can be either*.

I think it follows that Hegel's law is in effect a statement, not about facts, but about language; and could be re-stated less metaphysically as "some processes which can (without going contrary to accepted usage) be classified as changes of quantity can *also* be classified as changes of quality"—the method of classification depending of course on the object in view.

Hegel could not have been an idealist without hypostatizing his abstractions (thus ignoring the vagueness of their meanings), and therefore it never occurred to him that his law was a law of language. He took it for granted that it was a law of nature.

Hegel's philosophy is, I think, a very good example of a "tempting" one, in that it asserts an idealist Unifying Formula, and, in doing so, adopts numbers of Comfortable Concepts about the meanings of words. It is significant that Marx specifically denied the idealist part of Hegelianism, thus denying his followers the Hegelian Comforts. But it seems to me that some of his followers have not been quite ascetic enough. They keep being incommoded by the way in which the materialist part of their belief obstinately asserts the baffling diversity and complexity of nature.[1] And, in spite of the fact that this is its most important point of divergence from metaphysics, they implicitly deny it by trying to establish a Unifying Formula. This is, I think, because they feel an inner necessity to believe that things are simpler than they are, so that they can feel they understand. Professor Haldane himself is quite aware of this point. He states, in *Science and Everyday Life*, that he has managed to get rid of longstanding gastritis caused by worry and anxiety. "I had it for about fifteen years," he says, "until I read Lenin and other writers, who showed me what was wrong with society and how to cure it. Since then I have needed no magnesia."

Unfortunately, the chase after a Unifying Formula translates the Dialectical Materialists into the world of subjective opinion already inhabited by the metaphysicians, and lays them open to criticism which would otherwise be quite irrelevant. If they want comfort as well as accuracy—if they want faith

---

[1] "All nature, from the smallest thing to the biggest . . . is in a constant state of coming into being and going out of being, in a constant flux, in a ceaseless state of movement and change." Engels. *Dialectics of Nature.* "It is, of course, absurd to say that materialism ever . . . professed a 'mechanical' picture of the world, and not an electro-magnetic or some other, immeasurably more complex, picture of the world as matter in motion." Lenin. *Materialism and Empiricism.*

and science—they will get the worst of both worlds and only a part of either. On the other hand, it must be admitted that, if what they want is converts to their philosophy, they have chosen the best method. For it is clear enough that the purely rational materialist attitude is uninviting unless it is tempered by some comforting simplification. Perhaps after all Professor Haldane remains, in practice, an uncompromising materialist, and it is only in his public writings that he tempers the wind to the shorn lamb.

I have dealt with this example in detail partly because it illustrates some of the effects of the desire to understand, as well as some of the methods used in satisfying it, and chiefly because, what applies to a fundamentally materialist *Weltanschauung* applies all the more to those which are asserted by idealists and metaphysicists; for the temptations of the former are as nothing to the temptations of the latter.

My choice of example, I must repeat, is consequently not to be taken as a sign of disagreement with the general principles upon which Dialectical Materialists base their approach to scientific problems nor with the objective conclusions they reach (and certainly not with those of Professor Haldane); but only as a suggestion that the attempt to combine these with a metaphysical outlook is probably a form of fantasy-thinking. In fact, as will have been gathered from my general thesis, the materialist approach appears to be the only one open to anyone who wishes to be rational (in the sense of " wishing to form correct opinions about the objective world ") while, according to a number of modern scientists, the dialectical approach, in so far as it emphasizes the view that reality is a flux, and counteracts the old-fashioned tendency to regard it as made up of self-subsisting entities, is essential to an understanding of recent research, especially in physics. All the more pity is it then that the clear-headedness of Dialectical Materialism should have been fogged by metaphysics. For, though the Unifying Formula may bring in some converts, it may also scare away some rationalists. And, what is worse, the Marxists' evident desire to prove the universal validity of their formula gives a handle to their opponents by lending weight to the fallacious and tempting view that failure to prove it will demonstrate the falseness of any particular aspect of Marxism.

(3) THE QUESTIONS OF METAPHYSICS

What is important is that every inference be a tested inference;
or (since often this is not possible) that we discriminate between
beliefs that rest upon tested evidence and those that do not, and be
accordingly on our guard as to the kind and degree of assent or belief
that is justified.—John Dewey. "How We Think."

Alice sighed wearily. " I think you might do something better with
the time," she said, " than waste it asking riddles with no answers."

" If you knew Time as well as I do," said the Hatter, " you
wouldn't talk about wasting it. It's him."

" I don't know what you mean," said Alice.

—Lewis Carroll.

The belief that words have a true meaning is the first and
necessary step towards the metaphysical attitude and towards
the idealist type of philosophy. One cannot be happy trying
to investigate the nature of reality or knowledge or goodness
without believing that these labels stand for definite concepts.
I have already suggested that such problems, when stated in
this way, are irrelevant, and that they ask questions to which
there are no objective answers, since such answers must depend
on an arbitrary definition of the concept being investigated.
I can now, to some extent, clarify this statement.

A large number of philosophies—and, as far as I know, all
metaphysical philosophies—are concerned with enquiring into
the nature of some abstract concept (of the type of " reality ",
" truth ", " goodness ", etc.). This being so, it follows that
such a school or system of philosophy attempts to show that
certain things are (say) " real "; and its opponents attempt
to show, conversely, that these things are not really real; but
that other things are. Such an attitude towards the concept
" reality " is only justifiable on the assumption that there is
such *a* concept. In other words, it must be assumed that it
has a true meaning, even though no one has yet agreed as to
what this true meaning is.

Thus, in trying to establish that " reality " or " truth " or
" goodness " *is* something or other, a philosopher is stating a
personal opinion, which can have no objective value as a
statement about the world outside his brain. To go back to
our original terminology, it can have no relation to reality-
thinking. As such, there is nothing wrong with it. People
are at liberty to take pleasure in discussions of this kind—to
imagine an abstract thing called " reality " or " goodness "
and to say what they would like it to be, just as they are at

liberty to paint pictures or to write poetry.   They are also at liberty, like the poet and the painter, to try and induce in other people a parallel experience of their own subjective emotion. On the other hand, they cannot expect their methods to give them, as well, a true picture of the concrete world—" true " being here used as it would be used by a scientist who said that the laws of dynamics gave him a true indication of what will happen when a bat hits a ball.

We come back here to the two worlds, the concrete world and the world of fantasy, distinguished by Pareto.[1]   The metaphysicians are like other people in having a strong desire to believe that they have a rational understanding of the universe.   They want to have the best of both worlds and, in consequence, they believe and assert that their propositions are applicable to the objective world as well as to their own subjective one.   As a further consequence, they take it for granted that there is some way of proving or disproving these propositions.   They do not realize that they might just as well try to prove the truth or falsity of my statement that I think my spaniel should be called " Fanny ".   No wonder they argue !   " But that isn't a *Fanny!* " they expostulate.   And, if it so happens that they like the name, " *This* is a Fanny," they say, pointing to their own dog.

This is one of the points at which the confusion between logical and practical certainty fogs the issue.   The metaphysicians' insistent search for logical certainty in their judgments about the objective world seems to be stimulated by the fact that the statements of mathematics and logic can be " logically " or " absolutely " certain.   For example, such an axiom as " Things which are equal to the same thing are equal to one another " is logically certain ; but it is certain

---

[1] Pareto applies the label " logico-experimental " to those sciences which deal with what we are calling the concrete or objective world ; and the label " non-logico-experimental " to those sciences which deal with the subjective or fantastic world.   But in acknowledging the existence of these two types of sciences, he emphasizes that they have nothing whatsoever to do with each other.   Reality-thinking, as we have been defining it, is thus logico-experimental ; while metaphysics and some philosophies are non-logico-experimental. " The mysteries of metaphysics," says Pareto, " stand on a footing with the mysteries of any other religion."   Paragraph 1,535, *Mind and Society*.

If I had used Pareto's terminology throughout, I would have achieved more exactness than is possible with familiar words, since a word only becomes familiar through acquiring a number of mental associations which diminish its exactness.   But, conversely, it is difficult to remember the meanings of unfamiliar words.   As I have said before, I have therefore tried to avoid too many of them.

merely because it is a re-statement of the fact that, if A, B and C are all identical (say) in area, we have agreed to describe the situation by saying " A and B are each equal to C and they are equal to each other." It is thus a re-statement of the definition of " equal "; it is a statement about how we use language, *not a fact about the objective world*. The propositions of mathematics and formal logic are themselves deductions, by a chain of reasoning, from axioms; and are thus more complex re-statements of definitions. For example, the statement—" Two and two makes four " is certainly true because it follows with logical certainty from the definition of " two " as the label for " one-and-one " and " four " as the label for " one-and-one-and-one-and-one ". Such propositions are sometimes classed as tautologies. They do not tell us new facts about the world. On the other hand they are useful because they re-state in various more convenient forms the implications of already known facts. Given the fact that a cistern is ten by six by four feet we can work out with the aid of our system of numerical terminology how many gallons of water it will hold. Similarly the syllogistic form of reasoning starts from two premises and deduces an inescapable conclusion. *If* the premises are correct, the conclusions must be correct. If all men are mortal, and if Hitler is a man, then Hitler is mortal. The conclusion does not involve the observation of a new fact; it brings to view a fact already implicit in the original premises or observations. When the premises are axioms, the conclusions can attain absolute certainty; when the premises are objective (i.e. " practically " certain) statements about the world, the conclusions cannot aspire to more than the same degree of practical certainty.

Because there *is* such a thing as absolute certainty to be found in the restricted field of statements about language, the metaphysicians expect and demand it in all fields. There are, I think, two main motives behind this demand. The first, as I have suggested, derives from the desire to understand and to lessen anxiety. The second depends on a wish to avoid the necessity of finding evidence for statements about the world— a necessity which is a bother to philosophers and forces them out of their ivory towers. In consequence, they seize upon the fact that axioms are " self-evident " and, by persuading themselves that these axioms *do* tell us things about the objective world, they imagine that it is possible to find out what the world is like without looking to see.   The knowledge provided by axioms they call *a priori* knowledge and, they say, it conveniently tells us logically provable things about the objective world for which no evidence need be collected.   I hope I have made it clear that objective knowledge can neither be absolutely certain nor dispense with objective evidence.

This confusion between logical and practical certainty is very useful to the metaphysician.   For it gives him an excuse, when faced by awkward questions, to appeal to science—to reality-thinking—for support, and to select all the evidence in his own favour.   Naturally, among the various opinions backed by science, there will be some which incidentally back his own view.   There will also be many which tend to upset it.   In order to deal with this difficulty the metaphysician has manœuvred himself into a beautiful position.   He can leave unquestioned all the opinions which favour him.   But, because *any* objective judgment or opinion can be shown to be only " practically " certain, he is able to pounce on the inconvenient ones and show—to his own and many other people's satisfaction—that they can be ignored because they cannot be proved with his kind of logical certainty.   (This controversial device is referred to again later with examples.)

There is a school of philosophers which admits the impossibility of absolute definitions and absolute certainty and devotes its time to the construction of a system of definitions " in use " which will reveal, with greater accuracy than does ordinary language, what exactly it is that we are saying when we state a proposition that is presumed to be true (cf. the chapter on " The Nature of Philosophical Analysis" in *Language, Truth and Logic*, by A. J. Ayer, and, for a short introduction, *Philosophy and Logical Syntax*, by Rudolf Carnap, in the series of Psyche Miniatures).   But it remains true that most of the different systems or schools of philosophy appear to differ only because they are trying to establish absolute definitions.   The various theories of knowledge (or schools of Epistemology), for instance, depend largely on arbitrary definitions of the word " know ".   The Empiricists say that we can only know what we gain from experience. The Nominalists say that we can only know the words and symbols used to talk about things, the things themselves being only conjectured.   Again, the Solipsists, carrying the chase after logical certainty to its logical extreme, created an ideally nonsensical philosophy by assuming that we cannot know anything unless it is absolutely certain, and thus denying any reality outside the individual Solipsist's own brain. (They challenged anybody to refute their theory and naturally refused to accept Dr. Johnson's "practical" method of kicking a large stone and saying, "I refute it thus.") And so on. What else does this mean than that the Empiricists are using the word "know" in one way and the Nominalists and Solipsists are using it in other ways? When the Nominalists say that what we gain from experience is different from what we gain from words, they are perfectly correct. But when they say that the former is not knowledge, while the latter is, they are merely asserting their dislike of anyone else's presuming to use the label in a different way from their own.

The trouble would, of course, be at once cleared up if all these types of experience or knowledge or what you will were admitted as phenomena from whose observation it is possible to make inferences of varying probability. The various types could then be given special labels for convenience in referring to them ; and the philosophical problem would disappear into thin air. The problems that would remain would turn out to be scientific ones rather than philosophical or metaphysical ones. For, once you have decided to label a certain class of phenomena as "real" (in a certain sense) you can then get down to the task of examining and describing the phenomena in this class and of searching for other phenomena which can be appropriately put in the same class. Similarly, it is perfectly legitimate to discuss whether certain things can be known, once you have defined exactly what you mean, for present purposes, by the word "know". Similarly again, it is nonsensical to enquire as to what "life" is, but it is sensible, having once adopted a certain definition of this label, to classify the phenomena of the world as accurately as possible according to whether they come into this definition or not, and then to observe and describe their characteristics. But what are all these activities? Clearly enough they are scientific— they come under such headings as physics, physiology and biology.

Any further illustration of this point is outside my scope. I must therefore refer anyone interested in a fuller treatment of it to Mr. Ayer's discussion in *Language, Truth and Logic*. In the meantime Lewis Carroll's Alice has already epitomized what I would like to have said, as will be seen from the quotation at the head of this section. Notice, incidentally, that the Hatter has not only hypostatized time but also personalized it. He was, after all, more than usually irrational.

However, it is not outside my scope to enquire into the problem of why philosophers should choose one meaning rather than another from the many which an abstract word possesses. It seems probable that their motives in so doing must often be similar to those which I suggested in Part III when discussing this habit from a general point of view. From what we saw then, it is clear that the adoption of a special meaning for a word, combined with copious use of the Utraquistic fallacy[1] will be a great help to a philosopher in proving—or at least believing—that his own *Weltanschauung* is the correct one. This suggests that his view may be formed *before* he starts to examine the evidence, and not after. In fact it appears that, in addition to the simple desire to understand, there may often exist a desire to construct an elaborate rationalization which will justify an opinion formed, not rationally, but at the behest of some obscure mixture of ingrained preferences and aversions.

If such may be the case with a philosopher, it may also be the case with a sociologist, economist or psychologist—with anyone, in fact, whose job it is to investigate phenomena which are not in their nature susceptible of the exact observation, measurement and verification that the physical sciences are able to apply. In such cases, theories cannot be verified with scientific accuracy; conversely, irrational or erroneous theories cannot easily be disproved. Though this means that the work of sociologists and psychologists is scientifically rather inexact, it does not, as some people contend, mean that nearly all their theories—especially the unpalatable ones—can be dismissed as mere guesses. They cannot, after all, be such wild guesses as would the theories of someone who had not troubled to study his subject at all, and they are at least potentially capable of objective verification, since they deal with objective phenomena. On the other hand their relative

---

[1] The fallacy of using a word in more than one sense. Examination of the writings of philosophers will show that this fallacy is the *sine qua non* of most of their arguments. "The Utraquistic subterfuge has probably made more bad arguments plausible than any other controversial device which can be practised upon trustful humanity." *The Meaning of Meaning,* by Ogden and Richards.

inexactness leaves a door wide open to temptation. If an opinion cannot be easily disproved there is little to stop it from being as irrational as its holder likes. And, in the case of sociologists and economists especially, there is the perennial temptation to believe that what they want is what the world in general ought to want. Thus, whenever we catch any of these people assuming that some word has a one and only true meaning, we can begin to suspect things.[1]

I have suggested that it is fatally easy for systems of philosophy and sociology to be in reality elaborate systems of rationalization. If it is easy, it is also likely. This is a conclusion which has been reached, though from different directions, by a number of people. "And now the astonishing and perturbing suspicion emerges", says Professor James Harvey Robinson, "that perhaps almost all that had passed for social science, political economy, politics and ethics in the past may be brushed aside by future generations as mainly rationalizing. John Dewey has already reached this conclusion in regard to philosophy (in *Reconstruction in Philosophy*). Veblen and other writers have revealed the various unperceived presuppositions of the traditional political economy, and now comes . . . Vilfredo Pareto, who . . . devotes hundreds of pages to substantiating a similar thesis affecting *all* the social sciences. This conclusion . . . is by no means fully worked out, and it is so opposed to nature that it will be very slowly accepted by the great mass of those who consider themselves thoughtful. As a historical student I am personally fully reconciled to this newer view."[2]

Here again, perfectionism raises its Gorgon head. Those who dislike the implications of an inexact science will seize upon such a view as Professor Robinson's as justification for ignoring them. But these sciences are still very much better than nothing, especially since the scientists themselves have become aware of the danger of rationalization.

[1] See Chapters XIV, XV and XVI of *The Tyranny of Words*, by Stuart Chase, for a large number of examples taken from the writings of economists.

[2] *The Mind in the Making*. See also *The Flight from Reason*, by Hector Hawton, which develops the theory as it applies in ancient history to ideologies (i.e. combined systems of art, religion, politics and morals). F. H. Bradley's famous remark on the same subject is seldom quoted in its proper—and significant—context. "Metaphysics," he said, "may be the finding of bad reasons for what we believe upon instinct; but," he added, as if in justification, "to find these reasons is no less an instinct." Precisely! Metaphysical speculation satisfies a human need, but this in no way proves that it tells us everything about the objective world.

(4) THE COMPLEXITY OF CAUSES

" I have finished another year," said God. . . .
Then he: " My labours—logicless—
*   You may explain : not I ;*
Sense-sealed I have wrought, without a guess
That I evolved a consciousness
*   To ask for reasons why."*

—Thomas Hardy. " New Year's Eve."

Metaphysical systems always end up, even if they do not begin, with hypostatization of abstract words. They are thus assuming the existence or subsistence of immaterial entities, though some of their propounders try to avoid the fact by clothing their hypostatizations in the vaguest possible terms. With this assumption, they have taken the first step towards a belief in some sort óf diety. The second step is greatly facilitated by applying a mental process rather like hypostatization to the causes of objective phenomena, the stimulus to the process being the desire to understand these causes.

As we have seen, the word " mind ", though originally a label for a complex of mental events, often becomes hypostatized into an entity. Similarly, when the causes of some phenomenon are too complex to be detailed, we naturally give them a single label for purposes of reference. We say that an apple falls to the ground because of the effect of gravity on it ; or that someone's kind action is due to his innate generosity. In such cases, we realize when we come to think of it that our " causes " are inadequate by themselves as explanations and that the whole thing is really more complex ; we know, in effect, that these things, gravity and generosity, are not entities.

This is a fact which we acknowledge easily enough whenever the causes in question are not too complex to be at least roughly apprehended by our minds. Though the fundamental explanation of gravitational force, for instance, may be still a mystery to most of us, we at least understand enough about the general laws of the mutual attraction of bodies for the behaviour of the apple not to seem miraculous. In other words, though we may not understand the ultimate causes we find that we can understand the proximate ones. And therefore we are quite prepared to believe in them. What is more, we are not at all surprised to find that they are " material " causes ;—we should indeed be most distrustful of anybody who tried to foist off on us, in their place, some immaterial entity—some miracle—as the real explanation.

But what happens when we cannot understand even the proximate causes ?—when, as far as we can see, there is no explanation ? Similarly, what happens when we trace our causes back and come up against those ultimate ones which even the Einsteins of this world have not yet understood ? I suggest that the same sort of thing happens as in the case of abstract words whose meanings are too varied to be easily grasped.

But before amplifying this suggestion I must, at the risk of tediousness, define the senses in which I am using the words " cause " and " material ", since the confusion of their meanings plays a large part in setting people at loggerheads over such questions as Vitalism and Materialism and even has an indirect effect in fostering irrational ideas about morality. In the case of the word " material " I need only emphasize that it has no connection with matter (in the ordinary sense of solid substance) but typifies any phenomena which exist in the objective world and which have observable relations with other phenomena. Thus, though some people would say that electrical forces are immaterial, they are—in the sense here used—" material " ; and so are the processes (whatever they are) that send messages along a nerve. The word " cause " is more of a problem. I can best indicate the sense in which I am using it as follows: Take two objective phenomena, A and B. Suppose that it has very often been observed that whenever A happens B happens also, and that up till now B has never been observed to happen without A. If, then, it appears extremely probable (as the scientists would say) or certain (as the ordinary person would say) that *whenever* A happens, B will also happen, this pair of phenomena is described and classified by labelling it a case of cause and effect ; and if A happens before B, then A is called the cause. (Although the flux of events cannot logically be divided up into discrete phenomena, we have to attempt the division in practice—as when, for instance, we say " There's a new moon to-night ". My arbitrary division is thus valid for practical purposes.)

At this point the reader will perhaps object that this is very obvious and that he knew it all before. I hope he does, for he will then be agreeing that the words " cause " and " effect " are very commonly used in the sense I have indicated. This sense, it is important to note, is a definitely restricted one and should not be confused with any imitations passing under the same name. In the first place it emphasizes that the word " cause " is only a label used as an aid to classification, the corollary being that the phenomena labelled " A " do really exist in the objective world and will go on existing even if some metaphysician chooses to use the word " cause " in a different way and then to prove to his own satisfaction that the things *he* means by it don't exist at all. (This is what metaphysicians often do.) In the second place, the definition does not imply any *necessary* relationship between the phenomena concerned ; it merely indicates the observed fact that they appear always in conjunction, and the very high probability that they will continue to do so. It is, in effect, though disguised, a statement similar to that of a scientific law, which does not—and cannot—aim at absolute certainty. The general " law of universal causation " is likewise a scientific law in that it affirms, not a certainty, but merely the extremely high probability, based on thousands of years of observation of phenomena which have been associated in the way labelled " cause and effect ", that all phenomena are so associated. Thus, though not absolutely certain, it is as certain a law as any that can be formulated about the objective world, since its application tells us things even more certain than the statement that the sun will rise in the east tomorrow.

This long and pedantic definition must seem at first sight a waste of time. But it is necessary because it is my justification for assuming the validity of the law of universal causation (which is the basis not only of my whole argument but of all reality-thinking and of all scientific research), and because there are some philosophers who assert that a true cause must have some necessary relation with its effect (i.e. that *their* meaning of the expression " cause and effect " is the only correct one), who then show that this necessary relation cannot be proved and, having demonstrated that the law disobeys their rules, imagine that they have denied its validity.[1] The basis of this attitude (which is essentially the metaphysical attitude in its confusion between the two kinds of certainty) is of course the desire to understand, with its imperious demand for absolute certainty, and its consequent refusal to admit that this may be unattainable. Thus, for these philosophers a law is not a law unless it is absolutely certain (again the one true meaning) and any inconvenient theories which are based on the law of universal causation can be safely ignored. If this attitude were confined to meta- physicians and philosophers it would hardly concern us here. But, as will be seen later, it unfortunately spreads with deadly effect into the fields of morality and politics, lending weight to the suggestion that immaterial entities may exist and that the rational approach is incapable of producing a correct view of the objective world.

When the word " cause " is used in the sense I have indicated, it is of course redundant to call it a material cause. However, for safety's sake, I will occasionally use the word " material " to indicate *this* kind of cause, as opposed to the immaterial somethings that are so frequently postulated.

I think it is clear, from what we have just seen, that the law of cause and effect (as defined by the scientists) is not only valid but is a " practical " certainty. Few things, then, could be more rational than to assume, for the purpose of understanding the objective world, that all phenomena have material causes, even though we may not yet know what these causes are. I think it will also be agreed that there is no rational basis for postulating a limit to the complexity of the material causes of any phenomenon ; there is certainly good reason for thinking that this complexity must often be immeasurably greater than can be grasped as a whole

---

[1] See pages 55 ff. of *Language, Truth and Logic*, by A. J. Ayer, for an elucidation of Hume's treatment of the subject. Hume is widely supposed to have denied the law of causation, and this supposed denial is one of the main-stays of the philosophers' argument. Mr. Ayer however points out that he was merely denying, as I have tried to do, that there is any logical necessity in the relation between cause and effect and " in fact he was concerned only with defining it (causation). So far is he from asserting that no causal propositions are true that he is himself at pains to give rules for judging of the existence of causes and effects." The philosophical associations of the word " cause " have now led some of the advanced sciences to replace the notion of cause by the less misleading notion of " functional dependence ". However, for my purposes it is the thing that matters, not the name. The attempts of certain modern scientists to deny the law of universal causation on scientific grounds are referred to later.

by a single human brain. It is therefore *possible* that a
phenomenon which seems to us completely unexplainable may
in fact have causes too complex for us to understand.
However, though it may be possible, this is difficult and
uncomfortable to believe. If we want to understand the
world, what sort of satisfaction will we get from a *Weltanschauung* which suggests that our desire may be unattainable?
Which asks us, not to affirm something already proved and
certain but to refrain from denying something which is merely
possible? The temptation is obvious. If only we could find
some concept which would present to our brains a less uncomfortable picture of the world ! Is it perhaps possible after all,
we ask ourselves, that there may be immaterial causes—or,
better still, one Immaterial Cause? Unfortunately, in the
sense in which we have been using the word " cause "—no !
And yet, for many people, it seems easier to believe than the
alternative—easier than if it had been merely improbable.
Certum est, quia impossibile est.

This is where hypostatization comes in so useful. It
makes such a belief seem more plausible by providing labels,
already conveniently simplified, for the causes whose complexity we wish to overlook. Why does a man strive to satisfy
his appetites? The proximate causes, complex enough in
themselves, are usually labelled " instinct ". But what is it
that gives the instincts their impulsive power? What, in
effect, are the ultimate causes? They are unknown. They
are possibly too complex for us to understand. But we cannot
talk or think about them in comfort without giving them a
name, so we call them (say) " purposive energy ". And,
after we have got used to this name and provided it with a set
of associations all its own, it becomes a unified concept in our
minds all ready to be transformed into a self-subsisting—and
necessarily immaterial—entity, complete with capital letters.
Since such an entity is just what we are looking for, the
temptation is irresistible ; the transformation is effected ; and
there we are !—comfortably set upon the path which leads to
Vitalism. The process is paralleled by (and probably an
aftermath of) the child's tendency to justify at all costs any
phenomenon he comes across. He has no appreciation of the
idea of chance (i.e. of causes too obscure or too complicated
to be unravelled) and will therefore assume the existence of a
simple, but not necessarily logical, explanation of anything

which strikes his attention, e.g. " Why is that stick lying there on the grass ? " the child asks, assuming that there exists a brief and complete explanation.[1]

The actual label used in this process of hypostatization is unimportant, the prime consideration being that it provides a unified concept. Thus William McDougall, who was admittedly a vitalist, used the label " hormic energy " and pointed out in his *Outline of Psychology* that " Schopenhauer's ' will-to-live ', Professor Bergson's ' *élan vital* ', and Doctor C. G. Jung's ' libido ', are alternative expressions for the purposive or hormic energy that is manifested in human and animal behaviour ".

It is outside my scope to examine in detail the various arguments which have been used to support the Vitalistic view. I should, however, point out that since this view supposes some sort of *quid* (i.e. indefinable what ?) which is a principle of life or a purpose in the world, it not only satisfies by simplification the desire to understand but also provides a comfortable refuge for the many people who have an aversion to any idea which suggests that they may not be completely free agents. The believer in Free-Will is thus a Vitalist, in this sense, because Vitalism implicitly denies the law of cause and effect and leaves him free to deny all the unpleasant implications of what *he* understands by the concept of Determinism.

The situation is analogous in the so-called Vitalism-Mechanism controversy. Here the issue is clouded by the way in which any view which merely tries to deny Vitalism is associated with such words as " Mechanism ", " Materialism ", " Determinism ", etc., which have various and confused philosophical or scientific implications, not to mention the extraneous implications introduced by their use in more collo-quial senses. In particular, such words have often been used as names for theories which were themselves philosophical over-simplifications. The difficulty here is once again the baffling complexity of the world. Unless we assume " the existence and operation of a non-material entity or causal agent as an essential factor in the regulation of form, behaviour, and evolution of organisms "[2] we must think of any living organism as being an unimaginably complex system

[1] Cf. particularly *The Language and Thought of the Child*, by Jean Piaget, Chapters IV and V.
[2] This is from the definition of Vitalism given in the *Dictionary of Psychology* (Ed. Howard C. Warren).

of interactions between chemical, physical and electrical (i.e. material) processes. (This is, in itself, much too simple a statement; but it serves to indicate briefly the inordinately lengthy statement that would be reasonably adequate.) It is clear that an *unimaginably* complex system cannot have any close resemblance to any system with which we, in our ordinary lives, are familiar. On the other hand, the only way in which the characteristics of such a system can be described in general terms is by relating them to something that is already known. The consequence is that anyone who wishes to deny the Vitalist view must either give his theory some negative name like " non-metaphysical non-vitalism " or, if he wants to typify it more positively, must adopt some label whose purpose is to indicate, roughly and by extremely remote analogy, the *kind* of thing he considers a living organism to be.

Thus Professor Lancelot Hogben, in discussing the imperfections of the Vitalist approach to problems of biology[1] advocates a form of " non-metaphysical non-vitalist " approach which he calls Mechanism. He uses this word not because he thinks a living organism has the attributes of a machine, but (if I understand him correctly) merely because it helps to typify his approach by suggesting that it is in some respects similar to the old-fashioned Mechanism. He makes it clear, however, that it is by no means so simplified as the older Mechanism. He specifically qualifies it by calling it " the new mechanistic or ' *publicist* ' standpoint ",[2] using the word " publicist " to indicate roughly what I have been calling the standpoint of reality-thinking, which tries to form correct opinions about the objective world and is not concerned with subjective opinions or emotions. He also takes great pains to point out that " the principle of mechanism, that a complex system is interpretable only by reference to the properties of its constituent parts, is not urged in the spirit of dogmatic assertion, but because it has served us well in the past ".[3] In other words, it is essentially scientific. At the same time it in no way implies that a living organism is anything else but what it is; it does not suggest that such an organism is comparable to a piece of machinery, nor that consciousness is a form of matter, nor that a human being is unable to choose

---

[1] In *The Nature of Living Matter* (1930).
[2] Page 100, op. cit.
[3] Page 97, op. cit.

between two alternatives (in the ordinary sense of this phrase). What it does suggest (apart from the futility of trying to increase our knowledge of living organisms without invoking the law of universal causation) is only to be understood by reference to the methods of enquiry which it advocates, and cannot be compressed, from Professor Hogben's thousands of words, into a *Weltanschauung*. Thus Professor Hogben might say—like Humpty Dumpty when referring to the word " glory "—that the concept " Mechanism ", in this context, means just what he chooses it to mean—neither more nor less. And any attempt to saddle it with another meaning more consonant with the colloquial or philosophical usage will naturally lead to all the muddles characteristic of metaphysical juggling with words. And yet this is just what people do attempt. There are, I think, two reasons for this. In the first place, they are unable to stomach the enormous complexity and the lack of absolute certainty implied by a non-vitalist view, with the result that they conceive it in terms of the simplified certainty which they demand of all concepts and make it out to be more repugnant than it really is, this alone being sometimes enough to drive them into the Vitalist camp. In the second place, they often have—as I have suggested—additional motives for wanting to join this camp. And a little juggling with meanings enables them, once arrived there, to consolidate their position by demolishing a nonsensical theory which they fondly imagine is that of their opponents, but which is really their own invention.

Professor Hogben himself notes several examples of this controversial trick.[1] But it is not only against Professor Hogben's Mechanism that it is directed. Since it is tacitly based on the assumption that there is one true meaning for such words as Mechanism, Materialism and Determinism, it can be equally useful in proving first that any and all views called by these names are nonsense and then, with equal logicality, that some sort of Vitalism must be sense. (The fact that *some* forms of Mechanism, for instance, have been nonsensical

---

[1] See pages 91, 99 and 100 of *The Nature of Living Matter*. The fallacy upon which it depends is known as the Fallacy of Extension. One " extends " one's opponent's statement by making it out to be more extreme or more comprehensive than as originally stated. "It can be done," says R. H. Thouless in *Straight and Crooked Thinking*, " either by luring him on to extend it himself in the heat of argument or, more impudently, by misrepresenting what he said. It is a very common trick, often done involuntarily." The fallacy is further illustrated in the Supplement.

over-simplifications naturally makes it all the easier.) For example, Professor T. P. Nunn[1] says, "A supra-human spectator . . . would see that they (purposive processes) all differ from purely mechanical processes by the presence of an internal 'drive'." The adverb "purely" gives him away. Who has suggested that such processes are purely mechanical in the sense that he implies?

Whatever the rights and wrongs of the actual debate and whatever the motives, the fact remains that there are people who postulate the existence of immaterial forces or entities— who, in other words, decide that, as they don't know what the causes of some phenomenon are, they will invent something else and call it a cause. To those whose attitude is naturally materialistic the irrationality of such a postulation is shown by the fact that it abjures what we have called reality-thinking and assumes the existence of something for which there is neither objective necessity nor objective evidence. But to others the opposite view seems much preferable and therefore practically obvious or "self-evident" (which merely means that there is no independent evidence for it). Here we see again the same mental process occurring as we have found to operate in the human attitude towards all natural phenomena. There is no reason to postulate a limit to the complexity of these phenomena ; it is therefore a necessity of the human mind rather than of the objective world which impels us to take it for granted that something immaterial (unreasonable) steps in to help us out of our difficulty in understanding and to preserve for us that belief in human independence of action which has been instilled into us by our cultural and religious environment.[2]

This mental necessity is so urgent that it brooks no denial. It ignores the lack of evidence in favour of its postulations ; it also ignores a significant amount of indirect evidence against them. This evidence is provided in the first place by the fact that, in past attempts to explain the unknown, innumerable such postulations have been confidently made and, with the

[1] Quoted by William McDougall in *An Outline of Psychology*.
[2] "In making the world He brought into existence vast numbers of things which always have to obey His law for them—from stars and planets to atoms and electrons ; these have no choice but to obey. But He also made creatures—men and women—who could disobey His law for them, and do so ; He did this in order that there might be some who gave Him a free obedience. . . ." *Christianity and Social Order*. William Temple. I suggest later an explanation as to *why* this belief has been instilled into us by our environment.

advance of knowledge, have subsequently been shown to be unwarranted (e.g. witchcraft, spirits, Thor, magnetism, etc.) ; and secondly by the fact that the size and capacity of the average human brain has not perceptibly varied for thousands of years, so that it is by no means unreasonable to suggest that many human beings are to-day trying to explain the unknown in the same way that their predecessors did three hundred years ago. (The increase of *knowledge* during the interval need not, of course, be taken as a sign of increased mental powers, since it can more plausibly be attributed to the fact that the results of scientific research have become increasingly useful to the advance of industry.)

(5) THE FREE-WILL OF PHYSICISTS

These men (the Authorities whom men nowadays follow) set down whatever is unknown or unattained by themselves or their masters as beyond the limits of possibility ; and, as if on the authority of their art, declare that it is impossible to be known or done, most presumptuously and invidiously turning the imperfection of their own discoveries into a libel on Nature herself, and the despair of everyone else.

—Francis Bacon. "Novum Organum."

Science, being human enquiry, can hear no answer except an answer couched somehow in human tones. Primitive man stood in the mountains and shouted against a cliff ; the echo brought back his own voice, and he believed in a disembodied spirit. The scientist of to-day stands counting out loud in the face of the unknown. Numbers come back to him—and he believes in the Great Mathematician.—Richard Hughes. Article on " Physics, Astronomy and Mathematics " in the " Outline of Knowledge for Boys and Girls and their Parents."

Sir, we know *our will is free, and* there's *an end on't.*

—Samuel Johnson.

A large public, urged on by intimations of free-will, has greeted with delight the writings of such modern physicists as Sir James Jeans and Sir Arthur Eddington, who bring all the authority of their mysterious knowledge to reinforce the suggestion that, after all, the law of universal causation may be denied—or, to use a more up-to-date terminology, that the principle of Scientific Determinism is invalid. The basis of their contention is, very roughly, that, though electrons and particles in the mass behave in a predictable manner, individual electrons do not do so ; they appear to move completely at random. In other words, scientists do not know how to discover—much less measure—the forces or processes (or whatever they are) which make an individual electron move one way rather than another, and which we would call causes (in the sense here used).   There seems also to be a fairly general opinion that, owing to difficulties of measurement, scientists may *never* be able to predict the actions of individual electrons; i.e. they may never discover any causes.   But does this prove that causes do not exist?   I think not.   No more than it proves that they do exist.   The question, like all scientific ones, is a matter of assessing probabilities upon the basis of experimental evidence.   We have already seen how enormous is the evidence in favour of the law of universal causation.   (We might incidentally add to it the evidence provided by every occasion on which Jeans and Eddington themselves, as physicists, have used the law as the foundation of a successful piece of research.)   We must also take into account the fact that, in all situations which have practical significance for us, we are dealing with electrons in the mass, not as individuals, so that the implications of their individual behaviour can in any case be ignored in our attempts to apply reality-thinking to the universe.   We then have to set against all this the evidence provided, firstly, by the fact that individual electrons appear to move at random and, secondly, by the fair probability that they will always appear to do so. In my opinion, the preponderance of evidence in favour of Determinism is overwhelming.   Nor is it made appreciably less overwhelming by the indirect evidence supposed by Eddington to arise from the implications of the Law of Entropy, which makes it possible for mathematicians to introduce the idea of time into their equations.   As Professor H. Levy points out in *The Universe of Science*, Eddington's arguments are based on laws which are not laws of nature but laws of mathematics and thus tell us nothing about the objective world.   Miss Susan Stebbing[1] also suggests—very pertinently to our subject—that one reason for Eddington's confusion is that he " seems temporarily to have forgotten that the second law of thermodynamics is not an *a priori* principle but a well-established *experimental* law ".   To put it into our terminology, he has confused logical and practical certainty. A final point, brought out by Joseph McCabe in *The Riddle of the Universe To-day*, is that, contrary to the general opinion,

---

[1] In her chapter on " Entropy and Becoming " in *Philosophy and the Physicists*.

the scientists who take the anti-determinist view are in a minority. Their pronouncements are much publicized, but they are not representative—their voice is loud but misleading.

However, this short outline of the question is so over-simplified that I must refer interested readers to Professor Levy's and Miss Stebbing's books already mentioned, as well as to Bertrand Russell's chapter on "Scientific Metaphysics" in *The Scientific Outlook*.[1]

If this is—as it appears to be—a case of Selection of Evidence on a large scale, it is probable that it is motivated by some mental necessity. The probability is confirmed by the fact that both Jeans and Eddington have carried the implications of their indeterminacy into the field of philosophy. It is also confirmed by the way in which, for both of them, a very important implication is that " our intuition " (Eddington) and " our innate conviction " (Jeans) of Free-Will must be justified. " A few scientists ", says Pareto, " use scientific language in their specialities, outside of which they reason as badly as the plain man—and often worse." In this connection, I would refer the reader to Miss Stebbing's chapter on " The Rejection of Physical Determinism ", in which she demonstrates, among other things, that many of the philosophical conclusions of both Eddington and Jeans are dependent on the Utraquistic Fallacy, with frequent use of non-scientific words in several senses at once. We can only hope that—like Humpty Dumpty—when scientists make words do such a lot of work, they always pay them extra. As employers of this kind of labour, they certainly make a good enough profit.

As the consequence of asserting an immaterial cause is to deny the possibility of a material one, so the consequence of denying a material cause is at least to suggest some sort of immaterial entity in its place. The entities of Jeans and Eddington are carefully protected, by the verbosity of their creators, from a too curious examination of their anatomy, and it is difficult to find out just what they are, apart from

---

[1] " How is it ", says Professor Levy, " that Eddington can see in this (unpredictability of the electron)—a form of indeterminacy so fundamental in Nature that he is prepared to sweep aside all previous prediction and apparent determinism on the larger scale and assert, ' We cannot find a particle of evidence in favour of Determinism ' ? " Page 162, op. cit. Thinkers' Library, 1938.

Sir James Jeans' latest book, *Physics and Philosophy*, takes up a much less extreme position, though it is careful to leave the door open to indeterminacy. This door is a Trap for the Unwary, as I suggest in the chapter " Pigs Might Fly "

being perhaps Unifying Formulae of the type that we have already seen to be eminently desirable. But it appears that Eddington's at any rate, proud of its scientific stock, disclaims any relationship with the older and larger entities of orthodox religion. Can this disclaimer be taken seriously? I do not think so. Once an immaterial entity is born it is surely futile to excuse it by saying that it is only a little one. Once you have admitted the principle of doing without a reasonable explanation, you might as well give up trying to find *any* reasonable explanations—and incidentally give up acting reasonably at all (except that, if you did you would soon be dead). For it is clear that if you can produce an entity which can cause a certain phenomenon without any perceptible or verifiable means of doing so, there is nothing whatsoever to stop it (or some other entity of the same sort) from causing any phenomenon you like. From this stage the logical step is to an Entity which can break all the rules—which can equally well hear a prayer or work a miracle. However, luckily—and paradoxically—such an Entity hardly ever chooses to work awkward miracles, like impelling the floor of one's house to collapse without material cause. The reason for this is of course that—being made in man's image or vice versa—it has a Mind similar to that of man, and understands man's desire for reasonable and predictable behaviour at least in his work-a-day surroundings.

(6) MORALS

It (science) embraces the whole history of man and, by studying the evolution of modes of conduct and their effects upon individuals and communities, it arrives at generalizations which are the expression of moral values vindicated by human experience. The fundamental difference between the scientific and the non-scientific approach to ethics is that science regards such vindication as adequate, while its critics seek some absolute standard—generally of supernatural origin. Those who feel the need of an imperative to define and vindicate their moral values may be dissatisfied with ethics based on science but they should realize that anthropology, psychology and sociology do not pursue their researches in an ethical vacuum.—Adam Gowans Whyte.

Orthodoxy is my doxy—heterodoxy is another man's doxy.
—Bishop Warburton.

Most systems of morality, whether or not they are avowedly religious, have as their object the formation of a code which will act as a sort of ready-reference to be turned to for guidance in conduct. Such a code has two basic functions. Thus, if I wish to decide whether some action is a "good" one, a moral code will help me to decide, firstly, what end I wish to attain, i.e. how I am to define the *noun* "Good"; and secondly, whether this action is an efficient means to the desired end, i.e. how I can be consistent in my definition of the *adjective* "good".

This pedantic distinction between the adjective and the noun—between the means and the end—is of great importance. For the question of defining the abstraction "Good" is, like that of defining such words as "reality", "truth", etc., a matter of subjective opinion, whereas, once a definition has been adopted, the further question of deciding which actions are good resolves itself into a scientific one—into a matter of reality-thinking.

The distinction serves to emphasize those aspects of the problem of morality which come into the scope of our present investigation—this being, briefly, to find out in what way the adoption of a typical system of morality can be used to satisfy irrationally the desire to feel good and the desire to understand, with its subsidiary the desire for certainty. Once again I must forestall an obvious objection; I do not mean to suggest that *all* systems of morality and all moral beliefs are irrational. On the contrary, it will, I think, become clear that reality-thinking can indicate what might be called a scientific basis for an ethical system—an important point, since so much is now being said of the content as well as of the methods of education.

I think I have shown that, from the point of view of reality-thinking, no statement about objective phenomena can be regarded as self-evident. If, therefore, someone were to say "Adultery is a Good Thing" and to claim that this statement were rational, he would have to be prepared to back it with objective evidence. (Incidentally, the same thing applies to the converse statement.) But what sort of evidence could he produce? Obviously, none—unless first he were to make it clear for whom, or for what purpose, he thought adultery was a good thing.[1] It follows that, when we apply the adjective

---

[1] It may be necessary to repeat here that the evidence of tradition or of authority (i.e. of other people's statements of what *they* mean by "Goodness") is not what we have here been calling objective evidence. For one thing, authorities and traditions differ so much! Cf. *Ethical Relativity*, by E. A. Westermarck.

" good " to some action, we are in effect saying that the action is an expedient means to some approved end.   It also follows that no action can be intrinsically good.   To continue with the illustration, when the protagonist of adultery has produced his evidence, his statement resolves itself into a prediction that adultery will have certain effects.   From which it again follows that any judgment of value about an action is (if rational) a form of prediction—a fact which has the important corollary that any such judgment which cannot be translated into the form of a prediction is necessarily an arbitrary statement of personal opinion with no relation to reality-thinking; for, if it does not predict anything, there is no way in which it can be verified.[1]

A moral code does not always apply its judgments directly to actions.   It may for instance classify as bad or good such things as political systems, or individual people, or ideas. The goodness or badness (i.e. expediency or inexpediency) of these things is, once again, not intrinsic, but depends on the results which they produce.

This means that forming a moral judgment is essentially a matter of trying to form correct opinions about the objective world, and is subject to all the irrational temptations that we have already seen to apply to opinions in general.   In the case of actions, for example, our assurance of doing the right or expedient thing depends directly on the amount of trouble we take in thinking out their results.   But, as with any action, life is too short for lengthy indecision.   It is reasonable to compromise, partly by making relatively hasty decisions and partly by setting up or adopting a rough and ready code which tells us at a glance which actions are likely, *in most circumstances*, to produce the desired results.   However, if such a compromise is to remain consistently reasonable, it entails a constant openness of mind about the validity both of the decisions and of the code, and, the more we give in to our desire for simplicity and ease by over-simplifying the code, the less can we be reasonably certain that we have acted rightly.   The whole thing is in fact most inconvenient.

[1] As it happens, all objective judgments or beliefs (as opposed to experimentally observed facts) are similarly—though very indirectly—predictions, in that they can be translated into the form, " I predict that observation of the facts will (or could conceivably) confirm that such-and-such was, is, or will be, the case."   The point is unimportant, however, except as a confirmation of the general argument that beliefs which cannot conceivably be verified have no place in reality-thinking.

The consequence is that, for the comfort of our minds, we are always being tempted to increase the rigidity of any code we have adopted, while at the same time allowing ourselves to forget the need for caution. Up to a certain point, this may have few practical disadvantages (if any). For the code may have been well-worked out in the first place, either by ourselves or the leaders of the religious, or political, party whose ends coincide with ours. But once we get to the stage of regarding an action as an isolated concept—as an item permanently dubbed bad or good in the code—we have undoubtedly started to be less rational even though we may have made things apparently easier for ourselves. We are already on the path which leads to the comforts of absolute certainty. Our state of mind is the same in kind as, though perhaps different in degree from, that of a nation which blindly follows a dictator, confident that the code he has set up is infallible.

We see then that, even if we ignore completely the moral aspect, there are considerable temptations to irrationality in the formation of judgments of value—in the application of the word " good " as an adjective. The moral aspect itself introduces yet further temptations, since it provides almost unlimited opportunities for satisfying the desire to feel good as well as the desire for certainty. This is, I think, the main reason why systems of morality present on the average more glaring inconsistencies and absurdities to the dispassionate eye than do systems of philosophy; they have double the amount of mental comforting to do.

There are two very popular methods of satisfying the desire to feel good by adopting a moral code. Both of these methods culminate, more or less indirectly, in the belief that there is an Absolute Good—a Good which everyone will agree (or ought to agree) is the only end worth attaining. However, they approach this belief from different standpoints. The first is mixed up with the desire for certainty and involves ignoring or overlooking the fundamental distinction between the good as a means and the good as an end. In doing this, it also overlooks the fact that any judgment of value about objective phenomena is, as we have seen, a form of prediction. When our desire for ease and simplicity makes us increase the rigidity of our moral code, we tend to become more and more sure that certain things and actions are good (or bad) in all circumstances. The logical extension of this tendency is that we finally regard the thing as certainly good—as self-evidently good. And from this it soon follows, with apparent obviousness, that it is intrinsically good, quite independent of the end.

For example, many people will talk about the sanctity of family life, implying that it is self-evidently a Good Thing, and will not only be shocked by the suggestion that the question is debatable but will even refuse with asperity to explain precisely (a) to whom it is beneficial, (b) what these benefits are and (c) how it produces them; in other words, they will refuse to translate their judgment into a potentially verifiable prediction. The field of sex, of course, provides innumerable examples of things or actions which are considered intrinsically bad.

From this confusion of the good as a means and as an end, it appears to follow that there *must* be an Absolute Good; for to say that a means is good in itself implies that it is a chip off an Absolute block.

The other method of establishing a belief in an Absolute Good is by starting directly from the Comfortable Concept that abstract words have a one true meaning, i.e. an " absolute " meaning.

With either method, once the Absolute Good is established it tends to be arbitrarily defined so as to be consistent with the particular individual's pre-conceived ideas, these ideas in turn being often closely, though unconsciously, connected with what happens to be to the individual's advantage. This has a most satisfactory result; for it means that, once a man has adopted a moral code which includes the concept of an Absolute Good (suitably defined) he has only to do an action which is ticketed in his code as " good " to be absolutely certain of his own virtue. Even more important, it means that, so long as he does not do anything ticketed " bad ", he has nothing to worry about. There were many people in the last century whose sense of virtue remained unimpaired by making children work twelve and fourteen hours a day in their factories. And, in this century (to avoid invidious particularity) there are many people whose actions are curiously at variance, to an impartial observer, with their sincere belief that what they desire is universal good. There is yet another, more horrifying, advantage of a rigid moral code. It allows the persecution of anybody who refuses to obey it. The

Spanish Inquisition and the concentration camp are extreme examples from the many available.

We come here to a point which, at first sight, appears to support the suggestion that there may be a universal or Absolute Good.

There are many abstractions, such as " efficiency ", " reality ", " truth ", etc., which can be used in an ethically neutral sense, i.e. they need not imply any moral approval or disapproval of the things to which they refer. In such cases the abstractions can refer to a number of different and incompatible things. But when they are used with an ethical tinge, they imply that the things to which they refer, have, in addition to their other qualities, the quality of being good or bad. And " goodness ", although it can—like other abstractions—refer to different and incompatible things, always has as part of its meaning the common element of moral approval. In other words there may perhaps be said to be an element in the meaning of " good " which is common to all communities. It is much too often overlooked, however, that this common element *refers to the emotions of human beings and not to the phenomena which arouse these emotions.* It implies that human beings tend to feel certain emotions in common, and that communities need some word which will express approval ; it does not imply that there are any things in the objective world to which the word " good " consistently and universally refers or which constitute " goodness ". The same thing applies to the various classes or subdivisions of goodness. Surely, we will be inclined to think, there is *something* that has always been considered good—kindness, for instance— surely at no time and in no community has kindness been condemned ? And we will be quite right ; but, here again, " kind " is a label applied to certain kinds of actions of which the community approves—the approval *does* in fact remain constant—what change are the actions to which it is applied. The preservation of someone's life, for instance, is kindness if he is a friend, but weakness if he is an enemy.

I have underlined this point because a misunderstanding of it, combined with the indispensable Utraquistic fallacy, is the basis of some very persuasive attempts to establish an Absolute Good. The common emotional tone which attaches to the word " good " is of course established easily enough. But it is never referred to as " emotional tone " ; it is always called " the meaning " of the word. Then, because " meaning " can also be a label for the " referent " of a word (i.e. the outside thing to which it refers), the argument assumes without further ado that the referents also have a common element —that there are certain things universally agreed to be good.

However, although one cannot give an absolute meaning to " good " nor establish any universal agreement as to which qualities it should describe, it is clearly nonsensical to say that it has no useful meaning in any one community. Thus, in England, there are innumerable discussions which argue what is the best thing to do in the field of politics (say) or education or health, and which can be called reality-thinking, but which do not first of all go to the pedantic length of defining the end—the " good "—in view. The " good " implied in the majority of such discussions may be taken as the meaning " in use " of the word " good " in our community. In other words, it is the kind of meaning which " good " should be given *when it is used without qualification*. I think it can be shown that this meaning in use is a very down-to-earth one, and that it implies the desirability of attaining ends very different from those of many eminent moralists.

Let us look at it this way. In the first place, from the point of view of reality-thinking, statements are of no practical value unless they can be objectively verified or refuted. It follows that the only way in which the word " good " can be given an objective meaning is to identify it with something objective, i.e. with the attainment of some state of affairs which has " material " aspects and can therefore be checked. In the second place, if such a word as " good " (or any word which expresses an attitude, for that matter) is to have practical value as a means of communication, its most frequently used sense must have as wide an application as possible. To put it differently, the word " good " as an expression of approval must, *unless specifically qualified*, express the approval of the community in general—not that of individuals or separate classes of individual. To take an obvious example; if an individual is to be allowed to live in a herd, he must to some extent subordinate his personal interests to those of his companions, and therefore the general view of the herd will be that selfishness is anti-social; the herd will deny selfishness its moral approval and will call it " bad "

This down-to-earth aspect of the word " good " is indeed implied in nearly all economic and political discussions (i.e. in discussions about action to be taken)—again, unless the word is specifically qualified. For example, in discussions of the Beveridge Report on Social Security, the Conservatives have happened to disagree with the Beveridge plan as a means, but have strenuously identified themselves with the Socialists on the question of ends. " Nothing is nearer to our hearts ", they have said, " than the happiness and well-being of the people of Great Britain ; but . . ." And, if taxed, they will always assert that by " the people " they mean, all appearances to the contrary, the majority of the people.

The same appears to be true of most discussions of practical questions. One can hardly imagine anyone who, having advocated perhaps Birth Control or Socialism or Prohibition, would not resent an accusation that he was thinking of the interests only of a minority.

In so far, then, as the word " good " has a reasonably objective meaning " in use ", it seems to be identified with the happiness and well-being of *people* and of as many of the people as is practical.[1] This does at least show the futility of asserting that " the good "—*tout court*—must be identified with the advancement of a particular hypostatized nation, or with the attainment of any sort of spiritual ideal, divorced from consideration of the material and emotional needs of ordinary *living* men.

It also suggests the basis for a rational system of ethics, very similar to Utilitarianism ; that is to say, one which decides in a scientific spirit to take as objective a view as possible of what its " end " should be, and, having decided on this end, approaches the question of attaining it in a similarly scientific spirit. It unfortunately happens that, as we have seen, many of the sciences which deal with this question of means (such as economics, both social and political) provide excellent opportunities for their practitioners to persuade themselves that the correct answer to the question is that which incidentally ensures their own well-being. But I think these opportunities would be slightly restricted by a clear realization

[1] Unfortunately it has for thousands of years been widely held (perhaps rightly) that it is impractical for any class of people to be well-off unless a lower class of slaves or workers was unhappy and over-worked. There seem to be some people who still believe this, in spite of the fact that there are now machines to do the work of slaves.

that the desired end is the well-being of people rather than some vague and arbitrarily definable " Good ".

All the same, the problem of deciding, with any useful precision, what the desirable end should be, remains one of the thorniest and most difficult of all problems. I hope I have not appeared to imply that, because it cannot be decided with " logical " certainty, it cannot or should not be discussed at all.[1] Some sort of ethical system is desirable, if only because it helps with the problem of educating people to live in a community. But the better the education (i.e. the more people are taught to think objectively) the less necessity there is for a dangerously arbitrary code. The aim of education in fact should by no means be destruction of moral values, but the sowing of a healthy seed of scepticism. For scepticism is—in the world of ideas—one of the most creative of emotions.

This seed of doubt is, however, regarded by many people as a vicious weed—for two main reasons, both of which have been made fairly clear. It is for these reasons that so many people cannot stomach the scientific attitude towards questions of ethics. This attitude does in fact accept the importance of moral values. It also attempts, not only to explain their biological function, but also to assess the relative worth to us of the different standards which have at one time or another been set up. In doing so, as Adam Gowans Whyte says in the quotation at the head of this chapter, " it arrives at generalizations which are the expression of moral values vindicated by human experience ".

But the trouble is that the scientific attitude obstinately refuses to claim absolute or logical certainty for these generalizations. This is what seems inadequate to many people, and, to lovers of the Absolute, with their desire for perfection and for the restful certainty of immutable authority, it is a half-loaf which is worse than no bread.

The quotation from Mr. Gowans Whyte was taken from a letter to the *Times Literary Supplement* referring to a review

---

[1] A stimulating discussion is to be found in *Science and Ethics*, by C. H. Waddington and others. Its basis is an essay by Dr. Waddington in which he suggests that we should define our " good " in terms of what conduces to " evolutionary advance ", this advance being held to imply also advance in the physical and mental health of men. Since the argument is about " ends ", it naturally leads to a great variety of comment, among which that of Dr. Burniston Brown puts forward something similar to the Utilitarian scheme. Dr. Waddington's suggestion is further worked out in Dr. Julian Huxley's *Evolutionary Ethics.*

of Dr. Julian Huxley's *On Living in a Revolution*. It is interesting to note how naïvely the reviewer's answer to the letter begs the whole question.   In the review it was asserted that " Science may observe the emergence of moral values: it cannot vindicate them ".   (Yet another case of the metaphysical mind's confusion between the two kinds of certainty, with consequent refusal to allow any but its own " absolute " kind of proof.)   In questioning this assertion, Mr. Gowans Whyte specifically questions the absoluteness of moral values.   After which the reviewer calmly answers: " No doubt history (which is also a science) throws light on the moral development of mankind, but only on condition that moral values are accepted as binding realities in themselves, and not explained away as mere psychological habits or mere instruments of survival."   Not only is the question begged ; the choice of words is also emotively suggestive—suggestive, with its " explained away " and its double " mere ", of the reviewer's emotional need for certainty.

(7) MORALS FOR THE MASSES

For to say that a blind custom of obedience should be a surer obligation than duty taught and understood, it is to affirm, that a blind man may tread surer by a guide than a seeing man can by a light.—Francis Bacon.   " Advancement of Learning."

What we must look for here is first, religious and moral principles ; secondly, gentlemanly conduct ; and thirdly, intellectual ability.
                                                    —Dr. Arnold of Rugby.

We have already seen how great are the mental comforts of believing in a Universal Good (suitably defined) and of constructing a moral code designed to attain that goal.   But these are as nothing to the physical comforts of inducing a sufficient number of other people to adopt the same code for themselves.   For then they will all believe that it is right to do the things you want them to do, and they will often do these things even when they are against their own interests. This is, of course, quite understandable, since they have been persuaded (or taught) not to think things out for themselves, but to accept your code as their guide, a process which, when applied to the young, is generally called " building up character ".

The advantages of such a course are so overwhelming that, in fact, the history of the world provides a long series of examples of the way in which a small ruling class has controlled and restricted the education of the remaining majority so as to ensure its unthinking adoption of a prescribed code. The fact that the ruling class has usually maintained its ascendancy for quite a long time, and has fought savagely when it was finally threatened, is, I think, evidence that this prescribed code must, as a rule, have been based on a conception of " the Good " which was in effect the " good " of the ruling class, however much it may have been *said*—and however much the ruling class may have deceived itself into believing—that it was the universal good.

Such a code will of course be immensely more efficient if it is incorporated into a religion. For (a) it becomes more rigid ; (b) the penalties for questioning it or disobeying it are increased by extension from this temporal world into the eternity of the next; (c) the ultimate Good is so firmly identified with suprahuman interests that there is no chance of anyone's suspecting that he is sacrificing his own interests for those of a small group of other men ; (d) if the world is as God made it, the way it is arranged should not and cannot be altered ; and (e) men should not expect happiness in this world, but in the next.

Whatever other functions a religion may have, and however beneficent these may be, this short and incomplete list of typical religious tenets shows that it can be in practice a most useful instrument in the hands of a ruling class. And it seems most unlikely that any ruling class could be so foolish as not to take advantage of it. Indeed, history provides evidence that, in fact, ruling classes have *not* been so foolish. Hector Hawton (in *The Flight from Reality*) demonstrates that, in ancient and classical history, ruling classes have defined " good " as they wished by making their God in the image of their King and then ingeniously letting it follow that the ways of Kings and ruling classes can be justified as the ways of God. The evidence from modern history is less obvious and less direct, since, as Archibald Robinson has recently pointed out, it is provided by such things as " the injunction by New Testament writers and Church Fathers of passive obedience to the powers that be ; the establishment and endowment of the Church by the Roman emperors from

Constantine on; the wealth and temporal dominion of the Catholic hierachy in the Middle Ages; the savage suppression of peasant revolts and heretical movements; the anti-clerical and finally anti-religious character of all the revolutionary movements of the eighteenth, nineteenth and twentieth centuries. . . .'' These and other facts suggest, he continues, that " the recognition of (human) rights is of secular origin, and has been pressed for generations in defiance of the Church ''. I think they also suggest that the ruling classes have gone on as of old (unconsciously, it is true) making and re-making God in their own image and then trading on the resemblance.[1]

When a state sets up or consolidates a moral code, it does not as a rule incorporate this code entirely into the State religion. Some of it is left outside the religious field and spreads its fundamental principles into the whole ideology. For, of course, the ideology in general must, if it is to serve a useful purpose, be adapted to the mental and physical comfort of its exponents. I propose now to suggest how the desire to feel good, when combined with the adoption of such an ideology, would be likely to affect the attitude of an upper class towards philosophical and scientific questions.

It is generally true that the preservation of the *status quo* is in the interests of the class which is in power. As we have seen, one of the most efficient means of doing this is to induce the mass of the people to adopt a prescribed ideology, part of which consists in a belief in a vague sort of Absolute Good. From the point of view of their physical comfort, the ruling class need do no more than this; there is no reason why they themselves should also believe in the propaganda of their own ideology. On the other hand, from the point of view of mental comfort, there are considerable temptations to do so. No man with a kind heart can enjoy thinking that he might be responsible—even indirectly—for slums. In practice the majority of the ruling class usually does believe its own propaganda—sometimes with disastrous results to its own

---

[1] Cf. the resolutions (quoted by Mr. Desmond MacCarthy in the *New Statesman and Nation*) of the first settlers in Connecticut, who were troubled in their minds about dispossessing the Indians: After examining the Scriptures—that the earth is the Lord's (voted); that the Lord can give the earth to His saints (voted); and that we are His saints (voted). Incidentally, it is significant that it should be considered bad taste, in ecclesiastical circles, to mention the difference between the teachings of Christ and the present practice of the Churches.

safety.   Witness the state of mind of the French and Russian courts before their revolutions, and the way in which the policy-makers of Great Britain during the 1930's believed in their own wildly erroneous propaganda about the military and industrial efficiency of the U.S.S.R.

Now let us see what a belief in his own ideology involves for a member of a ruling class.   The main object of the belief, it must be remembered, is comfortable assurance of virtue. The first step therefore is to persuade oneself that what is in effect the good of one's own minority is really nothing of the sort.   For the unreflective man this is done fairly simply by taking all his innate prejudices and beliefs absolutely for granted.   "Right is right," he says, "and Left is wrong— that's all there is to it."   But for other people, some sort of rationalization is necessary.   The "Good" must be arbitrarily defined in so vague a manner that it can somehow be assumed to be a sort of Absolute or Universal Good.   For the religious man, this again is simple enough; it has already been done for him.   But, even for religious people, religious arguments are not always wholly satisfactory.   Those of the upper class who spend any of their comparatively ample leisure in rumination are inclined to demand the kind of argument that will at least have the appearance of being rational.   The consequence is that they will eagerly accept any view which seems able to *prove*, independently of religious authority, that such a thing as Absolute Good can exist.

But, as we have seen, this can only be "proved", with the absolute certainty so desirable, by taking up the metaphysical attitude rather than the materialist one—by imagining that word-juggling can provide that knowledge of the objective world that can be provided only by the experimental observation of objective phenomena.   The temptingness of the metaphysical attitude, already powerful, is thus further re-inforced.   When one considers that the cultural, the religious and particularly the educational environment (i.e. the pattern of the ideology) add their effect, it seems only to be expected that the metaphysical attitude should, in spite of its irrationality, prevail over reality-thinking.

With the metaphysical attitude (in the sense of "metaphysical" that we have been using) there goes hypostatization of abstractions, since this follows naturally from the belief in Absolutes.   And once hypostatization is allowed, the

Immaterial Entity is only just round the corner. The Immaterial Entity, in its turn, goes hand-in-hand with Vitalism—and Vitalism, as we have seen, with a belief in Free-Will. Here we come full-circle to another belief which has powerful temptations for those who wish to keep the *status quo*. The importance of the Free-Will view is that, in denying the necessity of the law of causation, it imagines that it has denied its validity and shown that it is, in consequence, futile to search for inconvenient causes. At the same time, it appears to confirm the view that when things go wrong (e.g. unemployment, poverty, war, etc.) the causes are to be found in man's or God's incalculable freedom of action, rather than in economic, predictable, and therefore possibly *alterable* factors—factors whose control would, by definition, be the responsibility of the ruling class. ("If there are no material causes, then it is nobody's fault, and if it is nobody's fault, then it certainly can't be mine.")[1]

Thus the Free-Will view acts as a bulwark against the materialist view that the search for causes will show economic conditions to be relatively important and the *status quo* to be by no means the " natural order of things ".

Finally, the Vitalist attitude, with its anti-Determinist belief in an underlying Purpose or "hormic energy" or "élan vital" can have an important psychological value. If one has a number of unacknowledged motives for one's beliefs and if it is essential for one's mental comfort that these motives should remain unacknowledged, one will naturally shy away from the Determinist view, which suggests that there may be unconscious causes for one's actions. For, if there is Free-Will—if one's actions are guided by the conscious exercise of *free* choice, independent of pre-determining unconscious factors—one need not look further than the surface of one's mind for one's motives; there is no necessity to start delving below in the search for desires which, being one's own and being till then unrealized, can hardly be said to display that conscious altruism which is the distinguishing mark of virtue.

This brief statement of the mental temptations which can

---

[1] Cf. "Vansittartism" as a mental attitude possibly symptomatic of a desire to evade the materialistic view of the causation of wars. "The origin of this war (the 2nd World War) is not to be sought in any financial system, but in the ambitions of the German heart." Lord Vansittart, speaking at a London Rotary Club Luncheon, quoted in the *Daily Telegraph*, July 30th, 1942.

be expected to appeal to members of a ruling class serves, in spite of its over-simplification, to suggest that what might be called the Idealist (in the philosophical sense), the metaphysical, the vitalist, the semi-religious attitude, is more likely to be characteristic of middle and upper class thought than is the opposite materialist one. Conversely, anyone who wants to change the *status quo* will necessarily have questioned some of the assumptions of the prevailing ideology. He will try to show up its irrational elements and thus will tend to take the materialist attitude, whether or not he clothes it in a philosophical Unifying Formula and starts being irrational himself.

I hope I will not be taken as asserting that this broad division between mental attitudes is characteristic only of class divisions. It corresponds roughly with Wilfred Trotter's division between the stable and unstable mentality, in which the stable mentality is described as susceptible to the suggestions of the herd (i.e. inclined to absorb the traditional ideology without questioning it), and is opposed to the unstable mentality, which is inclined to be " sceptical in such matters as patriotism, religion, politics, social success ", and when carried to extremes tends to be weak in persistence of energy —to be flighty and variable in enthusiasms. Trotter poses the question as to whether the qualities of these two types are inborn—and declines to answer it. However, this division between mental attitudes also corresponds roughly with William James' division between the tender-minded and the tough-minded philosophical types, which has in turn been suggested by Jung to be characteristic of a preponderance respectively of the introvert and of the extrovert tendencies. Jung, who is himself a Vitalist, clearly assumes that these tendencies are inherent in the human temperament.

Whatever the facts in individual cases, the broad division I have outlined does suggest that, other things being equal and on the average, the metaphysical and vitalist attitude will be symptomatic of the forces of reaction, while the materialist attitude will be symptomatic of the forces of change. Once again, history provides confirmatory evidence. A large amount of this evidence is detailed in Hector Hawton's *Flight from Reality*, and also in Professor Benjamin Farrington's *Science and Politics in the Ancient World*. I will quote only two further examples. First, Jung points out (in *Psychological Types*) that, in Plato's time, " it was precisely the

proletarian philosophy that adopted the inherency principle "
(which he identifies with materialism and Nominalism in
philosophy). Secondly, in eighteenth century France, where
the distribution of power was still arranged on feudal lines, the
old idealist and religious views were challenged by the relative
materialism of the Encyclopédistes and other writers who,
as members of the middle class, identified themselves with the
demand of the middle and lower classes for their rights. The
materialism of the latter half of the nineteenth century in
England appears at first sight to provide an exception; for
the middle class were already part of the ruling class and had
consolidated their position with the passing of the Reform
Bill. But one must remember, first, that this materialism
was confined to intellectual circles, and secondly, that the
idealist and metaphysical view is valuable, less for its objective efficacy, than as a bulwark against the dangerous thoughts
of materialists. And, as a result of the industrial revolution,
the ruling class were so firmly entrenched in power that
thoughts of danger were almost inconceivable; it seemed
perfectly safe to reject the metaphysical view in favour of the
(much more industrially useful) material view. Even so, in
Europe generally, advocates of the theory of evolution found
themselves widely and violently attacked as politically sub-
versive forces. In the case of Haeckel, " his opinions ceased
to be a matter of merely academic concern; they, and his
right to express them, had become the symbol of a struggle of
the people for emancipation ".[1]

However, by the turn of the century, danger had begun to
loom much closer ahead; the bulwark began once more to
have its uses. We have here perhaps a further explanation of
the flight from reason which is so marked a characteristic of
this century. We also have another example, almost too
obvious to mention, of our broad division between mental
attitudes. Few modern points of view can have roused more
ire in respectable breasts than that associated with Marx and
Materialism.

Into the minds of those who are inclined to extend my
argument into the assertion that all members of a ruling class
are self-deceiving oppressors, there will by now have popped
such names as Bacon, Shaftesbury, Wilberforce, etc. They
will, I hope, realize that to take such cases as counters to

[1] B. Farrington. Op. cit., page 17.

my argument would be selecting the evidence as and with a vengeance.

At this point the question arises: " Even though a man may be deceiving himself as to his own motives, if he sincerely believes himself to be good, can he be said to be a bad man ? " Since it all depends on what you mean by " bad " in this context, I leave the question unanswered, merely pointing out in passing that there are innumerable such men in the world who are charming, cultured, honest, kind and just. It is such as they who have made the world what it is.

CONCLUSION

After a hundred or so pages of unmitigated emphasis on man's unreason, the reader may feel that the picture has been badly distorted. But I do not think it has. Our desire to feel that we are reasonable is strong enough to make us shift our gaze whenever we are presented with those really disconcerting bits of evidence which involve us personally. Perhaps the most universal of these emerges from the answer to a simple question. How many times during (say) the past three months can you, my reader, remember having had an argument or discussion in which you were unreasonable? What?—you cannot remember a single one? Surely. . . . And yet, now I come to think of it, I cannot remember an occasion when *I* have been unreasonable, either. Can *none* of us do so? . . . Who, then, were all those people we argued with?

What, again, did the Democrats and Republicans in the U.S.A. think when they read the results of the Gallup Poll (reported in the *News Chronicle* of August 30th, 1944) which took place shortly before the Presidential Election? The poll was on the question of whether President Roosevelt's health would permit him to carry on until 1948. Of the Democrats 84 per cent. thought it would do so, and 16 per cent. thought it would break down; whereas, of the Republicans, 47 per cent. thought it would permit him to carry on, and 53 per cent. thought it would break down. Was it always, in the thoughts of individual Democrats and Republicans, the *other* fellow who had allowed his political opinions to affect his judgment on a non-political matter of fact?

President Roosevelt's health was a matter on which no one but an expert—a doctor—could hold an opinion with any reasonable assurance. It is extraordinary to reflect how many of our opinions are held with considerable assurance about matters which are similarly the province of the expert. "In matters that really interest him," says Wilfred Trotter, "man cannot support the suspense of judgment which science so often has to enjoin. He is too anxious to feel certain to have time to know." I cannot do better than quote Trotter's own list of examples:

" If we examine the mental furniture of the average man, we shall find it made up of a vast number of judgments of a very precise kind upon subjects of very considerable variety, complexity, and difficulty. He will have fairly settled views upon the origin and nature of the universe, and upon what he will probably call its meaning; he will have conclusions as to what is to happen to him at death and after, as to what is and what should be the basis of conduct. He will know how the country should be governed, and why it is going to the dogs, why this piece of legislation is good and that bad. He will have strong views upon military and naval strategy, the principles of taxation, the use of alcohol and vaccination, the treatment of influenza, the prevention of hydrophobia, upon municipal trading, the teaching of Greek, upon what is permissible in art, satisfactory in literature and hopeful in science.

" The bulk of such opinions must necessarily be without rational basis, since many of them are concerned with problems admitted by the expert to be still unsolved, while as to the rest it is clear that the training and experience of no average man can qualify him to have any opinion upon them at all. The rational method adequately used would have told him that on the great majority of these questions there could be for him but one attitude—that of suspended judgment."

Glory!—as Humpty-Dumpty would have said.

The great trouble about all our opinions on important matters is that, if they are wrong, their wrongness does not have immediately uncomfortable results. There is nothing to bring us up short—to show us inescapably or painfully that we have misjudged reality, as there is when we misjudge the speed of a bus or tread on the step that is not there. As a matter of fact, when the results of our judgments *are* immediately apparent, we are capable of thinking with remarkable clarity, as witness so many marvels of civilization. We must hope that, with further advances in civilization, we will so understand our minds that we begin to behave in our more abstract thinking as rationally as we do in our concrete actions—in the chores of everyday life like washing-up dishes, distempering walls, writing letters and posting them. As things are now, if we were to decide whether to cross a road on the basis of the kind of thinking we often use when deciding between capitalism and socialism, we should all end up in an ambulance.

What are the conditions for an improvement in our thinking? Since the chief temptation to irrationality derives from frustrated desires, one solution would be to diminish our frustrations—to improve our social conditions. If we can achieve this, we will not diminish the strength of the desires. But at least we may manage to give them more satisfaction than they get now. For instance, our desire to feel good must be constantly dissatisfied—in most Christian countries—by the extraordinary conflict between what we are told to do by our religion and what we are impelled to do by our economic circumstances and the customs and traditions that they inspire. There must surely be many children whose thinking is pitifully confused by the answers they receive from their elders to such questions as, " Why *don't* we give all our goods to the poor ? " In some book (I am afraid I have forgotten which) there was an Australian aborigine who never could understand why white men seemed so worried and drawn, until finally he visited England. Then he found out. It was because the English had two Laws—two mutually hostile Laws—to both of which they owed obedience.

Quite apart from the way it would help clear-thinking, it must be pleasant to live in a country where the two ethics do not conflict.

If one solution to the problem of irrationality is to decrease our frustrations, another is to increase our awareness of its tempting comforts—to steel ourselves to the discomforts and to the relative dullness of reality-thinking. But a state of suspended judgment, like one of suspended movement, is not very stimulating ; on the other hand, enthusiasm is infectious, passion is convincing, and conviction is sustaining. Indeed, the comforts of unreason have turned out to be so enormous as almost to suggest that we might as well give in and wallow in the enjoyments of fantasy. But we have done this for a long time already, and *do* we enjoy ourselves? *Is* the world, for most of us, as pleasant a place as it might be? Is it even (in 1944) passably pleasant? The social argument in favour of reality-thinking (in its place) seems overwhelming. He who dwells in an ivory tower, supported by independent means, can perhaps afford to replace reality-thinking by subjective muddle. But we who dwell co-operatively in a community must co-operate or bust. In 1940 we nearly did bust.

So far this has been a depressing conclusion. It has emphasized that, although there are many people who can think clearly on almost any subject, there are millions more who seldom do so except when concrete circumstances force them, or when it does not matter much anyway. On the other hand, the prospects are perhaps encouraging. There seems no reason for assuming that these millions would remain incapable of thinking clearly once they understood their own mental processes. At any rate, this book has gone on the assumption that, even for intelligent people, a clearer understanding of the motives for irrationality will make those motives less insidiously tempting. (Incidentally, the book has re-grouped already-held ideas into a new system of classification based on the whys of our thoughts, not on the hows. It is not suggested that this is the only correct classification, nor that thoughts and other phenomena " are "—in any absolute sense—the labels here given them.)

It is a platitude that the techniques of science are outrunning our ability to deal with them sensibly. If this is so, the knowledge of which we are now most in need is knowledge of our own minds. But luckily this is what we appear to be on the verge of getting. As Raymond Mortimer has said, " in this age the most notable advance achieved by human reason has consisted in a fuller understanding of human unreasonableness ". If the speed with which the principles (at least) of modern psychology have been accepted since 1900 is any indication, it seems possible that before long we may have the principle—and even the practice—of psychological teaching accepted in our schools. Together with this we may have the universal practice (now only sporadic) of teaching, as a part of " Eng.Lit.", the ability to distinguish—both in reading and in listening—between objective and subjective, emotive and informative and ultimately rational and irrational.

All the same, a fuller understanding of psychology is not a panacea. Our present knowledge seems to indicate a cul-de-sac at the end of the road. (Not that this matters to us now. If we advance even a fraction of the way towards it we shall be doing well.)

The cul-de-sac is suggested by the theory that the main tendency of a man's thought is decided—and as a rule unalterably decided—by what happens to him in childhood, or even perhaps by what happened when the genes and chromosomes mingled at conception. On this view, a man's attitude towards authority is decided, in essentials, by his attitude as a child towards his father. Again, his views on discipline in education are conditioned by the way in which his parents treated him, this in turn being dependent on his and his parents' inherent make-up. In details his opinions about authority or discipline in schools may be modified by personal interest or by the impact of objective evidence. But the modifications will always vary around a predetermined line (say) of rebelliousness or of harshness. If this is so, there is a certain point beyond which even the clearest brain cannot progress—there are fundamental and inescapable prejudices which it cannot exorcize.

I think it probably *is* so. In some way or other, most of us arrive at maturity already firmly gripped by sentiments formed in childhood, even if we are not born into a set position in some scale such as the introvert-extrovert scale. At first sight this presents a nasty problem—a problem which seems to be currently in the air. (This was written in 1944 ; but the problem of course remains.) For instance, Arthur Koestler poses it very skilfully—and pessimistically—in his *Arrival and Departure*, where the hero, after being analysed, finds that his patriotism is due to guilt feelings derived from very early childhood, that his self-sacrifice satisfied an inner demand for restitution, and that he was on the side of the poor and the weak because his whole life was a " pilgrimage of atonement " for an early sin in jealousy against his infant brother. How, then, it seems, can anyone decide what is reasonable ?

Surely, to be halted by such disillusionment is the reward of one who has been whoring—since early childhood—after perfection ? It would certainly not become me, who have written this book, to hold that there is any wholly satisfactory and absolute answer to the problem thus posed. I maintain only that, if we discover our motives—if we discount them in proportion to their strength, then at least we will become more, rather than less, reasonable than we were before.

This is a platitude, but it is a platitude which is catastrophically ignored.

SUPPLEMENT

TESTS, DANGER SIGNS AND TRAPS FOR THE UNWARY

(1) THE DANGER DEFINED

Truth, this metaphysical being of which everybody imagines he has a clear conception, seems to me to be a confusion of so many diverse phenomena (to all of which the one name is given) that I am not surprised people have difficulty in recognizing it. . . .

The word "truth" suggests only a vague and formless idea. It has never been precisely defined; and the definition itself, taken in its widest and most general sense, is nothing but an abstraction which in turn depends for its existence on a mere assumption. Instead, then, of trying to work out a definition of truth, let us try to make an enumeration of it; let vs examine closely those things which are commonly called truth, and endeavour to get a clear view of them.
—Buffon. "Histoire Naturelle."

In a dispute between two chemists there is a judge; experience. In a dispute between a Moslem and a Christian, who is the judge? Nobody.—Vilfredo Pareto. "The Mind and Society."

Knowing and feeling are equally essential ingredients both in the life of the individual and in that of the community.
—Bertrand Russell. "The Scientific Outlook."

In the main part of this book we have examined the motives for irrationality. This supplement will deal with methods of diagnosis and prevention. Before we can go into the question, we need to summarize and codify some of the conclusions as to the scope and function of rational thought which have emerged piecemeal from the preceding pages. In particular there will be misunderstanding unless we recall the restricted (and yet unexpectedly wide) definition which was given to "reality-thinking" in Part I. This chapter, therefore, will inevitably contain a certain amount of recapitulation.

The word "truth" is used to refer to a number of very different concepts. If, by one's thinking, one wants to acquire knowledge of all the different kinds of truth, one will have to indulge in all the different kinds of thought process that are characteristic of man, including some that would ordinarily not be called thinking at all.

Among these different things called truth, there are some that are with difficulty describable, but which I will indicate as the Xs that people experience when they say they have grasped the true nature of beauty, or felt the truth that Beethoven was trying to express in his later string quartets. There are also Xs which, for most of us, are always beyond reach, though they may have been attained by a few—by the mystics who gain contact with ultimate reality or by such as Henry Vaughan who " saw eternity the other night, like a great ring of pure and endless light ". These Xs are unlikely to be confused with the kind of truth that we have been calling " objective ", and they may therefore be left out of account.

However, the word " truth " is not as a general rule hypostatized in this way; it is more often used to describe the quality *of* some proposition; in other words, the truth of a belief or judgment is supposed to depend on its correspondence with some standard. As things are, the standard most often taken is objective reality, since this is the most useful standard in practical life. When, therefore, we say that some proposition is true we are taken to mean (unless we qualify it) that it gives us reasonably accurate and *objective* information. But, as it turns out, there are surprisingly few propositions which can safely be taken at their face value.

Let us therefore examine some types of statement which are often called truths (without any qualification). For convenience, we will divide them into five classes, arranged, not according to their rationality or their usefulness (in this respect the items in any one class may differ widely) but according to the type of truth they express. Thus, in Class A, both the examples give us information about the same sort of phenomena and their truth or falsity is verifiable by reference to the same sort of standard. Similarly with the examples in any one of the other classes. On the other hand the kinds of information given by (and the standards relevant to) the different classes are by no means always the same. And yet, as everyone will agree, the world is full of people who take it for granted that propositions or judgments of all these classes (except the last) are capable of being true or false in the same way—who assume that, if they are true, they are true in the commonly accepted sense that they give us information about the objective world.

I contend that it is this unfortunate assumption (reinforced

by the belief that there is one " true " meaning of the word
" truth ") which is at the bottom of an enormous amount of
fundamentally unnecessary controversy—controversy about
aesthetics, ethics, politics and, in particular, about the conflict
between science and religion. This contention is certainly
not original (see Pareto, Hogben, Ogden and Richards,
Britton, Bacon, Hume, Rignano and others). But it is a
contention which, in spite of (or rather because of) its importance, will always be unpopular ; for its acceptance involves
the clear realization that the world of fantasy-thinking must
be divorced from the world of reality-thinking, and that most
of the judgments and beliefs of religion, art and morals have
no objective value, the unwelcome implication being that it
is never incumbent on the rest of mankind to agree with what
you or I think about God or beauty or Right and Wrong. I
have tried, in the foregoing chapters, to show how powerful
are the motives, derived from the desires to understand, to
feel good, and to conform, which will tempt people to run
away from this last implication.

We will, then, examine our classes with the particular
purpose of establishing what *kind* of knowledge they give us,
and by what standards (if any) they may be verified :

Class A. Tautologies and Axioms.

1. All white clouds are white.
2. 2 plus 2 equals 4.

These statements both give us the same sort of knowledge
as would, say, "An area of 4,840 square yards is
called an acre." This tells us that, in the English-speaking
community, the symbol currently used for referring to a
certain area is " acre ". It does not tell us anything new
about objective phenomena—about a particular field or kind
of country. Similarly, " All white clouds are white," shows
how we use, as part of our system of communication, the
symbols " white ", " all ", etc., but it does not tell us anything new about clouds. It is what is often called an *a priori*
truth ; that is to say, it is a truth which is self-evident—a sort
of axiom, which does not need to be verified by observation
of the objective world. " 2 plus 2 equals 4 " is also an *a priori*
truth, since it follows with absolute (i.e. logical) certainty

from the accepted mathematical usage of the symbols 2, 4, plus, and equals. Statements of this type, in fact, tell us things about how we use language, not about how the phenomena of the objective world are related; and the standard by which they are verifiable is linguistic custom. As I have already pointed out, given agreement as to the usage of symbols in any one community, such statements can be proved or disproved with *absolute* certainty; and in this they are to be sharply differentiated from statements (i.e. predictions) about objective phenomena, whose certainty can never be more than practical, though it may be so great as to allow us, in practice, to ignore the element of doubt.

There have been many eminent thinkers who have assumed that *a priori* truths are objective truths. Upon this assumption they have based, first, the theory that it is possible to attain knowledge of the world without observing it and, secondly, a rationalization of the satisfying belief that it must somehow be possible to attain logically certain knowledge of the objective world. They have, in effect, wanted to believe that their mare's nest existed; they have then asserted that it does exist, and have managed to persuade themselves that there is no point in looking to see if they are right. What is more, when some scientist with his eyes open actually observes a wren's nest (a " practical " certainty), they feel quite at liberty to keep their eyes shut and say that mares' nests are the only ones that are any good.

It is important to note that propositions in this class are the only absolute certainties with which all sane members of the community will agree.

Class B. *Metaphysical and Mystical.*

1. Jesus Christ is the Son of God.
2. There is nothing in the Whole beside appearance, and every fragment of appearance qualifies the Whole; while on the other hand, so taken together, appearances, as such, cease.[1]

Propositions in this class are often put forward as absolute certainties; and it is true that they cannot possibly be confuted by experience. But the trouble is that people happen not to agree about them. This is of course because they tell us things

[1] *Appearance and Reality*, by F. H. Bradley.

about the beliefs and emotions of the individuals who state them; and because there are no generally accepted rules as to what we should all feel, as there are about how we should use language. It is, I know, a shocking suggestion to some people that the two examples given here inform us only of subjective matters. But its very shockingness to those who take the opposite view, is a sign, though not a proof, that those who are shocked are being irrational.

It may, for instance, be impossible to confute Bradley's remark, but equally it is impossible to produce any objective evidence to support it. There is in fact no conceivable way in which the observation of objective phenomena by independent witnesses could provide any facts which are relevant to its truth or falsity. The operative words themselves are all abstractions of the kind which have many possible meanings. Bradley's particular choice of meaning is then arbitrary, and tells us how *he* likes to feel about a mental concept of his own; it does not tell us a fact or hypothesis about some objective phenomenon. To put it baldly, the whole statement comes into the realm of fantasy-thinking. As such it is all very well; some speculations of this sort—if perhaps not this one—often have considerable beauty. But if Bradley or anyone else imagines that it has objective validity as a specimen of reality-thinking, he is being irrational. (I hope that anyone who is disposed to doubt this will refer back to the definitions on pages 7ff.)

From this point of view similar considerations apply to No. 1 and also to such a statement as "I feel bewildered." In neither case is there any conceivable way in which the observation of objective phenomena could provide evidence for or against the probability of their being true.[1] Consequently they are not objective statements. If I say that I feel bewildered I cannot be denied; neither can it be objectively proved.

The only standard by which propositions in this class can be tested is that of individual and subjective emotion or faith.

[1] Observation of objective phenomena can provide evidence for the truth of the statement that many people, including men in positions of the highest authority, have believed that Jesus Christ was the Son of God; it can also provide evidence for or against the probability of Jesus Christ's having existed as a material human being. But such evidence is, of course, irrelevant to the truth or falsity of the original statement, since this proposition remains unverifiable unless the words "Son" and "God" are defined in terms of objective phenomena.

Class C.   Aesthetic and Moral.

1. Epstein's *Genesis* is a monstrosity.
2. *Wozzek* is the greatest modern opera.
3. Communists are wicked.
4. We are the greatest people on earth.[1]

These statements are, *in their present forms*, similar to those in the previous class, in that they tell us only of the feelings of individuals. For, as we have seen, unless the definitions of such words as " monstrosity ", " wicked " and " great " are first agreed, there is no way of deciding by what standards statements containing them can be verified. When such words are not explicitly or implicitly defined, statements of this class tell us no more than would such statements as " I like beefsteak " or " I disapprove of Sunday opening of cinemas." On the other hand, in No. 2 for instance, once it is decided how the word " great " is being used, the statement will become equivalent (in informative value) to, say, " Most people like beefsteak." Even then it remains rather vague and difficult to verify; but at least it is conceivably verifiable (by, let us say, a Gallup Poll) and it does potentially tell us something about the objective world in that it makes a statement about the reactions and emotions of human beings, apart from those of the speaker himself.

In Nos. 3 and 4, similarly, once it is decided how the words " wicked " and " great " are being used, the statements become equivalent to (say) " Sunday opening of cinemas has harmful effects on the physical welfare and happiness of most of the population." Once again, the statements remain difficult to verify, since they relate to very complex subjects. But at least they have become scientific in form—they have become amenable to experimental observation. This is, as a matter of fact, truer of 3 and 4 than of 1 and 2, since it is relatively difficult to isolate definite facts about people's aesthetic emotions. Indeed, there are some who consider that all aesthetic judgments of value are devoid of objective validity. But I am inclined to follow such people as Karl Britton[2] in holding that, in any one community or group there is sufficient homogeneity of feeling and emotional response to give general statements about the group-feeling some validity,

---

[1] Mr. Duff Cooper broadcasting to the English race in May 1942.

[2] *Communication.* Cf. pages 8ff. and 47ff. for a fuller discussion of these points.

though, to quote Mr. Britton, " we do not know enough about human beings in general, or about particular persons (not even about ourselves) to be able to assert many of these propositions with any *reasonable confidence* ".   Since it so happens that people are constantly making such assertions with boundless confidence, the assertions remain largely irrational even when the words have first been defined.   And it remains true that, when the words have not been defined, the assertions are completely irrational if they imply that they are telling us an objective fact about the world rather than, as in " I like beefsteak," a fact about the feelings and opinions of the speaker.   In practice, of course, such words are very seldom defined, chiefly because their main function is emotive ; i.e. they are designed to arouse (in the hearer) an emotional response of agreement, and (in the speaker) a comforting impression that his own opinion is objective, reinforced by the suggestion, implicit in their apparent objectivity, that they have the sanction of the herd.

Class D.   Reality Thinking.

1. Napoleon I was born in A.D. 1769.
2. Mr. Duff Cooper said in May 1942 that the English were the greatest people on earth.
3. This kettle is boiling.
4. There are millions of people who believe in a deity.
5. Water boils at 212 degrees.
6. If we put an import duty on wheat this year, there will be less unemployment among agricultural workers next year.

Statements in this class will all, on examination, be seen to be translatable into the form of predictions which can potentially be verified by observation of objective phenomena. Even statements like Nos. 1 and 2, though about past events, are translatable into such forms as : " I predict that observation of documents and MSS. will show that it is extremely probable that Napoleon I was born in 1769." It is with such propositions and statements as these that rational (or reality-) thinking is concerned. Even when true, none of them is an " absolute " certainty, like the tautologies and axioms in Class A, though they may in favourable circumstances be either " practical " certainties or alternatively exact enough approximations for practical purposes ; they all tell us things about the objective world ; and, since the evidence which would verify them is available to independent observers, they can all provide a basis for discussion.

Class E. Poetic Truths.

1. All the world's a stage.
2. How wonderful is Death, Death and his brother sleep. . . .

Statements of this kind tell us about individual and subjective emotion, as do the metaphysical and mystical ones in Class B. But they do not confuse us by pretending to do more. They are equivalent in informative value to a statement like—" I have a feeling—a new and illuminating idea —about death ; and I want someone else to keep me company by sharing the same feeling." Admittedly this statement fails to suggest the way in which poetic truth can illuminate aspects of the world. But this quality of poetry is beside the present point, for the aspects thus illuminated are not reality-thinking and extremely few people pretend for a moment that they are.

But—and this is the present point—people constantly fall into the trap of imagining that, because all the different kinds of proposition just enumerated can be called " true " or " false " they can all be judged by their correspondence with the same standard ; and, as I have said, it is persistently taken for granted that this standard is objective reality—and therefore that the propositions can be objective truths.

I have tried to make it clear that, in fact, there are at least five different kinds of " truth " involved. (See Table.)

As we have seen, reality-thinking is concerned with propositions of the types in Class D, because these are the only ones which tell us things about the objective world (apart from things about the way we define words). Now in Part I of this book we saw that irrational thinking included thinking which imagines itself to be reality-thinking but which is in fact nothing of the sort ; and, during the foregoing chapters, we have come across a number of examples of this form of irrationality. I have made this careful enumeration of types of proposition in order to summarize and clarify the situation, and to indicate a fairly simple method of detecting a large part of the irrationality in the world. In brief, the method is this : whenever somebody makes a statement of the type shown in Classes B, C and E he is being non-rational ; if he implies that his statement is of the same type as those in Class D—if, further, he implies that his statements can afford a basis for

FIVE TYPES OF TRUTH

Class	Type	Criterion	Degree of Certainty	Examples
A. Tautologies and Axioms	Non-objective	Linguistic custom	Absolute or Logical	All white clouds are white. 2 plus 2 equals 4
B. Metaphysical and Mystical	Subjective	Individual or subjective emotion (expressed sometimes as the dogma of authority)	Pseudo-absolute	Jesus Christ is the Son of God. There is nothing in the whole besides appearance . . . etc.
C. Aesthetic and Moral	Subjective except when defined	Subjective feelings of pleasure and pain (aesthetic). Ditto of approval or disapproval (moral)	Depending on definition and restricted to culture pattern	Epstein's *Genesis* is a monstrosity. Communists are wicked, etc.
D. Reality Thinking	Objective	Experimental observation	"Practical" certainty	Napoleon I was born in 1769. Water boils at 212 degrees, etc.
E. Poetic Truths	Frankly subjective	Same as B	"Fractional" truths	All the world's a stage. How wonderful is Death, Death and his brother sleep. . . .

discussion and objective agreement—he is being irrational.
(I am using the words " irrational " and " rational " here as
they were defined in Part I. These are the definitions used
in practice by every person who wishes to assert that his
statements are sensible and well-founded; he would say that
" Napoleon I was born in 1769 " is a rational statement,
and he would claim the same kind of rationality for his own
statements.)

It is astonishing to reflect how much writing and speaking
is immediately branded by such a test. In the case of conversation it does not matter so very much; for only a very
small proportion of our pleasure in conversation springs from
the exchange of useful information. But the printed word
carries greater weight; unless it is written (and read) openly
as a contribution to fantasy-thinking (e.g. fiction, poetry, art
and some of its criticism) it tends to be taken for granted as
a contribution to our knowledge of the external world. The
spoken word—the political speech, the after-dinner speech,
the sermon, the " message to the nation "—also carries weight
in proportion as the words used are emotive rather than
informative, i.e. in proportion as they are stirring, pregnant
with meaning and evocative of higher thoughts. One can
seldom open one's newspaper without finding that someone,
in a speech or letter, is earnestly asking us all to agree with a
statement which he fondly imagines to be informing us of some
objective truth, but which in fact informs us only of what he
himself believes and feels.

It cannot be too often emphasized that propositions of the
types shown in Classes B, C and E are subjective; that there
is no universally accepted basis for discussion of them; and
that in consequence it is irrational to demand *as a right* either
agreement or disagreement with them. From this there
follows the important conclusion that a large part of what is
now taught to children as objective truth is in fact no more than
dogma. It would not matter if it were made clear to the
children's potentially clear minds that it *was* dogma. But,
as it is, we do not even explain to them the difference between
dogma and scientific statement; and, as a result, we practice
on them a cruel and dangerous deceit which may permanently
addle their reasoning powers.

Tautologies and axioms were left out of the last paragraph
partly because they are non-objective rather than subjective

and partly because the layman finds it impossible to mis-interpret them. It is only the trained mind of a metaphysician which can produce a sufficiently intricate muddle from such small beginnings. The distinctive feature of tautologies and axioms is that they re-state definitions in a more convenient form, and they help us to see new aspects of already estab-lished or assumed facts. In the former capacity they are called *a priori* truths ; in the latter, they form the greater part of any chain of reasoning. In the former they are absolute certainties and self-evident ; in the latter, their practical certainty and objective value depend on how closely they follow the rules and on how correct are the assumptions from which they start—these assumptions themselves being by no means self-evident. The greater part of this book is made up of such axioms and tautologies.

As for the higher truths—the ultimate realities—of the mystics, it is hardly necessary to point out (except to the mystics, and then it is useless) that they have no objective meaning.

I must not be misunderstood as suggesting that such " truths " have no value. I would as soon suggest that poetic truths have no value—that there is nothing to be got from art and all other forms of fantasy-thinking. It is very clear that we need these things in our lives and that we need the kind of writing and speaking which will tell us about them and will help us to experience them. It is also clear that the scientific attitude of reality-thinking does not and cannot tell us any-thing about them (though it does seem to be on the way to explaining how and why they come to be experienced). This fact is often held against the scientific attitude. It is suggested that because it does not provide us with the " higher " truths, the truths it does provide us with are a low sort of fraudulent imitation, to be rejected whenever they lead to inconvenient conclusions. Again the one true meaning !—it is assumed that somehow " truth " is all one species, and that, in conse-quence, all kinds of truth can be placed in higher or lower grades. Then the most satisfactory kinds are labelled the " higher " ones (on the principle of grabbing a word with an admirable aroma for something one likes) and the whole question is successfully begged.

The matter resolves itself into what kind of knowledge we want. When we want knowledge of certain kinds of emotional truth, we should turn to poetry and art and metaphysics; when we want knowledge of the objective world (usually for the purpose of action) we will fail to get it unless we confine ourselves to reality-thinking. We may fail even then if our reality-thinking is incompetent; but at least we are using the right tools.

Where then does the conflict between science and religion come in ? We appear to have established that it is illusory— but, for an illusion, it is extremely vociferous. The trouble, I think, is that, though science admits freely that it can tell us nothing about those "truths" of revealed religion whose acceptance is "an act of faith", religion on the other hand refuses to admit that it can tell us nothing about the objective world. It continually asserts that its dogma and beliefs have equal validity, for the same purpose and in the same field, with the laws and hypotheses upon which scientists base their knowledge and their plans for action. In other words, the believer in religious truths continually claims for his statements the same kind of rationality as he would claim for "Napoleon I was born in 1769."

Moreover, it is not only for the religious type of subjective belief that this rationality is claimed; it is claimed for almost all the subjective beliefs, particularly those to do with ethics and politics. In fact, it is claimed much more passionately for these than for the objective ones to which it correctly refers. As I have suggested, this is probably because it is primarily on questions of ethics and religion that we instinctively desire the approval of the community, combined with the assurance of our own rightness and righteousness. The paradox is that objective knowledge is least attainable in just those fields where it is most desirable and thus most "natural" for us to believe that we can have it.

(2) TESTS

INTRODUCTION

Earthly minds, like mud walls, resist the strongest batteries ; and though, perhaps, sometimes the force of a clear argument may make some impression, yet they nevertheless stand firm, keep out the enemy, truth, that would captivate or disturb them.
—John Locke. "An Essay Concerning Human Understanding."

One of the uses of language is to persuade people to take opinions on trust; we state an opinion and we bolster it up

with arguments designed to appear so convincing as to require
no further evidence to support them. The art of oratory—
particularly in politics—is essentially the art of so manipulating
words that they can disguise the exiguousness of the evidence
they purport to be providing—or, alternatively, can rouse the
audience to such a pitch that it ceases to demand evidence at
all. The art of oratory has been practised assiduously for
thousands of years. For about five hundred years the printed
word has been put to much the same uses. It is not surprising,
therefore, that language as we now know it is well adapted
for deception, nor that this deception should be practised as
often on the speaker as on the hearer. The last chapter was
designed to afford a method of smelling out the deception in
a large number of cases. But the manipulators of language
have thought up disguises infinitely more subtle than any that
I there displayed. I will therefore try, in this chapter, to
indicate some further tests for irrationality. A very few of these
will be fairly certain tests; the rest will be more in the nature
of signs whose recognition serves as a warning of *probable*
irrationality. Whether the reader will accept these tests and
signs as valid will depend largely on whether he has accepted
the main contentions of this book. Nearly all the signs and
tests are in fact logical conclusions from what has already
been said, and they are classified and named here because it
is primarily through classification by naming that our minds
manage to recognize any phenomenon and thus decide how
best to deal with it.

The majority of irrational arguments depend for their
plausibility on logical fallacies; and the detection of a fallacy
in an argument is a certain sign that the argument is irrational
—though not necessarily, be it noted, that the conclusion
arrived at is false. People are often right for the wrong
reason, and even more often they are right (or wrong) for no
reason at all. At the end of this supplement I shall describe
one or two fallacies which are particularly prominent in
discussions of the main subject of this book. But, in general,
fallacies are outside my province. Their detection is, however, an almost indispensable accessory to the signs and tests
given here, because it is not much use suspecting or accusing
someone of irrationality if you cannot discover where his
reasoning is at fault. As Schopenhauer has said, " it would
be a very good thing if every trick could receive some short

and obviously appropriate name, so that when a man used this or that particular trick, he could be at once reproached for it ".[1] *Logic in Practice* (particularly Chapters IV and V), by L. Susan Stebbing, and *Clearer Thinking*, by A. E. Mander, both give excellent untechnical expositions, with names, of the main fallacies. For political fallacies I have not found anything better than Bentham's *Book of Fallacies*, but, as Bentham's own style is heavy going, these are more easily digested by reading Sidney Smith's witty summary, given in his notice of the book in the Edinburgh Review and included in his collected essays.

(1) Word-substitution

This is primarily a test of reality-thinking. It is not, I must emphasize, a test of general value; a piece of writing or talking which does not fulfil the test requirements is thus shown to be faulty only *qua* reality-thinking; it may remain perfectly satisfactory *qua* poetry or drama or aesthetics. In the case of many expressions of fantasy-thinking there would anyway be no point in applying the test. For one thing, they make no pretence that their object is to be informative rather than emotive. For another, the object of fantasy-thinking is to express ideas, mental concepts, emotions and feelings for which (since they are largely subjective) there are no defined word-symbols; and there is thus no question of talking about " things " as objectively conceived.

But one form of irrationality occurs as fantasy-thinking which purports to be reality-thinking. And it is this form that the test is designed to diagnose.

The theoretical foundation of the test is as follows: In reality-thinking we are dealing with objective phenomena; and in discussion we have (on pain of aborting the discussion) to refer to phenomena which (a) can be clearly identified, through the word-labels used, by all parties to the discussion, and which (b) can or could conceivably be observed experimentally by these parties. Since then it is phenomena which are being discussed, it does not matter what they are called, *so long as* it is clear which phenomena are being referred to. Naturally, in order to save time, we tend to use the familiar labels for our phenomena; we do not fancifully call a motor-car a " pobble " or the curious behaviour of a crowd of people

[1] *The Art of Controversy*, quoted in the *Meaning of Meaning*, op. cit.

at a football match "engorgitation". It would be no use, first because our hearers have not yet come across any phenomena so labelled, and secondly because we have not told them beforehand what we intend the labels to refer to. On the other hand, if I wished to talk about a particular type of car with five wheels and a propellor, I would first describe it clearly enough to differentiate it (for the purpose of the particular discussion) from other cars and then I would refer to it, later on, as "this type of car" or "the Thingumijig I'm talking about"—if I wanted to be pedantic, I could even call it "X" or "A" or "the pobble". The point is that the actual name I used would not matter; my argument would remain equally valid which ever of these labels was used. Similarly in the case of the curious behaviour of the crowd. After having described and differentiated it adequately, I could perhaps call it "a sort of mob-hysteria"; later on, to save time, I might call it "mob-hysteria" *tout court*. But the behaviour I was talking about would be the particular behaviour in question; it would not necessarily be what you thought mob-hysteria to mean. You could not therefore legitimately draw conclusions about it based on your own definition. All the same, the fact that we were using a common label would be very likely to mislead either of us in to drawing false conclusions. And the safest way of detecting any such false reasoning would be for the behaviour *I* was talking about to be called "X"; there would then be no chance of confusion. In practice, of course, one seldom goes to such pedantic lengths. But the fact remains that, if an argument is suspected of being confused in this way, the confusion can be detected by the process of replacing doubtful labels by colourless letters of the alphabet, with the object (a) of getting rid of pre-conceived associations and (b) of making sure that one really is arguing about the phenomenon in question and not about the meaning of words.

Examples of the use of letters of the alphabet as labels are to be found in the field of psychology. Investigators engaged in working out tests of mental qualities have established that certain tests definitely measure specific qualities or factors of mental behaviour. One of these factors is very near to what most people mean by "pure intelligence". But all the same the label "intelligence" is too vague—it has too many previous connotations, with the result that people are inclined to object, "But this factor isn't intelligence; it's cleverness" (or "quickness of reaction" or "brightness"— according to how they severally define these labels). So the psychologists have decided to call the factor the "g-factor"; and there is now no trouble, for there is no temptation for people to think the label applies to anything else but the specific factor (whatever it is) that is measured by the tests. In the course of further experiment the functions and correlations of this factor have been gradually established and it has become unnecessary to disqualify it by thinking of it as "whatever it is"; it has, in fact, become an extremely useful concept to the psychologist. A quotation from Dr. Cyril Burt[1] gives a specific example in the field of testing for character-qualities:

"It was expected that such methods (of testing) would measure what was supposed to be a kind of mental momentum or inertia, and so bring to light any marked liability to obsessions. Actually, however, this theory proved to be too simple; and the characteristic tested now seems to be a definite but somewhat specific factor for which the best name is an entirely non-committal term—the 'p-factor.'"

The scientific method, in fact, is to examine a thing and then to hunt up a name for it. (The metaphysical method is to examine a word and then to hunt up—or even invent—a thing for it to denote.) To paraphrase Pareto (from *Mind and Society*) the objective sciences never quarrel about names. They quarrel about the things that the names stand for. A scientific argument retains its full value if the names it uses are replaced by letters of the alphabet or by numbers. Thus, if things are designated beyond possibility of doubt or mis-understanding, the names given to them matter hardly at all.

We have already seen that one of the most prolific sources of doubt and misunderstanding is the Utraquistic fallacy, in which the same name is given to several different things. Its prolificness is such that the word-substitution test is much too tedious as a means of diagnosis. However, under a later heading I will suggest a way in which, once the fallacy is suspected, letters of the alphabet can be extremely useful as an aid to clarifying the argument.

The main value of the word-substitution test lies in its adaptability to cases where abstract words are being used, not to refer to clearly identified concepts, but to conjure up

---

[1] *The Subnormal Mind.*

vague and misty sentiments, tinged as a rule by association with "higher", more spiritual, levels of thought. In discussions of Social Security I have recently come across the following words used in this way: "strength of character", "initiative", "independence", "the Will of the People", "National Pride"; other words constantly met in current reading are: "Freedom", "justice", "culture", and so on. Now, such words are inevitably rather vague in their meaning, and this vagueness is even to some extent a blessing; for it provides them with what William James called a "fringe of meaning", so that when people are talking one does at least get a hazy idea of what they are talking about—and a hazy idea (so long as its haziness is recognized) is better than no idea at all.   It is extremely seldom that two people, discussing abstract ideas, have precisely the same ideas in mind.   Consequently, if we were demanding that words should have exact meanings, we should need an immeasurably vast number of separate labels for all these different concepts.   In practice, we make do with relatively few words, relying on the fringe of meaning to cover most of the useful variations.   We cannot therefore indict abstract words merely for being vague.   If, on replacing them by letters of the alphabet, it remains fairly clear that they do still (and must, from the context) refer to concepts which have a logical place in the argument, then they pass the test.   On the other hand, if the letters of the alphabet show no signs whatever of referring to anything clearly definable; if, further, any attempt at clear definition reduces the validity of the argument; then the words do not pass the test. The test will, in fact, have shown that the words are not being used to refer to anything objective but are trading on their vagueness of meaning in order to invoke in the reader either a feeling that something has been logically stated or an emotion associated with a group sentiment.[1]

Typical group sentiments invoked in this way are those centred on the concepts of love of country, justice, foreigners,

---

[1] I use the word "sentiment" here in the psychological sense, as involving —in Professor MacDougall's words—"an individual tendency to experience certain emotions and desires in relation to some particular object".   A group sentiment is one which is common to most members of the group, the "group" being anything from a clique to a class to a nation.   Sentiments are, as a rule, established in childhood and are so much taken for granted that their genesis and rationality are never afterwards questioned.   The group sentiments are largely conditioned by the already prevailing ethical traditions and culture pattern of the child's parents.

cowardice, fair-play and so on. And the object of thus invoking them is partly to surround the general tenor of the argument with an aura of socially approved emotion (this is when a point of view is being upheld ; otherwise it is vice versa) and partly to invest the argument with a high-sounding nobility of phrase. The speeches of Lord Halifax, in my opinion, provide quite excellent examples, with their use of such phrases as " the eternal and immutable verities ". It is interesting to note how often his speeches or writings are described as " noble " or " profound ".

There is such an abundance of writing and talking in this category that it is difficult to recognize it on sight. We have come to take it as part of the natural order of things and anyone who tries to keep up with current affairs tends to find himself skimming over it, in newspapers and periodicals, humbly assuming that it all means something, and that, if only he had time to read it with due care, he would find out what it was. There is indeed every excuse for believing, at first sight, that there is a meaning to be found ; the abstract words make it all sound very deep—but too often it is about as deep and clear as the mud at the bottom of the pond.

It should therefore be helpful if I give first a very obvious example :

" Fascism henceforward has in the world the universality of all those doctrines which, by fulfilling themselves, have significance in the history of the human spirit."[1]

Here is a less obvious example—less obvious because there is a chain of reasoning hidden beneath the verbiage ; and, when one draws aside this verbiage and finds the chain actually there, one is inclined to cry Eureka without bothering to see whether in fact the chain leads where it is supposed to lead. The words " mere ", " sincere ", " conviction ", " self-knowledge ", " continuity ", " threatening decay ", are suspect :

" We are not led by mere conservatism to wish to preserve for the future the study of the Classics because their study is traditional in the Grammar Schools of the past ; rather we would say that it is traditional, not from accidental reasons, but from a sincere conviction, however variously expressed,

---

[1] " La Dottrina del Fascismo " (1932), article by Mussolini in the *Enciclopedia Italiana*, quoted in *Social and Political Doctrines of Contemporary Europe*, by Michael Oakeshott.

that, unless a culture attains to and preserves self-knowledge, its continuity is not assured; failure in self-knowledge is a symptom of threatening decay."[1] Replace "sincere" and "conviction" by A and B; in my opinion, they stand for something like "strong opinion". They are thus allowed to pass the test, though incidentally they have been shown to be carefully selected so as to invoke a favourable reaction in the reader towards the opinion in question. But now let us take the word "self-knowledge"; replace it by C. The passage then reads, "unless a culture attains C, its continuity is not assured". We begin now to see that C is so vague in meaning as to be incapable of referring to concepts which will be effectively the same for all readers. (If anyone doubts this let him ask a number of people what they think C should refer to.) We see also that any attempt to give it a clearly defined meaning will make the argument much less plausible. If we try to imagine what kind of self-knowledge will assure continuity of a culture, we can get a *relatively* clear concept. Again, if we try to imagine what kind of self-knowledge a study of the Classics will ensure, we get a relatively clear concept. But are these concepts the same? I doubt it. One seems to have something to do with Great Britain; the other is expanded to include also something to do with Greece and Rome. There may perhaps be something significant in common. But this is clearly a debatable point. In any case, the argument has lost a lot of its glory. Further, I myself find that, if I make a guess at the sort of thing the writer of the report intended, and if I also ignore the emotionally approving aura he has set up, his chain of reasoning appears to lead, in fact, to the conclusion that what we need in our schools is not a course of the Classics but a course of anthropology and group psychology (which of course would include a study of the effects on our culture pattern of Roman and Greek ideas).

The words "threatening decay" can be tested similarly. But there is no point in elaborating. The passage quoted has all the characteristics necessary for inducing the reader to *feel* that somehow something of import has been said and that it deserves assent.

One of the primary difficulties with this test is to decide which words to apply it to. But this is made easier if one

[1] *Curriculum and Examinations in Secondary Schools*, The "Norwood" Report, H.M.S.O. (1943), page 119.

remembers that the words whose meanings are most numerous are the abstract ones. In books whose argument relies on discrediting the efficacy of scientific thinking, for instance, the suspicious words are such as "knowledge", "reality", "validity", "ultimate", "essence", etc. In books whose object is to defend some political system, the suspicious words are such as "democracy", "freedom", "culture", "state-control", "enterprise", "order", "race", and so on.

The test is often useful—and comparatively easy to apply—in cases where an ostensibly rational argument is relying for its force, not upon objective evidence combined with valid reasoning, but upon the emotive power of the words used. In such cases, it will be found that the argument is not necessarily shown to be meaningless, nor is it shown to be false; it may in fact state a perfectly sound opinion. But when the phenomena or concepts referred to are divorced from the words with which they are labelled, it turns out that the arguer has produced no independent evidence, and as a rule has begged the question either by implying that he *has* produced evidence or by assuming in his choice of words that the point at issue has already been settled.

Queen Victoria's letters are italicized all over with examples of the latter kind of begged question, most of them so obvious that even if the Queen had not considerately underlined them for us, they would need no test for their diagnosis. One of the most delightful is from a note of March 13th, 1880, to Sir Henry Ponsonby, her private secretary:[1] "The Queen is *no* partizan & *never has* been since the 1st 3 or 4 years of her reign. . . . But she has . . . most *deeply* grieved over & been *indignant* at the *blind* & *destructive* course pursued by the Opposition wh. wd. *ruin* the country & her great anxiety is to *warn* them not to go on committing themselves to such a very dangerous & reckless course."

Another note, written in 1885,[2] gives a mild example of the other kind of begged question:

"Sir Henry shd. tell Mr. Goschen that she hopes he & those he hopes to act with will be *truly patriotic* & will not be in a hurry to try & turn out this Government which is doing its best in a most difficult position."

[1] *Henry Ponsonby; His Life from His Letters*, by his son, Arthur Ponsonby, page 183.

[2] Op. cit., page 194.

Here again Her Majesty has kindly underlined the suspicious words. Replace them by A and B and see what happens: "Sir Henry shd. tell Mr. Goschen that she hopes he . . . will be A-ly B & will not be in a hurry to try & . . ." We gather from the context roughly what the labels stand for; they are being used to describe the qualities which would attach to the negative action of "not turning out the Government". This negative action would naturally have effects on the course of events in Great Britain—i.e. it would be (we could say) "effective"—though whether harmfully or beneficially is a question of some complexity; we should certainly need some evidence before we accepted the conclusion that it would definitely be either. In fact, *without further evidence,* "A-ly B" appears to be a completely neutral qualification of Mr. Goschen's suggested action; whereas the patent intention of the note was to imply that "patriotism" provided evidence in favour of the course of action suggested.

As in so many cases of this sort, the argument when analysed turns out to have no more validity than "I think so-and-so, and therefore everybody should agree." The substitution of letters of the alphabet for the emotively coloured words has got rid of the logically irrelevant emotions associated with them and exposes the fact that the argument depends, not upon evidence or reason, but upon persuasion; it is, in fact, not a piece of information but an exhortation.

In this case, the exhortatory quality is fairly obvious; but the test works as well—and more usefully—with subtler examples of the confusion between the informative and the emotive functions of language. I must, however, repeat that a positive reaction is not an indication that the argument tested comes to a false conclusion; it is merely a sign that the conclusion, whether true or false, is backed by very much less evidence than it implies and that its acceptance is demanded on emotional rather than on rational grounds. For this reason, there is little point in applying the test to political speeches; they will nearly always show a positive reaction and will not be any the less excellent for it. The more a speech relies on emotional persuasion (through the use of fine words, phrases, diction and rhythm) the better it is as a piece of oratory and, so long as it is not for one moment confused with reality-thinking, it can have valuable effects.

Newspaper and magazine articles are, of course, fruitful experimental territory, especially as they usually set themselves up to be pure reality-thinking. I will give one or two random examples from current reading. In an article in the *News Chronicle* on " Teaching Religion in the Schools ", Lord Elton said: " In these uniform State schools the Christian religion would find no place. ' The ethics of social responsibility must take the place of religious dogma,' explained Mr. Chester, on behalf of the General Council (of the T.U.C.). It was clear from the sentimental materialism of this and other speeches that for these worthy folk the fabric and equipment of the schools are more important than the beliefs of the teachers."

In this passage the obviously emotive words, in my opinion, are such as " sentimental" and " worthy "; they need no test for their detection. More insidious, however, are " uniform ", " materialism " and " beliefs ". I have found that the passage loses much of its emotive force and some of its plausibility when these are, so to speak, deflated by means of the test.

In an article " On the Fall of France " in *Life* for February 1st, 1943, General Henri Honoré Giraud said:

"From 1918 to 1940 France luxuriated in every kind of regime that might be called republican—from horizon blue to the red Popular Front." (Suspicious word—"luxuriate".)

In the issue of *The Week* for February 4th, 1944, there occurred the passage:

"Demands raised by the Polish Patriots in Moscow in relation to East Prussia, Silesia, and Pomerania, have been received with enthusiasm in genuinely patriotic Polish circles. . . ." " Genuine ", like " true ", is hardly ever an innocent word. A trick which is common to Her Majesty, Queen Victoria, and to *The Week* can, however, at least claim a wide usage.

*   *   *

All this is to approach from another direction a point already touched upon. There is much writing and talking associated with what we have been calling fantasy-thinking which depends for part of its value on the emotive and ethical associations of the words it uses. These associations are so important that the words have to be very carefully chosen and cannot of course be replaced by other words without detracting from the effect. This is particularly the case with poetry—and even with much prose fiction. There are emotions and intuitions (i.e. poetic truths—aspects of sub-jective experience) which cannot be expressed *accurately* by words; they can only be hinted at, and the hints are made by means of the fringes of meaning and emotional associations of the words used. As these associations are not to be found in any dictionary, but agglomerate by custom and change subtly from time to time, they are always peculiar to the language community in which they are current. (They are also to some extent peculiar to each individual.) Hence the difficulty of translating poetry from one language into another; and hence the obscurity of some English poets (such as James Joyce, T. S. Eliot, etc.) except to those Englishmen who know intimately the poet himself or at least his immediate circle.

Thus it is only natural that, in translating any form of fantasy-thinking from one language to another, a loose inter-pretation should be more successful than an exact one. It is only in reality-thinking that language is intended to mean no more than it actually states, and that it is illegitimate to include any extraneous associations of the words used. In fantasy-thinking, on the other hand, any attempt to render literally the words used—to assume that the poet meant no more than what he literally stated—would be absurd.

Now it is important to acknowledge that there can be degrees of euphony—of vitality, of readability, etc.—not only in poetic writing but also in pure reality-thinking. A com-pletely logical argument can be written in such a way that it is too boring to read. But the fact remains that its validity is independent of the form of words used and of the particular words used, so long as it is clear to what those words refer. It follows that a piece of reality-thinking will always be potentially translatable from one language to another without there being any loss of its scientific or informative value, however much its readability may be impaired.

We have here another form of the word-substitution test, particularly appropriate incidentally to philosophy which argues about words instead of things. But it is subject to the proviso that a work on (say) economics or thermionics could hardly be translated into Zulu without completely losing its readability in the process of trying to define each unfamiliar term. Life is short, and we have therefore to hope that, when we make noises like "statistics", "capitalist" and "frequency-modulation", other people will understand well enough what we are getting at. However, if we are talking sense, it should always be possible for us to explain, ultimately in terms of "things", what those noises really refer to. The literature of economics and physics must, in order to save time, use words that refer to concepts unfamiliar to a Zulu. But all the same, unless it can be translated into terms which make sense in any language once the reference of those terms is established, it is saying nothing of any use as reality-thinking.[1]

A skilful translator can do much to nullify the disinfectant properties of translation, since he will choose, in the new language, words whose emotive and other associations are very near to those of the original words. For this reason translation into a language which restricts as far as possible the number of its words and thus makes it extremely difficult for the same concept to be expressed with varying emotional tones, will act as a more searching test than usual. Emotive writing will emerge from the process a colourless skeleton of itself with all the warm emotion removed and the bones—if any—exposed to the naked eye. Basic English and Inter-glossa are both such languages; indeed, their protaganists specifically state that they are not primarily designed to deal with emotive and imaginative writing.

Though this test is intended to aid us in distinguishing between the emotive and the scientific (or informative) uses of language, I do not wish to imply that it is always irrational to combine the two uses. In fact, a great part of writing about aesthetics quite legitimately does so. But this means that it is often very difficult to determine precisely where one begins and the other ends.

(2) "Your evidence, please?"

This test, though very simple to apply, needs skilful handling if relations with the person tested are to remain friendly.

---

[1] The task of translating current language into such terms is what the analytical philosophers have set themselves. The terms constitute the "physical language"—the language which refers to "things"—and the physical language is, in their view, the only really universal language.

It is designed mainly for use in discussion. The symptoms of an unfavourable reaction are usually insulted dignity, an imputation of bad manners to the tester or simple fury. The test does not apply to written arguments except in the obvious way that inability to produce evidence for a statement detracts from its value. The object of the test, in fact, is not so much to produce evidence as to see what happens to our opponent. From his behaviour we can generally judge whether his argument or opinion rests upon objective evidence at all, or whether he is just airing, trying to bolster up, or trying to put across, a pre-conceived opinion. In such cases, inability to produce or refer to the evidence is usually combined with a strong reluctance to admit the fact, since this would of course entail suspending judgment on the cherished opinion. And the more warmly cherished the opinion, the greater the reaction, so that the strength of the reaction is some measure of the irrationality involved. After all, if we *have* got evidence what could possibly be more delightful than to throw it lump by lump at our suspicious questioner ?

By itself, inability to produce evidence is naturally no definite sign of irrationality; the opinion may be merely tentative, or it may not be strongly held and the holder may therefore be quite ready to suspend judgment, especially if he is genuinely interested only in getting at the truth—or he may simply have left the evidence in his other pocket. But if deeper and more fishy motives are at work, these will be largely unrecognized, and our opponent's reluctance to admit any slur on his opinion will show itself in various types of rationalization. Injured dignity is most useful, especially in the case of elders and betters. It draws an authoritarian red-herring across the discussion, " What do you mean ?— evidence ! . . . I know it for a fact I tell you. After all, I've had some little experience . . ." Some such remark, hinting at belligerence, ingeniously puts us in the position of having either to give way, or to suggest, even more clearly, that we do not regard our opponent's word as evidence. This of course is Rude, and the original argument is almost certainly forgotten in a heated discussion of what is rude and what isn't.

An occasional reaction is unadulterated anger in which there is hardly any element of rationalization, but which is resorted to partly instinctively and partly because it is found by experience that it acts successfully as a diversion, since fear of a breakdown of relations forces the tester to drop the subject and to leave his opponent in undisturbed possession of his opinion.

Anger is so often a probable reaction that the test has, as I have suggested, to be applied in a complicated and round-about way.   It would be quite simple if one were prepared to lose any friend who thought and argued irrationally ; but man, being a herd animal, is not fitted for a life of such loneliness.   One has, therefore, to learn the technique of hinting that one may be about to ask for evidence and of then hurriedly withdrawing before the hint has become too broad to be ignored.

My emphasis on the dangers and delicacies of this test may seem unnecessary.   One would surely think that, in any discussion, evidence upon which to base conclusions was a *sine qua non*.   But this is, I submit, an error.

There is one circumstance in which the test is vitiated. This is when our opponent is arguing from the particular to the general and triumphantly produces his particular fact with a sublime unconsciousness of its inadequacy.   In a discussion on (say) the colour question he will retort : " Oh, there's no doubt about it.   Why ! my old friend, Archie Pellagow, lived for years in South Africa, and he found that the only thing to do with them was to treat them just like children and to give them all a sound thrashing every now and then."   In such cases the wisest course is usually a change of subject (provided that the new subject is not that of Mr. Pellagow's conception of paternal responsibilities).   However, if it is thought safe, the test can still be applied in a gentle form by pointing out with utmost circumspection that our opponent is arguing from the particular to the general, and watching to see how he takes this.

It is perhaps hardly necessary to mention that a case of arguing from the particular to the general is almost impossible to diagnose if it happens to back up one's own point of view.

(3) Self-Evidence

This test is a corollary of the one just dealt with.   It consists in watching out for the use of such words and phrases as " obvious ", " self-evident ", " a fundamental fact of life ", " law of nature ", and so on ; and then seeing whether they are redundant for the purposes of the argument. If they *are* redundant (that is to say, if the argument remains valid without them) the test is negative. If, on the other hand, the argument relies upon them to any appreciable extent, it is once again an argument which is falsely pretending to be backed by objective evidence.

The basis of the test is that there can be no opinions (except tautologies or re-statements of axioms) which are completely self-evident; there are in fact no objective judgments which can dispense with objective evidence. However, as usual, we have not time to be too particular. There are thousands of judgments and opinions current in everyday discussion which are very sensibly taken as "obviously" or "self-evidently" true. Though they are not self-evident in the philosophical or intrinsic sense, they are evident in the same way as it is evident that the sun will rise to-morrow or that there are lots of spaniels in England. They are judgments which 99 per cent. of the parties to a discussion will agree upon; and they are therefore the natural foundation of any discussion. Consequently to describe them as "obvious" or "self-evident" is redundant; the persuasive effect of such words is merely to emphasize a statement without increasing its acceptability. That is why, in these cases, the test is negative. When, on the other hand, the statement in question is not generally accepted—when the speaker cannot legitimately assume its truth—the use of words like "obvious" and "self-evident" is then part of an attempt to persuade himself and others by emotional rather than rational methods.

The next step in the test is to challenge the implied assumption that no evidence is needed. "But it will always come back to the same old thing," says our opponent, for instance, "You can't change human nature; that's obvious." "But *is* it obvious?" we may counter, "What about the evidence collected by people like Ruth Benedict and Margaret Mead?" The rational response to this would clearly be, "Oh, I didn't know about that. What did they find out?" or some such. The irrational response, on the other hand, is some sort of diversion, or perhaps a begging of the question on the lines of, "But anyway people have never stopped having wars; it's not in them to do it—they're not made that way." Anything, in fact, to draw attention away from unwelcome imputations on the cherished opinion.

(3) DANGER SIGNS

As a general rule, everyone who contemplates the nature of things should distrust whatever most readily takes and holds captive his own intellect, and should use so much the more caution in coming to determinations of this kind, that his understanding may remain impartial and clear.—Francis Bacon. "Novum Organum."

But the greatest of all causes of non-observation is a preconceived opinion. This it is which, in all ages, has made the whole race of mankind, and every separate section of it, for the most part unobservant of all facts, however abundant, even when passing under their own eyes, which are contradictory to any first appearance, or any received tenet.—J. S. Mill. "System of Logic."

As I have already said, these signs are merely indications of probable irrationality. They do not deserve much space, but will be briefly listed as useful warnings to the earnest seeker after truth. The reasons for their inclusion will in most cases be clear from reading the earlier chapters of this book.

(1) Strong Feelings

Two quotations will suffice here: "The more strongly we feel about an opinion the more likely it is that it is held on irrational grounds" (Dr. Julian Huxley), and "When opinions are expressed with passion it usually means an absence of secure grounds for belief, except in the presence of over-action of the thyroid gland; and that exception is highly important" (Dr. Robert T. Morris).

Dr. Morris's exception is, for our purposes, not very serious, since over-action of the thyroid gland will tend to cause all opinions to be expressed with passion, whereas in cases of irrationality it will only be the most cherished opinions which are strongly held.

This sign has to be interpreted relatively rather than absolutely, because extremely few people are willing to hold opinions with really scientific detachment and in consequence even the most reasonable discussion usually shows some degree of heat—as indeed does any objective phenomenon; absolute zero is still a half-degree away even in the laboratory. Besides, heat is the result of friction—of frustration; and the heat which accompanies an opinion may sometimes be due, not to the frustration of being unable to produce the evidence, but to the frustration of being in a minority—of being, although on the score of evidence in the right, powerless against the might of opposition. However, one must, in any case, beware of expecting consistent reality-thinking from the human brain. Moreover the mental discomfort of holding moderate opinions has created, by long tradition, a sort of social sanction for strong opinions, so that "anyone who habitually speaks with moderation tends to be regarded either as an ignorant fellow or as incapable of effective action ".[1] We want to feel justified in holding strong views about matters which affect us personally; we cannot find good reason for doing so; we therefore rationalize by persuading ourselves that there is something wrong—or, by converse, weak—about anybody who does not do so. No wonder, then, that perfect moderation is rare ! Nor perhaps is it even desirable. A correct opinion is of no use to the world if it is held with such moderation that its holder never does anything about it. The perfectly clear-headed man may be like Paul Valéry's Monsieur Teste, who could see no sufficient argument against complete inaction.

All the same, passionate feelings about opinions (as opposed to facts) do tend to signify irrationality in proportion to their strength. We need to hold opinions with sufficient certainty to act on them ; but this is different from passionately defending a belief against all comers.

(2) Use of Emotive Words

This is a danger sign only when the user of the emotive words (a) imagines or pretends that he is being perfectly rational, and (b) either is patently unconscious of the difference between emotive and informative language, or, being conscious himself of the difference, hopes that his audience is not. Once again, it is a sign which cannot be interpreted too rigidly ; in ordinary conversation an argument couched in completely emotionless terms is too boring to gain a hearing ; but the emotive words should be the appetizing garnish applied to the evidence, not a substitute for it.

(3) Use of Absolutes

We have seen that a common form of irrationality shows itself in a tendency to set up absolute standards of value by

---

[1] Susan Stebbing. *Thinking to Some Purpose*, see particularly the chapter on "The Unpopularity of Being Moderate ", from which the quotation is taken.

which to judge the subject under discussion. It is not always easy to recognize this sign for, as always in conversation (and even in written discussion which hopes to avoid prolixity), judgments of value have to be put into shorthand form. Someone may say, "I think it is wrong to profess Socialist views and at the same time to have a butler and chauffeur." Such a statement is indistinguishable in form from one which assumes an absolute right and wrong; but in practice it will often happen that those present will have already agreed roughly on the end which they wish to attain and are engaged merely in working out the means to that end. In this particular case, for instance, the end agreed upon may be Socialism and the word "wrong" in this context would be understood by everyone to imply "wrong for this purpose", i.e. (perhaps) "likely to do harm by making potential converts suspicious of the Socialist's good faith".

Nevertheless, this form of shorthand is often a disguise for irrationality. The test is to ask the user "wrong what *for*?" If he can produce some practical end and show that by "wrong" he means something that is harmful to—or unlikely to produce—that end, the discussion can then proceed on that basis. But if he produces some absolute standard— some standard he professes to think "bad" or "good" in itself—then it is an ominous sign. To continue with the example—he may assert that it is wrong because it militates against the individual's "unity" or "wholeness" or "self-consistency", implying that abstract qualities of this sort can themselves be intrinsically "good". (These qualities again are "absolutes" in the sense intended here if they cannot be defined as conducing to some end.) The discussion then bids fair to become useless; for the participants are unlikely to agree as to what precisely they mean by these words; they will all have used them sufficiently often to have attached different references and moral values to them; and the original user will almost certainly turn out to be assuming that they have the "one true meaning" which happens to justify his own statement.

Under the heading of absolutes, in this connection, come not only such words as "good", "bad", etc., but also any ethically-tinged qualities, with their abstractions, e.g. freedom, justice, nature, essence, etc. One comes across innumerable arguments which talk about a completely vague sort of "freedom" or "justice" which is assumed to be intrinsically good. When concepts like these are used as adjectives they can always be punctured by asking, as before, "natural to whom or to what?", "free—what for?", and so on.[1]

When they are used as abstractions it is as a rule more convenient to ask why the quality in question is considered intrinsically good. Anyone who then observes carefully the course of the argument will notice that the advocates of such an absolute good as "integrity" of the individual (for instance) persistently contradict themselves (a) by asserting that integrity *is* good in itself and (b) when asked to prove this, by then being reduced to attempts to justify it as a means to an end, i.e. to show that "keeping one's integrity" has good results from (say) the point of view of propaganda, or efficiency, or personal happiness.

Perhaps the device of asking "What for" might legitimately have been put under the heading of Tests, for it gives a quite definite indication of irrationality. But, owing to the way it impedes the pleasant flow of conversation, it is usually impracticable to do more than privately suspect.

(4) The One True Meaning

I hope I have made it clear that the assumption that a word has one and one only true meaning is fallacious. As a support for bad argument it is almost as widely and devastatingly used as the Utraquistic fallacy. In fact, the two fallacies paradoxically work together; the first, by asserting that there is only one meaning, covers up the fact that the second is nefariously juggling with several meanings. The Utraquistic fallacy is dealt with later, but the One True Meaning is mentioned here because it is easy to detect and is a fairly reliable danger-sign. In addition to the epithet "true" (true democracy, etc), the following words and phrases are pointers: "real", "essence", "properly understood", "in the full sense", "strictly speaking", "fundamental meaning", "in the last analysis", and so on.

---

[1] Alternatively "Free—what from?" as in the case of the schoolboy who answered that the Atlantic Charter gave us Freedom from Want, Freedom from Fear, Freedom from Religion and Freedom from Speech.

The 1830 and 1832 revolutions in France and England provide some pleasant examples from the past. Guizot spent a lot of time talking about "vraie" or "légitime" *liberté*, meaning apparently liberty for the middle classes. And Brougham, when supporting the Reform Bill, said with evident sincerity, "The question is, how we may best make the people's House of Parliament represent the people." But he was up against a difficulty; he was a self-made man who sprang from the upper middle class; it would be against his own interests to allow *all* the people to have political power; at the same time he believed that the people should have political representation. How was he to reconcile the contradiction ? Quite simply ! By adopting a one true meaning, carefully chosen, for "the people". "I do not mean the populace—the mob," he says, ". . . if there is the mob, there is the people also. I speak now of the middle classes. . . ." And he goes on to say how wonderful they are.[1]

A recent and remarkable example comes from *Reason and Emotion,* by John MacMurray (1935, page 187):

"Knowledge is by definition the apprehension of the real —not the description of it, which is another matter. Strictly speaking, therefore, science is not knowledge. I do not say that it is not cognition, but simply that it is not knowledge in the full sense. . . ."

Finally, a comment from Aldous Huxley's *Eyeless in Gaza.* Anthony Beavis is speaking:

"The name counts more with most people than the thing. . . . And of course 'True Freedom' is actually a better name than freedom *tout court*. Truth—it's one of the magical words. . . . Curious that people don't talk about true truth. . . . You couldn't take it seriously. If you want to make the contrary of truth acceptable, you've got to call it spiritual truth, or inner truth, or higher truth, or even. . . ."

(5) Misuse of the verb " to be "

This sign is a corollary of the last two, since it goes with a tendency to believe in absolutes and in true meanings. It springs fundamentally from a misunderstanding of the classificatory function of words as labels, to which I have already

---

[1] I am indebted for these examples to Mr. Leonard Woolf's *After the Deluge,* Vol II (1939), page 138. Mr. Woolf's *Quack, Quack !* (1935) is very much worth reading as an expose of Fascist and Nazi nonsense and of Intellectual Quack Quack !

referred. And it shows itself in the form of a certain attitude towards questions like "What is so-an-so?" and statements like "Such-and-such *is* so-and-so." Naturally, in everyday life, we continually make statements and ask questions of this sort. Sometimes we are merely asking for the name of a particular thing (e.g. "what is this crystalline substance?") and we are given, as answer, the name of the class of thing to which this particular thing belongs (e.g. "arsenic"). On the other hand, we may sometimes be asking a question about a class of thing (e.g. "what is arsenic?") and then such a question is (or at least should rationally be regarded as) shorthand for "How should so-and-so be further classified for some purpose?" For example, the answer to the question, "What is arsenic?" will be "a poison", "a tonic", or "a steel-grey brittle crystalline element", according to the point and the purpose in view.

It cannot be too often emphasized that, when the same object (or class of objects) is described from various points of view—when arsenic is called a poison and a tonic and a crystalline substance—none of the descriptions is more real or true than another, nor does any one aspect exclude the others. (As an analogy—a mountain viewed from the north would look quite different if seen from the south, but neither view will be more "true" or "real" than the other.) Further, to put a thing in a class—to give it a class-name (e.g. arsenic, or poison, or mammal) is not to say that it *is* something; for a class is not *a* thing, but merely a man-made mental aid to the understanding of how to make use of things.

How many long-drawn and fascinating arguments have turned on the question of what a chair (say) "really" is— whether it is really solid or whether it is really a mass of moving electrons? And yet the answer, of course, is that it is both. For the purposes of the ordinary man it is solid (because the word "solid" classifies it as one of those things which have a certain effect on the sense of touch), while from the point of view of the physicist it is conveniently seen as analysable into a mass of moving electrons.

Such an uncritical attitude towards the verb "to be" has produced an extraordinary number of misconceptions of the scientific method of classifying phenomena and working out their behaviour by varied methods of calculation. A scientist is not concerned with what things *are*, but (to quote from

C. H. Waddington's *The Scientific Attitude*) with discovering "how things work as causal systems". Any method of calculation (i.e. any way of looking at things) which helps the scientist towards successful predictions as to how things will work is regarded by him as "true" for his purpose. Thus, some aspects of the behaviour of light can be worked out by using the mathematics of wave-motion, while other aspects respond only to calculations based on the mathematics of quanta. In other words, light behaves sometimes rather *as if* it were transmitted in some sort of wave-motion and sometimes rather *as if* it were transmitted in separate chunks of radiant energy. There is undoubtedly a difficulty here; scientists cannot feel that their present methods of calculation are likely to be completely successful unless some more consistent basis is found. (It appears that C. E. M. Dirac may now have found such a basis.) But this difficulty has nothing to do with the question of what light *is*. Similarly, the whole theory of electrons is a statement of the kind of assumptions that have to be made in order to explain the behaviour of things—particularly in their microscopic aspect. It does not imply that there are such things as electrons (in the usual sense of the verb "to be"). Again, the psycho-analysts find that their work is made enormously easier if they talk and act *as if* it were possible to isolate from the rest of mental phenomena what the Behaviourists would call a multitude of reaction-systems out of contact with the main directive system. For convenience they call this "multitude of reaction systems . . ." the unconscious. But this does not mean that there is such a thing as an unconscious.[1]

It has been suggested that similar misconceptions are at the back of such statements as that the universe is expanding or that it is running down or that space is curved and finite. The idea that the universe is running down derives from the Law of Entropy, which makes it possible to introduce the direction of time into the physicists' equations. In other words, certain scientific calculations and hypotheses about the

---

[1] Some Freudians do appear to have hypostatized the unconscious. On the other hand, the Behaviourists have been so frightened of the danger of hypostatization that they have condemned the use of such convenient labels as "unconscious", "ego", "id", etc., and have confined themselves to a terminology which is as cumbersome as if a gardener were to ignore the convenient but somewhat misleading trade-names of the different kinds of manure and to deny their separate existence, referring to them always in terms of nitrogen, phosphorus and other chemical constituents.

universe are made possible by regarding the universe as if it were running down, and—in the present state of knowledge— there are no phenomena in this field to which "winding-up" types of calculation are usefully applicable. Again, some of Einstein's work on the theory of relativity has been based on mathematical processes which necessitate the concepts of curvature and of finitude. I do not know enough about physics to have any valid opinion on such matters. But, from the philosophical point of view, the extension of mathematical methods of calculation into assertions of "being" seems highly suspicious.

The controversy between idealist and materialist is, from this point of view, seen to be a controversy about nothing. "What is Mind ? No matter ! What is matter ? Never mind ! " (I believe it was Lord Curzon who said this.) The suggestion that everything *is* either mental or material is nonsensical, since the question "What is Mind ? " is itself meaningless and resolves itself into a matter of definitions and of points of view. The phenomena of the universe are not divisible into mental and material, but are dealt with *in terms of* matter or *in terms of* mind according to the way in which they are approached. (This point is fully worked out in Bertrand Russell's *Analysis of Mind*.)

The implications of the irrational attitude towards the verb "to be" are best summarized in the words of I. A. Richards : ". . . science, as our most elaborate way of *pointing* to things, tells us and can tell us nothing about the nature of things in any *ultimate* sense. It can never answer any question of the form: *What* is so-and-so ? It can only tell us *how* such-and-such behave. And it does not attempt to do more than this. Nor, indeed, can more than this be done. Those ancient, deeply troubling, formulations that begin with ' What ' and ' Why '—as contrasted with ' How '—prove, when we examine them, to be not questions at all ; but requests —for emotional satisfaction. They indicate our desire not for knowledge, the indifferent and emotionally neutral knowledge which is yielded by science, but for assurance. ... ."[1]

---

[1] *Science and Poetry* (1935), page 58. I have been concerned here with only a small part of the confusions which are latent in the verb "to be". Those latent in its many other functions lead to erroneous rather than irrational thinking and are therefore outside my scope. They are fully expounded by Mr. Richards in his *Interpretation in Teaching*, Chapters XVIII and XIX.

(6) Reluctance to accept explanations

This is often a sign of fantasy-thinking, but not necessarily of irrationality. It appears in comfortable gossipy conversations and is significant merely as a warning that it would be both bad-mannered and futile to try and haul the conversation on to a higher intellectual plane.

The great disadvantage of explanations is that they kill such discussions stone-dead. Indeed, any fact or piece of evidence which tends to clear up the question is regarded with disfavour. There must have been innumerable meal-time conversations which have established a comfortable atmosphere by plunging into a leisurely discussion of the road the guests came by and of which is really the best and shortest route. These discussions are carried on with such persistence that the innocent onlooker sometimes imagines that the arguers are sincere seekers after truth. Full of a desire to be helpful he rushes out to fetch a road map—only to find that his help is subtly but definitely unwelcome. The company does not in the least want to know the facts; for the facts would deprive them of an excuse for comfortable conversation so arranged that each has a turn at evoking familiar country.

Similarly there are many conversations which are designed to allow fantasy-thinking, on the lines of either (a) wonder at some marvel or apparent miracle of life, or (b) indulgence of a pre-conceived opinion about other people's behaviour. In the first category come such things as the predictions of gypsies about the end of the war or of fortune-tellers in general, weather forecasts (e.g. Buchan's cold spells), gambling systems, well-known mysteries (e.g. the Mystery of the Marie-Celeste).[1] In the second category come remarks hypocritically phrased as questions, like "I wonder *why* Mrs. Robinson is so mean about her mangle?" or "What *is* it that has made the Germans start so many wars lately?"

The danger sign shows itself as a reluctance to entertain the possibility that there may be an explanation—i.e. in the first category, a material explanation or "explaining-away", and, in the second category, an explanation which will provide something more rationally satisfactory than a chewing over of the "badness" of Mrs. Robinson or the Germans. And, of

[1] I have sometimes made myself unpopular by recommending or quoting from *The Great Marie Celeste Hoax*, by L. J. Keating, which is a fascinating book, but unfortunately explodes the mystery with all the necessary documentary evidence.

course, there is no reason at all why the person should be blamed for refusing or denying explanations; nor why he should be forced to talk rationally.   His only inconsistency lies in that, if taxed, he will as a rule indignantly assert that he *does* want an explanation.

(7) Taboos and accusations of bad taste

This sign, like the last, does not necessarily indicate irrationality; it merely shows that it is unwise to expect reality-thinking in its presence.   It manifests itself in the form of reliance on social taboos and on conventional ideas of bad manners in order to prevent a conversation from questioning the foundations of a belief.

The respect due to old age has eternally been used for this purpose, the key-word of course being "impertinence".   The taboo on sex discussion has been used much less directly, though in practice it has acted as a powerful stabilizing influence for the moral *status quo*.   However, in the fields of ethics and politics, opinions are so strongly held that questioning of them is liable at any moment to lead to bad temper, if not to a breach of the peace.   And naturally, behaviour which tends to fracture the delicate texture of friendly conversation is socially regarded as bad-mannered.   For example, in certain circles, it is a sign of very bad taste to start analysing on psychological lines the sentiment of patriotism; in others it is il¹·bred to discuss the "goodness" or expediency of private profit; in others it is bad manners to suggest that Stalin may be a selfish dictator; in still others it is considered that only a cad would mention pimps.

In the field of religion there are naturally numbers of questions and topics which it is bad taste to raise.   In addition there is an understandable reluctance to "hurt people's feelings" (i.e. to undermine cherished beliefs).   It is at first sight curious that it should not be considered unkind to "hurt the feelings" of an atheist by talking to him about God.   But on second thoughts one sees that he is not in the vulnerable position of having beliefs to undermine.

I do not want to suggest that conventional ideas about manners are a Bad Thing; they are an invaluable set of rules designed to preserve the pleasantness of social intercourse. On the other hand the pleasantness of social intercourse is by no means in proportion to its content of reality-thinking.

A paradoxical corollary to all this is that it is safer and more practicable to point out a subtle twist in someone's argument than to expose a glaring and obvious fallacy. The reason is that people will seldom rationalize an opinion in a glaringly irrational manner unless they have been blinded to their mistake by a strong desire to cling on to that opinion—a desire so strong that exposure of their mistake rouses all the force of combined intellectual vanity and entrenched prejudice. Politics, as usual, will provide many examples ; less explosive examples are connected with, for instance, gambling systems, which ignore the fact that no toss or pitch or turn of the wheel can have any effect whatsoever on any succeeding toss or pitch or turn ; but any attempt to point out this quite glaring fallacy in the system to a devotee is usually received with hardly suppressed impatience. And this impatience is, of course, a danger sign—a sign that, at least on this particular subject, the devotee is impregnable to reason.

(8) Invocation of Nature

This is an almost infallible sign. Nature has always been regarded as a benevolent goddess ; and anything of which she approves is a Good Thing. Her name is therefore continually taken in vain and used as an endorsement (particularly by pseudo-scientific advertisers) of anything from aperients ("Nature's way") to social systems (Nature red in tooth and claw).

The fallacies here are, first : nature's way is not necessarily the best—not even in primitive circumstances and probably still less in civilized circumstances ; secondly, given the usually accepted meaning of "natural", nothing in modern life *is* natural, not even the beardless face of man nor the cultivated face of the land ; and thirdly, the accepted meaning is so ill-defined that it covers the usual multitude of logical sins.

"I once heard a man advocate", says Mr. E. S. P. Haynes, in talking of embalming and cremation (*Pages from a Lawyer's Note-Book*), "what he called the 'natural processes of burial.'"

(9) Argument by Analogy

I mention this here because it is a device often exploited by those who aim at persuading us to accept their views without offering us any grounds that would be acceptable to a reasonable thinker. An analogy is as a rule dangerous when the arguer tries to draw conclusions from his analogy instead of confining himself to illustration. But the task of safely diagnosing at what point an analogy has taken the bit between its teeth is too delicate for a short treatment; and I therefore recommend the chapter on "Illustration and Analogy" in Miss L. Susan Stebbing's *Thinking to Some Purpose*.

(10) Belief in the fundamental Goodness of human nature

This is by no means always a danger-sign. It has no significance here if it implies merely a refutation of belief in original sin or in the fundamental Badness of the human race. After all, given the usual meanings of "good" and "bad", the average of the human race would appear to be neutral. Again, the belief may be held perfectly sincerely and reasonably (i.e. without any ulterior motive). On the other hand, I think it is an important danger sign because it often acts as an outwardly respectable cloak for two types of wishful-thinking. (In these respects it acts similarly to a belief in Free-Will.)

First, a belief that human nature is fundamentally good gives backing to the assumption by each individual that his own nature is fundamentally good; it allows him to take it for granted—in all modesty—that when he *feels* good he *is* good, and so absolves him from any need to enquire into inner motives. The same sort of mental process is of course at work when people shy away from the (now accepted) psychological theories about unconscious motivation. (The excuse usually given here is that many of the more extreme Freudian or "gestalt" or "behaviourist" theories are still controversial.)

Secondly, a belief in the goodness of human beings acts subtly as a justification for the theory that it is in the best interests of a country to leave power in the hands of those who already hold it. If all men are good, then the members of a ruling-class must be good. (To suggest that it also follows that those who want to oust a ruling-class must be good too, is of course Rude.) There is, as it happens, something traditionally rather shocking (and highly uncomfortable) to the members of any community in the idea that their present leaders may not be altruistic. The tradition derives, according to some psychologists, partly from that belief in authority which is connected with the child's attitude towards his father. in any case, since to a great extent the leaders of a community regulate its tradition, it is hardly surprising.

The best way of clearing up a doubt about a particular example of this belief is gently to question it; the amount of shock or irritation registered is the surest measure of danger.

(11) Dislike of Reason

A very obvious danger sign—too obvious to be worth mentioning, one would think. But a dislike of reason (whatever its motive) will never appear undisguised; and "when reason is in opposition to a man's interests, his study will naturally be to render the faculty itself, and whatever issues from it, an object of hatred and contempt".[1]

We have already seen how often reason *is* in opposition to a man's interests. The disguises will take the form either of calling reason by some contemptuous name: Utopianism, starry-eyed idealism, gross materialism, intellectualism, etc., or of suggesting that some other "higher" abstraction is to be preferred, e.g. "sound common-sense"—as opposed to expert opinion, "character"—as opposed to intellect, "spiritual values"—as opposed to judgment on scientific lines.

However variously this attack on reason be expressed, the fact remains that, for the last twenty years or so, it has become increasingly vehement. Indeed, in its frank adoption of unreason. Fascism has found strange bed-fellows among many prominent thinkers and political leaders, who have attributed the world's present misfortunes to its undue respect for reason itself. To anyone watching the twenty years' progress of unreason these indiscretions must have appeared as unfortunately prophetic danger signs.

There are, of course, many people who quite openly express their dislike of reason when it is used to analyse—and in their opinion destroy the effect of—some types of fantasy-thinking. As we have seen, this is a perfectly legitimate point of view when the fantasy-thinking makes no pretence of being objectively true. Thus the first sentence of the following quotation[2]

---

[1] Jeremy Bentham. *The Book of Fallacies.*
[2] From a notice of *The Bible and Its Background*, by Archibald Robertson, which appeared in *The School Government Chronicle and Education Review* and which was quoted in *The Literary Guide*.

seems legitimate, while the second is true in substance though anti-rational in spirit:

" For those who like a scientific tearing away of all mystery, charm, and, to a large number, the sacredness of the Bible, this ruthless analysis of documentary evidence . . . will make considerable appeal. . . . There are countless thousands who will lose comfort if not something more serious by this casting of doubts on all they have hitherto believed."

A corollary of this danger sign shows itself as a vague dislike of "intellectuals" and of experts. Some intellectuals undoubtedly are very dislikeable ; but a generalized dislike is clearly irrational. Its uses are twofold ; first, it allows any uncomfortable piece of reason produced by an intellectual to be ignored ; secondly, it allows the "normal" man to feel that his equipment of knowledge is itself normal (the word "clever" is in England notoriously synonymous with "odd" or "peculiar"), and therefore that his contribution to a discussion is as valuable as anybody's. Naturally, it is in the field of politics that this tendency is most marked ; for, since our personal interests are affected, we like to believe that what we say will be worth saying and it never occurs to us that special knowledge is necessary. Many people will argue with an economist about labour conditions who would not think of arguing with an engineer about the inside of their car.

Hence the English tradition that a politician can be a country gentleman, who, as a boy, learnt and forgot little else but elementary mathematics, together with the elementary history and literature of England and of an ancient, unindustrialized civilization. Hence, also, the English tradition of pride in amateurism and muddling-through. It is probably nicer to be governed by a foolish country gentleman than a knavish intellectual, but it is at least possible that there are other alternatives.

One of the most dangerous and persistent of anti-rational arguments is that which suggests that scientists disagree among themselves as much as any other body of thinkers, the implication being that any uncomfortable scientific conclusion can be dismissed in the last resort as insufficiently established. (The argument runs parallel with the argument, already mentioned, that, since scientific laws lack absolute certainty, they are thereby rendered invalid.) It is a significant danger sign because it depends heavily on selection of evidence and is therefore associated with strongly pre-conceived opinions. In fact, it appears—to a neutral mind—patent nonsense. Naturally there are many matters (so many that the selectors of evidence have an easy task) on which scientists are not yet agreed. But these matters are generally acknowledged to be speculative. In any case they lie on the fringes of a vast area of present *agreed* knowledge and, as the area has become larger, the length of the fringe has naturally increased in proportion. The vastness of this area today is dimly comprehensible if we try to envisage the agreed knowledge which must underlie the marvels of the present age. And the point is that this knowledge is agreed in a way in which no matters of ethics or religion can claim. It is agreed in the same way that 99 per cent. of people would agree for instance on the fact that the British Isles are islands—because the evidence, though not directly perceivable by every one of those people, is in the aggregate conclusive. In addition, this knowledge passes an infallible test: upon it we base our dealings with the phenomena of the world, and, if it were wrong, our bridges and our ships would only occasionally stay up and our wirelesses would not work at all. We should remain to this day a primitive people. In this connection it is interesting to note how many fields of knowledge there are in which, before scientific method was able to investigate them, there was profound disagreement; but in which, now that science has invaded, all is peace and concord.

The expansion of agreed scientific knowledge presents another significant aspect. This is that it *has* expanded and that it goes on doing so, while it cannot be said that the philosophers and theologians, who have had just as long, if not longer, to try, have succeeded in increasing their mutual agreement.

There is one last bulwark of the anti-scientists. Again I think it is demonstrably false. But this time it appears to be based not so much on selection of evidence as on misconception of what a scientific theory is. Thus it is often claimed that Einstein's Theory of Relativity has shown Newton's laws to be all wrong after all—so what (is the implication) happens now to our agreed scientific knowledge ? But the matter is not so simple. Newton's laws are still valid in the restricted field for which they were first formulated. However, the new laws have introduced modifications in wider fields. In mechanics, for instance, the old laws are invalid if the velocity of the moving particle approaches that of light. And the new laws have been formulated to deal with these extreme cases. In general, the formulation (and verification by experiment) of new theories does not contradict those older theories which have similarly been verified by experiment and which form a part of the agreed body of knowledge. To use Einstein's own comparison,[1] "we could say that creating a new theory is not like destroying an old barn and erecting a skyscraper in its place. It is rather like climbing a mountain, gaining new and wider views, discovering unexpected connections between our starting point and its rich environment. But the point from which we started out still exists and can be seen, although it appears smaller and forms a tiny part of our broad view gained by the mastery of the obstacles on our adventurous way up."

(12) Change of heart versus change of conditions

I have already mentioned the various attempts that have been made to classify human psychological types, as a rule by establishing a sort of scale with degrees of variation between extremes, such as the introvert and extravert, stable and unstable-minded, etc. The applicability of these scales is still a matter of controversy; in any case the majority of people remain ambiguously near the border lines, displaying mixtures of many temperaments.

There is, however, one respect in which people seem to divide themselves from each other fairly sharply. I do not know how much connection the division has with these psychological types, but it does fit fairly closely to the division I have made between the fundamentally idealist (in the philosophical sense) and materialist points of view. I mention it because it has important effects on the course of almost any serious political or sociological discussion.

Most discussions are ostensibly attempts to find out the truth—to form a correct opinion. Thus, if a discussion starts with two people taking divergent views of the matter in question, we should on the face of it expect that one or other view will eventually be modified. Of course in practice this hardly ever happens—for reasons already given. However, there are occasions when final agreement is possible (if only as a result of finding that the argument was about definitions

[1] *The Evolution of Physics*, by Einstein and Infeld (1938), page 159.

of words instead of about things). On the other hand, there are occasions when agreement from the first is practically impossible. This occurs when the antagonists lie one on either side of the idealist-materialist division.

This danger sign is therefore designed to act as a device for quickly and accurately placing people on the appropriate side of the fence. It thus helps to save an enormous amount of time by showing when it is futile to continue with a discussion.

The title "change of heart versus change of conditions" suggests the method, which relies on the fact that, when people face the problem of getting the world out of the mess it is in, they ultimately resolve themselves into two camps. One believes that you cannot alter conditions without first inducing a different moral and social outlook in the human race in general; the other believes that the human outlook is so conditioned by its environment that conditions must first be altered and then hearts will be changed. Of course this second view clearly entails a "change of heart" among those who are to get the conditions altered in the first place, but the change can be restricted to a minority. In fact, the second view is to some extent a mixture. It does however differ sufficiently sharply from the first view for the shorthand titles "change of heart" and "change of conditions" to apply well enough.

These two viewpoints show themselves fairly clearly in relation to history, the second being of course allied to the "materialist conception". They also show themselves to some extent in biography and literary criticism, the first assuming the prime importance of the individual and of his free-will in controlling what he does and what he writes, the second tending to assume the prime importance of the individual's reactions to his environment.

If this fundamental division is borne in mind, it is easy to direct a conversation so that those taking part give an early indication of which side of the fence they are on.

(13) Subjective or Personal Signs

As a rule, our best chance of detecting our own fallacies is to know in what circumstances we are likely to argue fallaciously and to take note of the more obvious danger signs. These have all been covered in our general survey. They can, however, be applied to ourselves, and are summarized here for convenience:

(a) Undue pleasure or annoyance at the statement of some opinion. (See quotation from Bacon at the head of this chapter.)

(b) Anger at being asked for the evidence for a statement.

(c) Anger when convicted of fallacious argument.

(d) Shocked disapproval. (Not infallible; but may be a sign that preconceived opinions are being undermined.)

(e) The tendency to forget that, on a great many questions, there are the two points of view: the personal one (what would be good for me) and the communal one (what I believe would be good for the world). The two points of view diverge most in the case of members of a minority class, especially in the short run, since the immediate interests of the individual concerned are often different from those of the community in general.

(f) The assumption that one is always being rational when one thinks one is.

(g) The assumption that one is always being good when one thinks one is.

(h) The inability to remember any occasion during the last few months when one has been wrong or unreasonable in an argument—or has been selfish.

(i) The tendency to forget that, in respect of personal virtue, efficiency and sweet reasonableness, one is constantly putting up a façade to screen the horrid truth from the world. The danger of self-deception here is proportionate to the strength of the moral or other conscience (i.e. if one does not feel guilty one is less likely to hide oneself).

(j) In general—the assumption that one's motives are what they seem to be.

(4) TRAPS FOR THE UNWARY

Language is not only a means by which we hide our thoughts from other people ; it is a veil which helps to hide our own lives from ourselves.—C. K. Ogden. " The A.B.C. of Psychology."

In this chapter I shall refer to one or two fallacies which have particular relevance to my subject. The " Pigs-might-Fly " fallacy is especially important, for it is often the last —and formidable—resort of irrationality. I will also mention some points of view which tend to be overlooked by ordinary commonsense thinking and which are in consequence unrecognized obstacles to reality-thinking.

(1) The Utraquistic Fallacy

The prime difficulty in dealing with this fallacy is to detect it. Even when this has been done the task of keeping track of its variations in meaning is often so tedious that it seems easier to give up the struggle and just read on, feeling that one is at least getting somewhere—even if it is only to the end of the book.

However, there is a device which is very useful when detection of the fallacy seems really necessary. It works on the same principles as the word-substitution test, and consists in attaching to the doubtful word a sort of index which will show in what sense it is being used. For instance, the famous argument designed to show the existence of the unicorn can be analysed in this way. The argument, in simplified form, runs thus: "Anything I can think of must, by definition, be a thing. I can think of a unicorn. Therefore a unicorn is a thing" ("thing" here is something-about-which-I-can-think, or a subjective concept in my mind. This meaning we will index as "thing^s"). "A cow is a thing" ("thing" here refers to an objective phenomenon, outside my brain. This meaning we will index as "thing^o"). "A cow exists. Therefore a unicorn exists."

In this simplified form the argument has little chance of deceiving anyone; but, in more elaborate disguises, a similar argument is often used to prove the objective existence of "universals" (i.e. such relations as "roundness", "similarity") of "values" (i.e. "goodness", etc.) and of God.

Mr. J. W. Dunne uses it to establish the existence of the hypostatized concept of "redness" (in the second chapter of his *Experiment with Time*). "Now redness may not be a thing—but it is very certainly a *fact*," he says. He is here referring to the psycho-physical phenomenon which we experience when we look at things which are coloured in the way that we have agreed to call "red". And of course, he is perfectly within his rights in calling this phenomenon a "fact". However, for safety's sake we will index it as "fact^s", so as to indicate that it is a phenomenon existing subjectively in someone's brain. Mr. Dunne then proceeds to explain that "physics", in its task of describing and classifying phenomena of this kind, can do no more than "show us an alteration in the *positional arrangement* of the brain-particles, or alterations in the *tensions* acting upon those particles". The implications need not be followed in detail here, since we are not concerned with their particular validity. Suffice it that one of Mr. Dunne's conclusions is that "in the world described by physics there is no such fact [fact?] to be found", and that "we find, *after* we have abstracted therefrom [from such phenomena as 'redness'] every known or imaginable physical component, certain categorically nonphysical *residua*". "But these remnants", he goes on to say, "are the most obtrusive things in our universe."

How is that word "fact", which I have queried, to be indexed? The sentence which mentions "the most obtrusive *things* in our universe" gives us the clue. Mr. Dunne later makes it clear that he regards a "thing" as something which exists on its own—an objective entity. These *residua*—the remnants—are also being identified somehow with the "fact" we are querying, and, since this is so, this "fact" is being allowed to bear its more general and objective meaning. It must therefore be indexed, not as "fact^s", but as "fact^o" But Mr. Dunne has forgotten that, when he first used the word, it was in its restricted sense of "fact^s". He is thus able to persuade himself and many others that "redness" is a fact which exists objectively. And later he finds it comparatively easy to argue on the same lines that Time is also an objective fact.

It will be noticed that, in this short argument, Mr. Dunne has played the same Utraquistic trick on the word "thing" and has even, by implication, played it on the words "residua" and "remnants". This subtle and continually repeated shift of meaning is what makes an argument especially difficult to negotiate in safety. The pitfalls are so numerous and so well disguised that, by the time one has emerged successfully from the first few of them, one is too exhausted to struggle out of the rest.

The Utraquistic fallacy also infests the Free-Will—Determinism controversy. A belief in Free-Will or in some sort of vital principle involves denying that thoughts and actions are inevitable results of previous material causes ("material" being defined here as it was in Part III) and is therefore apt to be connected with a reluctance to admit that the universe and its inhabitants may be purposeless. This reluctance is often such that it is reduced to wholesale indulgence in the Utraquistic fallacy to make its arguments sound plausible. The word "purpose" is beautifully fitted to the purpose, for its purpose is to label a large variety of abstract concepts, and the purpose of its users is to shuffle these many purposes until they become as nonsensical as, by this time, the word "purpose" itself here sounds. The two main usages involved in such arguments are (a) as a label for the activity shown by human or other animals in striving towards some object—whether or not this striving is conditioned by previous environmental or hereditary factors (this is its colloquial or "lay" meaning), and (b) as a label used by philosophers for referring to the concept of "purposive energy", the distinguishing feature of this energy being that, in striving towards a goal, its actions are conditioned, not entirely by past events, but partly by a vision (so to speak) of the future and thus by some factor *independent* of material causation.[1] Since these two meanings of the word "purpose" complicate matters and confuse minds, we will index (a) as "purpose^m" and (b) as "purpose^v". Though this will not clear up the controversy, it will at least show when it is being misleadingly stated.

One of the most concise examples comes from Professor A. N. Whitehead. As it happens, it is a quotation whose wit and wealth of implication have made it beloved of vitalists. Here it is: "Scientists animated by the purpose of proving that they are purposeless constitute an interesting subject for study." I think it is clear that the first "purpose" here is "purpose^m", and that the other one is "purpose^v". If this is so, the implication falls rather flat! It is significant to note that, such is the value of the Utraquistic fallacy, Professor Whitehead's statement could not have been phrased so happily without its help.

The most insidious use of the Utraquistic fallacy is in

---

[1] An examination of such words as "energy" and "striving" (which are unavoidable in a reasonably short statement of the case) will show that they themselves can act as prolific sources of the Utraquistic fallacy—so much so that the controversy is extremely difficult to state at all without implying, in the associations of the words used, the existence of a vital principle (see the section on the Structure of Language below).

connection with such words as " explain " and " account for ".
Here is an example from page 131 of *God and Evil* (1942), by
C. E. M. Joad. " . . . a small unaccountable variation ",
says Dr. Joad, " is no less an outrage on materialist principles
than an unaccountable mutation." Dr. Joad is here implying
(quite rightly) that biologists cannot account for mutations
(though this of course does not prove that they will never be
accounted for, nor that there is no accounting for them), using
the word " account for " in the usually accepted sense of " find
causes on materialist principles " (account^m, say). Dr. Joad
then proceeds to *account for* them in his own way by " granting
that there is a principle of life in the universe, that the activity
of life is in part exempt from mechanical determinism . . ."
(note the question-begging use of the word " mechanical ").
Here " account for " is used in the sense of " explain on
vitalist principles " and can be indexed as " account^v ". But
Dr. Joad clearly implies that his " account^v " not only has the
same sound but also the same respectable qualities as
" account^m ". By doing so he misleadingly invests it with the
same common-sense rationality as that possessed by the
methods of the scientists. At the same time he disguises the
fact that it is as much a magical explanation as would be
the postulation that " four speedy Cherubim put to their lips
the sounding alchemy " and produced the winds. He also
disguises the fact that, by exempting his theories from
determinism, not only he, but even a poor biologist, could
" explain " anything whatsoever with the greatest of ease.

(2) Publicized authority

Since, in forming our opinions, we can seldom gather the
relevant facts for ourselves, we have to rely very largely on
the opinion of specialists in particular fields. The problem is
to know which specialists to trust. It is perhaps natural to
assume that the " well-known ", the " great " men in any
particular field are the most reliable—and also to assume that
the most popular and publicized of these great men's views
are similarly reliable.

This assumption is, in my opinion, a dangerous trap.

First; an expert's views hold good only within the limits
of the subject upon which he is expert. Outside those limits
they may cease to have any special value.

Secondly; the test of an expert's reliability in his own field is not the popularity of his views among the readers of news-papers and among the older and more respected (because more traditionally-minded) members of the community; on the contrary, it is the opinion of other experts in the same field which provides the only safe test.

Thirdly; the views which get most publicity are those (a) which are least like the dull, unemotive, undogmatic hypotheses of most scientific thinking; (b) which fit in with traditional ideas; (c) which support the views of the owners of the newspapers; (d) which allow loopholes for a religious (or at least vitalist) interpretation of the universe.

In this latter connection, it is interesting that the text books recommended for most University courses in psychology are those by William MacDougall, who is a vitalist; and that knighthoods and Orders of Merit have been conferred on the two physicists who have done most to spread the view that "science" has fallen into the arms of religion.

The abstraction "science" is itself a trap. It is too often used to refer to the views of a minority of well-publicized workers in particular fields of science, and its use implies (quite erroneously) the agreement of the great majority of scientists in all fields.[1] For example, C. S. Lewis, in *The Problem of Pain* (page 13) talks about "the arbitrary and idiosyncratic character which modern science is slowly teaching us to put up with in this wilful universe, where energy is made up in little parcels of a quantity no one could predict . . . where irreversible entropy gives time a real direction and the cosmos, no longer static or cyclic, moves like a drama from a real beginning to a real end" Incidentally one could hardly find a more compendious resume of those kinds of belief which I hope I have shown to result from mis-conceptions of modern scientific thought. Mr. Lewis is an extremely able and persuasive writer who emulates the greatest of our meta-physicians in his ability to make his views plausible.

In the fields of philosophy, logic and mathematics it has naturally happened that the classically "great" men have been the "idealists" Though Aristotle was less idealist than Plato, they were both, in comparison with the present range of thought and with such men as Epicurus and Heracleitus, thoroughly idealist and anti-materialist, especially in their

---

[1] Cf. *The Riddle of the Universe To-day*, by Joseph McCabe, for a comparison between the publicized and the expert view in most fields of science.

relative indifference to the value of experiment and their hypostatization of abstract words.   Similarly, Euclid's whole work
was the abstract pastime of a gentleman of leisure, and was
typically idealist in ignoring anything so suggestive of manual
labour as actual experiment.   "The cowboys", says Professor
E. T. Bell, in *The Search for Truth*, "have a way of trussing
up a steer or a pugnacious bronco which fixes the brute so
that it can neither move nor think.   This is the hog-tie, and it
is what Euclid did to geometry."

(3) Aesthetic and scientific treatment of subjects

This heading needs little comment.   It serves merely as
a reminder that subjects can be treated in either way—as
contributions to reality-thinking or as contributions to fantasy-
thinking, though sometimes the two ways are happily
combined, especially in those cases, already mentioned, where
imaginative writing can provide a more evocative and less
prolix picture of human emotion than scientific treatment
can yet attain.   But the purely aesthetic treatment often
masquerades as scientific treatment, and therein lies the trap.

(4) The Structure of Language

Under this heading I make a tentative suggestion ; it seems
plausible, but I have not come across any detailed study of
the subject—which in any case appears extremely complex.
The language of any community develops and changes
under the influence of the ideology of that community.   It
seems therefore likely that its structure gradually adapts itself
so as to make expression of that ideology implicit in the syntax.
This would produce, first, a tendency to unthinking acceptance
of traditional forms of thought, and, secondly, obstacles in the
language itself to clear expression of forms of thought which
are opposed to tradition.
Two elementary examples occur to me at the moment—
(a) the form of the imperative, first person singular and plural
—"Let's have a party," for instance, implies that we ourselves
must ask a superior being to allow us to have a party—a sort
of *deus vult.* ; (b) the fact that there is no concise form
of words for showing the distinction, in such a verb as
"determine", between "pre-determined" (in the passive
sense of decided beforehand by some outside entity) and

"pre-determined" (in the sense of theoretically pre-determinable, which merely implies that phenomena are the result of previous material phenomena, which need not, in the case of a human being, be "outside" phenomena). This peculiarity of our language leads to much misunderstanding of materialist statements of the theory of Determinism, especially in relation to human free-will.

The work of the Logical Positivists may possibly have a bearing on this subject. They point out that the form of our language continually leads us into formulating sentences about the way in which things are named *as if* they were sentences about what things are. For example, to quote from R. Carnap's *Philosophy and Logical Syntax*, "the statement, 'Friendship is not a quality but a relation,' is a sentence of the material mode [i.e. it takes the form of ordinary sentences about objective things] which can be translated into the formal mode [i.e. the language of classification and naming] as: 'The word friendship is not a quality-designation but a relation-designation.' By this translation it becomes clear that it is the *word* 'friendship' which is here concerned, and not friendship itself, as is falsely suggested by the form of the original sentence."

This clearly has a bearing on our misunderstanding of the verb "to be", since the much more natural sentence is the one which begins "Friendship *is* so-and-so . . ." and which suggests the existence of some thing—rather than word.

It appears therefore likely that our language preconditions in us our tendency to regard statements about the laws of language as being statements about the objective world, and to ask such questions as "What is Reality?" or even "What is the Unknown?" The fact that scientific method cannot pretend to answer such questions is thus a reflection, not on scientific method, but on the questions themselves.

(5) Dissociation of Opinions

Men find no difficulty whatever in holding contradictory opinions and in allowing sharp cleavages between their principles and their practice. The earnest seeker after reason will thus save himself disappointment if he freely acknowledges the fact. Every day and for thousands of years, leaders of thought have failed to practice what they preach and have contradicted their own pronouncements, the observed facts, and each other—and people have gone on listening to them with reverence and awe. Every day millions of people resort to special pleading—in two different contexts they will use mutually contradictory arguments. In such cases "it is useless to ask which (a man) believes. He believes both propositions and will employ either in different contexts. Men have a much larger power of believing inconsistent propositions than is commonly supposed."[1]

The trap here is that the unwary will be inclined to regard such contradictions as signs of a total and dangerous irrationality, indeed perhaps almost of insanity. But sanity is relative ; and in practice these contradictions are so universal that they have no diagnostic value. Enormous numbers of otherwise reasonable citizens will react with hostility to a demonstration of the contradiction between principle and practice in the social organization of their country (e.g. between principle and practice in education, between the principles of the established Church and the practice of commerce, and between the principle of democracy in England and the practice of imperialism in the Empire).

(6) Pigs might fly

" Can the man in the moon come down to earth ? "
" No, he can't."
" But how do you *know* he can't ? He *might*."
" Pigs *might* fly."

This conversation epitomizes the last line of defence—with its only concise answer—for the irrational opinion which has had to give way step by step before the evidence of reality-thinking. The basis of the defence is a controversial trick which is apt to be sprung on us just at the moment when we have at last forced our opponent to admit that the evidence is heavily against him, and when, to all rational appearance, the argument is over. The trick takes various extremely plausible disguises. However, in essence, what the user does is to hang on as long as possible to reality-thinking and its reliance on assessment of probabilities. But at the last moment, when it imminently threatens the cherished belief, he throws the whole paraphernalia overboard, and replaces it by the fantastic —and convenient—assumption that a belief which cannot be

[1] *Straight and Crooked Thinking*, R. H. Thouless.

"absolutely" certainly denied (however great the weight of evidence against it) may be allowed a place in reality-thinking. "Let us find out", he says in effect, "whether so-and-so is true," ignoring—as a last resort—the fact that, on the plane of reality-thinking, this question can mean nothing else but, "Let us believe so-and-so, *if the evidence is in its favour*."

Incidentally the trick is often immediately preceded by yet another, and kindred, device. When the objective evidence shows signs of leading to an inconvenient conclusion, the anti-materialist will ingeniously introduce the idea of intolerance. His opponent, he says, is constantly singing the praises of an open mind—of readiness to consider evidence from all sides. Why then does he so persistently show a bias against certain kinds of evidence and refuse to countenance any but *material* evidence ? When immaterial entities of any sort are involved, even if only by implication (as in the questions of Free-Will and of spiritualism for example) this accusation is difficult to counter, except by pointing out at boring length that "material" evidence is the only evidence that can be tested and thus can provide a basis for rational discussion.

A recent example of the "Pigs might fly" trick is to be found in Sir James Jeans' book, *Physics and Philosophy*, in which, though he takes up a less clearly anti-materialist and anti-determinist position than formerly, he is careful in his conclusions to leave a door open. On page 212 he says, in referring to Planck, Einstein and Schopenhauer:

"Modern philosophy also seems to have come to the conclusion that there is no real alternative to determinism, with the result that the question now discussed is no longer whether we are free but why we think we are free."

In spite of this, three pages later, he shows affection for the idea that *perhaps* our way of seeing things as determined is due to "the inability of our minds to imagine anything other than determinism". This seems a legitimate speculation ; but then what about the kind of thing his mind imagined only a few years before ? Incidentally, it is the sort of thing many people's minds imagine with extreme ease even now ; and there seems to be more than a trace left still in Jeans' own mind. For during the remainder of the book he makes a number of references to the open door, such as "the new physics . . . almost seems to suggest that the door may be unlocked—if only we could find the handle . . ." Finally, in his conclusion, he says, " Again we can hardly say that the new physics justifies any new conclusions on determinism, causality or free-will, but we can say that the argument for determinism is in some respects less compelling than it seemed to be fifty years ago."

This sentence provides a particularly appropriate example of the trap which I wish to expose. For one thing it is a subtly disguised example. For another, it summarizes the main theme of Jeans' book, which is that the new physics, so eagerly hailed by the bishops, has not after all produced any new positive evidence against determinism (Jeans now appears to agree that the negative evidence which I mentioned in Part IV has no value to speak of). From this it follows that the weight of probability in favour of determinism must still be enormous. It further follows, from the point of view of reality-thinking, that it is rational to regard determinism (or the Law of Universal Causation) as " practically " certain.

Now the insidiousness of Jeans' sentence lies in the fact that it implies something very much more than it actually states when taken literally. It is probably true that the logical (i.e. philosophical " quest for certainty ") argument for determinism is in some respects less compelling than it seemed fifty years ago. This fact in itself may be accepted, though it does not mean more than that anti-determinism, while still extremely improbable, is logically slightly less improbable than it used to seem. But what does the sentence imply over and above this ? Coming as it does among the conclusions of an important book, does it not suggest that we should take this hypothesis—this just noticeably anti-determinist implication —into account in our reality-thinking about the world ?

But if we do this, what does it entail ? It means that we must give it the same sort of validity as any judgment or opinion on which we base discussion and ultimately action. These judgments, like all those of reality-thinking, are based on assessment of probabilities (based in turn on experimental evidence) ; and *unless* the probabilities in favour of them are pretty high, we are not such fools as to entertain them seriously. We do not, for instance, fling ourselves unannounced from the top of a high building on the perfectly logical hypothesis that someone might by a millionth chance be holding a net underneath ; nor do we refuse to cross London

Bridge because it *might* fall down. We never commit such sins in the flesh; why then do we in the spirit?

To put it another way: if someone, in the course of what purports to be rational discussion, produces an opinion which he wishes to be taken seriously, he is implying that the probabilities are in its favour. It is therefore most misleading of Jeans to do this (by implication) with an opinion which he himself would admit has a very great weight of probability against it.

The point can be illustrated better, though less topically, by a quotation from F. H. Bradley's *Appearance and Reality*, which was hailed when it came out as one of the major contributions to English philosophy. Incidentally, Bradley himself points out in succeeding passages that probability is the test for valid judgments and opinions. One needs to know this in order to appreciate the full flavour of his argument.

" A future life ", he says, " is possible even on the ground of common crude Materialism. After an interval, no matter how long, another nervous system sufficiently like our own might develop; and in this case memory and a personal identity must arise. The event may be as improbable as you please, but I at least can find no reason for calling it impossible."

This statement—that something is possible though infinitely improbable—is perhaps amusing or titillating as a speculation in the realm of fantasy-thinking; but, for the purposes of reality-thinking, it is—if ever there was one—a patently useless statement (except perhaps as an indication of the wishes of the author). Its uselessness can be underlined by stating the argument in this way: Logically speaking, there might—or there might not be—a future life. Let us therefore try and decide, on the ground of common crude materialism, which of these two alternatives seems most probable. We start assessing the evidence, and we find that, on these grounds, the probabilities are enormously against a future life. We then conclude, not (as you might expect) by saying so, but simply by repeating hopefully, " There *might* be a future life."

Here again, the answer (the complete answer, for a metaphysician) is an indignant re-assertion that what Bradley says is perfectly correct—that he was doing no more than to deny an impossibility. But is this so? Was he not in fact doing more than this? Was he not by implication *suggesting a possibility*—and thus by further implication illegitimately claiming rationality for a non-rational hypothesis ? It seems so ; otherwise why would he have bothered to produce the argument at all ?

In ordinary conversation the platitudinous defence of a statement which flouts most of the evidence is "After all, there's no harm in my saying that it *might* be true," or, more often, "Well surely I've got a right to my own opinion." Once again, one has to agree. We all have a right to our private property and to our private opinions—as many and as fantastic as we like. But, unless we can produce enough evidence to give them value as reality-thinking, we have not got the right to offer them shamelessly to the general public without first clearly labelling them "NOT TO BE TAKEN as Reality-thinking."

The value of this kind of argument to anti-rational opinion is of course that, since a scientific hypothesis is always only an assessment of probabilities, it is legitimate to claim "possibility" (and, by insidious implication, rationality) for any hypothesis which contradicts an inconveniently rational one. Thus the trick derives inversely from the point of view which condemns scientific hypotheses for not being able to prove themselves "logically". Unfortunately its use is not confined to philosophers and metaphysicians ; it constantly appears as the last defence of theories whose plausibility ultimately depends on a denial of causation (e.g. attempts to suggest the intervention in human affairs of immaterial entities, such as a deity, or Free-Will, or hormic energy, or members of the spirit world). It is sometimes even used in the much more direct form of "But you can't *prove* it isn't so." To which —short of a disquisition on scientific probability—the only, if inelegant, answer is, "I quite agree. It *might* be so. Pigs *might* fly."

(7) The Fallacy of Extension

This is more a dishonest trick of argument than a fallacy ; for it is not a question of lack of skill in thought, as is (say) an undistributed middle in a syllogism, but depends on a motivated falsification—whether the falsification be done consciously or unconsciously. The opponent's position is extended beyond what he actually said *because* this extension will make the position untenable. Thus Professor Lancelot

Hogben's " Mechanism " is extended to untenable extremes by people who wish to contrast it with vitalism. Similarly, in arguments about public schools, it is sometimes suggested that it is inequitable that only rich men should have the opportunity to send their children (irrespective of these children's capacities) to a boarding-school. This suggestion is then extended into an assertion that the public schools are Bad Things ; i.e. are bad schools, or should be abolished, or have no virtues as compared with state-run schools.

I mention this fallacy, partly because it is very common and very difficult to spot, but chiefly in the hope that I may thus prevent some of my more controversial opinions from being extended until they burst. I do not, incidentally, claim that I must always be taken to mean no more than precisely what I say. That is a thoroughly dishonest controversial trick, used by the man who has said superficially neutral things with a world of underlying implications. Besides, there is, of course, no precise meaning to anything one says outside the field of the exact sciences. On the other hand, there is a limit to the implications which can legitimately be drawn from a statement. I have tried to be reasonably accurate and, except on one or two occasions when the temptation was too great, to argue unemotively. I hope then that I shall not be thought to have tried to disqualify for all purposes religious and idealistic feeling, nor to have written a diatribe against poetry, art, music and all such stuff as dreams are made on. Indeed, had I to sum up my theme in one tidy sentence, the nearest I could get would be, " A place for everything and everything in its place."

EPILOGUE

Whether or not I have made out a reasonable case for the views expressed in this book, I leave the reader to judge, confident that—if I am right—his opinions will probably remain unchanged whatever anyone says.

SELECTED BIBLIOGRAPHY

ALDRICH, C. R.: *The Primitive Mind and Modern Civilization* (Kegan Paul, 1931).

AYER, A. J.: *Language Truth and Logic* (Gollancz, 1936).

BELL, E. T.: *The Search for Truth* (Allen & Unwin, 1935).

BRITTON, KARL: *Communication* (Kegan Paul, 1939).

CHASE, STUART: *The Tyranny of Words* (Methuen, 1938).

CARNAP, RUDOLF: *Philosophy and Logical Syntax* (Kegan Paul, 1935).

DEWEY, JOHN: *How We Think* (Heath, N.Y., 1933).

————: *The Quest for Certainty* (Allen & Unwin, 1930).

EINSTEIN, ALBERT, and INFELD, LEOPOLD: *The Evolution of Physics* (C.U.P., 1938).

FARRINGTON, BENJAMIN: *Science and Politics in the Ancient World* (Allen & Unwin, 1939).

FROMM, ERICH: *The Fear of Freedom* (Kegan Paul, 1942).

HALDANE, J. B. S.: *The Marxist Philosophy and the Sciences* (Allen & Unwin, 1938).

————: *Fact and Faith* (Watts, 1934).

HAWTON, HECTOR: *The Flight from Reality* (Watts, 1941).

HOGBEN, LANCELOT: *The Nature of Living Matter* (Kegan Paul, 1930).

————: *The Retreat from Reason* (Allen & Unwin, 1937).

HUXLEY, JULIAN: *Evolutionary Ethics* (O.U.P., 1943).

————: *Religion without Revelation* (1927 ; Watts, 1941).

JEANS, SIR JAMES: *Physics and Philosophy* (C.U.P., 1942).

LEVY, H.: *Thinking* (Newnes, n.d., about 1936).

————: *The Universe of Science* (Watts, 1938).

LYALL, ARCHIBALD: *The Future of Taboo among the British Islanders* (Kegan Paul, 1936).

MCCABE, JOSEPH: *The Riddle of the Universe To-day* (Watts, 1934).

MANDER, A. E.: *Clearer Thinking* (Watts, 1936).

MANNHEIM, KARL: *Ideology and Utopia* (Kegan Paul, 1936).

————: *Man and Society in an Age of Reconstruction* (Kegan Paul, 1940).
(These two books each have a very large classified bibliography.)

NATHAN, PETER: *The Psychology of Fascism* (Faber, 1943).

NEEDHAM, JOSEPH (Ed.): *Science, Religion and Reality* (Sheldon Press, 1925).

OGDEN, C. K., and RICHARDS, I. A.: *The Meaning of Meaning* (Kegan Paul, 1936).

PARETO, V.: *The Mind and Society* (Cape, 1935).

PIAGET, JEAN: *Language and Thought of the Child* (Kegan Paul, 1926).

PLANCK, MAX: *The Philosophy of Physics* (Allen & Unwin, 1936).

RICHARDS, I. A.: *The Principles of Literary Criticism* (Kegan Paul, 1926).
———: *Interpretation in Teaching* (Kegan Paul, 1938).
———: *How to Read a Page* (Kegan Paul, 1943).
———: *Science and Poetry* (Kegan Paul, 1935).
———: *The Philosophy of Rhetoric* (O.U.P., 1936).
RIGNANO, E.: *The Psychology of Reasoning* (Kegan Paul, 1923).
RIVERS, W. H. R.: *Instinct and the Unconscious* (C.U.P., 1922).
ROBINSON, JAMES HARVEY: *The Mind in the Making* (1921 ; Watts, 1940).
RUSSELL, BERTRAND: *Let the People Think* (Watts, 1941).
———: *The Analysis of Mind* (Allen & Unwin, 1921).
———: *The Scientific Outlook* (Allen & Unwin, 1931).
———: *The Analysis of Matter* (Kegan Paul, 1927).
———: *An Inquiry into Meaning and Truth* (Allen & Unwin, 1940).
STEBBING, L. SUSAN: *A Modern Introduction to Logic* (Methuen, 1934).
———: *Thinking to Some Purpose* (Penguin, 1939).
———: *Philosophy and the Physicists* (Methuen, 1937).
THOMPSON, DENYS: *Between the Lines, or How to Read a Newspaper* (Muller, 1939).
THOULESS, R. H.: *Straight and Crooked Thinking* (English Universities Press, 1936).
TROTTER, WILFRED: *Instincts of the Herd in Peace and War* (Benn, 1919).
TUCKETT, I. LL.: *The Evidence for the Supernatural* (Watts, 1932).
VEBLEN, THORSTEIN: *The Place of Science in Modern Civilization* (Huebsch, N.Y., 1919).
———: *The Theory of the Leisure Class* (Huebsch, N.Y., 1918).
WADDINGTON, C. H.: *The Scientific Attitude* (Penguin, 1941).
———, and others: *Science and Ethics* (Allen & Unwin, 1942).
WESTERMARCK, EDWARD: *Ethical Relativity* (Kegan Paul, 1932).
WOOLF, LEONARD: *Quack! Quack!* (Hogarth Press, 1935).

The following, which have appeared since the book was written, are added because they deal with closely allied subjects:

BLACKBURN, JULIAN: *Psychology and the Social Pattern* (Kegan Paul, 1945).
BREND, WILLIAM A.: *Foundations of Human Conflicts* (Chapman & Hall, 1944).
MOORE, DORIS LANGLEY: *The Vulgar Heart: An Enquiry into the Sentimental Tendencies of Public Opinion* (Cassell, 1945).

INDEX

See also CONTENTS